CLARKEY
Mary Clarke Mohl, 1793-1883

CLARKEY

*A Portrait in Letters of
Mary Clarke Mohl
(1793-1883)*

MARGARET LESSER

OXFORD UNIVERSITY PRESS
1984

Oxford University Press, Walton Street, Oxford OX2 6DP
London New York Toronto
Delhi Bombay Calcutta Madras Karachi
Kuala Lumpur Singapore Hong Kong Tokyo
Nairobi Dar es Salaam Cape Town
Melbourne Auckland
and associated companies in
Beirut Berlin Ibadan Mexico City Nicosia

Oxford is a trade mark of Oxford University Press

Published in the United States
by Oxford University Press, New York

British Library Cataloguing in Publication Data
Lesser, M. J.
Clarkey—Mary Clarke Mohl 1793-1883
1. Mohl, Mary. 2. France—Intellectual life
—Biography
I. Title
944.06'092'4 DC33.5
ISBN 0-19-211787-4

Library of Congress Cataloging in Publication Data
Mohl, Mary Clarke, 1793-1883.
Clarkey—A Portrait in Letters of Mary Clarke Mohl
Bibliography: p.
1. Mohl, Mary Clarke, 1793-1883.
2. France—Intellectual life—19th century.
3. Intellectuals—France—Correspondence.
I. Lesser, Margaret. II. Title.
DC280.5.M65A4 1984 944.06'092'4 83-26813
ISBN 0-19-211787-4

Printed and bound in Great Britain by
Butler & Tanner Ltd, Frome and London

For Harry and Marcus

Sources and Acknowledgements

Although in the last half-century Mary Clarke Mohl has been, by and large, forgotten—or rather, has sunk from main text to footnotes—she is not entirely absent from the library shelves. Two collections of her letters were published within thirty years of her death. The first, *Letters and Recollections of Julius and Mary Mohl* (1887), was made by a (considerably younger) friend of hers, Mary Simpson. The second contains her correspondence with Fauriel and was published by M. Mohl's nephew, niece and great-niece, following instructions in Mary's will, in 1911. (They had previously requested the Swiss novelist Edouard Rod to present extracts from this correspondence and what survived of Mary's journal in the *Revue des Deux Mondes* of 1 December 1908 to 1 January 1909, and as some of this material was not included in the book of 1911, the two must be considered as one whole.)

A few additional letters are included in Kathleen O'Meara's inaccurate *Madame Mohl: her salon and her friends* (1885), Mary Elmina Smith's published thesis *Une Anglaise intellectuelle en France sous la Restauration: Miss Mary Clarke* (1927), and other printed sources, which are listed among the References.

However, all these sources leave considerable gaps. Mary Simpson's collection includes almost nothing from the first half of Mary's life, none of the Florence Nightingale correspondence (Miss Nightingale was notoriously unwilling to let the public into her private life), no letters which might wound surviving correspondents or their relations, few letters which show Mary in an unlovable light. The Fauriel letters (which have hitherto only been available in the original French; they are given here in my translation) naturally present a rather one-sided view of Mary's life before 1844. I am all the more indebted to the numerous institutions and individuals who have kindly allowed me to reprint unpublished letters which go some way to complete the portrait: Bedford College in the University of London, which owns the large corpus of letters to Mrs Reid; the British Library, which has a small number of letters to Florence Nightingale; the Institut de France, which possesses Mary's proposal of marriage and other documents; the

Leicestershire Record Office, which houses many letters to Mary's mother and great-niece Eleanor Martin; the Brotherton Collection at Leeds University; Trinity College, Cambridge, which possesses some of Mme Mohl's letters to Monckton Milnes, later Lord Houghton; and Frau Lisel-Charlotte von Siemens, a descendant of M. Mohl's brother Robert, who has kindly allowed me to use the letter from Florence Nightingale which appears on p. 207.

I owe a particular debt of gratitude to Mrs Elizabeth Bonython both for her friendly encouragement and for permission to use the extracts from the Mohl-Nightingale correspondence made by her mother Cecil Woodham-Smith when she was preparing her biography of Florence Nightingale. This was especially valuable, since nearly all the originals have been destroyed.

With great kindness, Chevalier Hay of the Clan Hay directed me to information about Mary's ancestors on her mother's side, and Captain John Binns, the present owner of Cold Overton Hall, allowed me to see round the house which left such strong impressions—good and bad—on her.

Finally, I am grateful to Gillian Hush, who took an instant liking to Mary's personality, to colleagues who have read my manuscript, and above all to my husband, whose patience, perceptiveness, and presence have been invaluable.

Contents

List of Illustrations

Introduction

I

'I must pop in two *clever* letters from a friend of mine, Madame Mohl,' wrote Mrs Gaskell to John Forster on 17 May 1854. 'Don't you like reading letters? I do, so much. Not grand formal letters; but such as Mme Mohl's, I mean.'[1]

Madame Mohl had unusual advantages as a letter-writer. Not only was her life—from 1793 to 1883—long and full, but she lived it among some of the most interesting figures on both sides of the Channel. She herself was 'English, in spite of her name'[2] (she had been a Mary Clarke before her marriage), but her home was in Paris—a circumstance which protected her from the more pompous insularities of the age.

I would die tomorrow thankfully for her [England], dear old thing! ... When I land there I am always on the point of kissing the dear free earth—only I'm afraid of being ridiculous. And yet I'd rather *live* here. Is it not absurd in the highest degree?[3]

For some sixty years she was the centre of a circle—or rather successive circles—which included Stendhal, Mérimée, Hugo, Sainte-Beuve, Tocqueville, Delacroix, Thiers, Renan, Turgenev.* Her English friends included not only Mrs Gaskell but George Eliot, Harriet Martineau, the Thackerays, the Brownings, the Trollopes, the Stanleys, the Russells,—statesmen and artists, scholars and journalists, pioneers of female emancipation. To Florence Nightingale she was much more than a friend: it is arguable that that extraordinary woman would never have got started on her career without Mme Mohl's encouragement, example and sturdy support.

She could be uniquely understanding; she could also be uniquely tart, and sometimes about the same people. As one of her friends observed, she was a mass of contradictions. Nevertheless, some of her characteristics were fairly constant. She always took a high

* See Biographical Notes on pp. 221-230.

hand with the conventions, and by middle age had tamed them altogether:

> Mme Mohl used to drop out of an omnibus, often into a mud-puddle, at our door, and delight us with her originality and freshness. I can see her now, just arrived, her feet on the fender before the fire, her hair flying, and her general untidiness so marked as to be picturesque, since she showed a supreme indifference to the details of dress. . . . If she came to urge me to go to the theatre or a concert with her, it was after her own fashion; she elbowed her way through the crowd with wonderful success and enjoyed the play, from some *balcon* or *fauteuil* that she had wrested from the box-office, in complete indifference to her surroundings. She cared for nothing but what she was seeing or hearing, and her racy comments were always worth remembering. . . .[4]

Her letters are equally unfettered. 'I could have thumped my spouse,'[5] she declares, when Mohl does not support her energetically enough in an argument; or, when she is told that a mother who has consistently exploited her daughter is bearing her death well: ' "The devil she does!" I could willingly write.'[6] Her thoughts and feelings spring off the page—rarely if ever distorted by caution, though sometimes by her hastiness, of which she was well aware:

> I should not judge from first impressions. . . . But dear me! if I don't, I forget, or cool down so much that everything is dead as a doornail! I suppose one should never speak out at all—that's the only way of never saying anything one don't mean.[7]

Often her pronouncements, startling to her contemporaries, strike the twentieth-century reader as self-evidently true; sometimes their penetration has yet to be generally accepted; sometimes they are as outrageous as ever—perhaps more outrageous now than then, since inhibitions have shifted from the sexual to other areas:

> We have only one vice which puts a female out of the pale of society . . . . Why one vice should be visited so much more sharply than any other in England—especially by religious people—is what I never could find out; they are all ranged together in the Decalogue, want of charity seeming to be the most unlaudable.[8]
> Melancholy is a luxury to the young, like walking to those who have a carriage. They use it and leave it when they like. Not so with the old.[9]

To a friend on her marriage:

> I hope you won't give up your translations to keep house; though house-

keeping is very laudable, the other's your best friend. One's pursuit always is; it sticks so close to one. No disparagement to the connubial tie, which I greatly esteem, but I have observed that *that* is improved by not being the only occupation in life; it is all *agrément* when one don't make it the sole stick to lean on.[10]

On the cotton famine, which caused great distress in Manchester:

I hear so much about the workers. . . . They have worn [Mrs Gaskell] out, and her children too. . . . So these human beings, worth so much, will be all sacrificed to the improvident good-for-little manufacturers [mill-hands], who used to earn eighteen pence a week and never laid by a sou! I would not stir a finger for them! Let them learn to think for the morrow, as other people do![11]

With her uninhibitedness and lively aspirations, she is for the most part so like what we think of as the modern woman that it comes as a shock when chance remarks, such as the last one quoted above, remind us that she did belong to another century. Within her own world she was obviously good-hearted to a fault. 'Despite the sharpness of your wit,' wrote Ferdinand Français, 'you are always kind. That is why we all love you.'[12] But the industrial working-classes did not 'count', and she could see no reason for bringing in universal primary education in the 1830s, since 'everybody' could read and write already. Throughout her life she loved music and was very sensitive to it, but Beethoven's works were too modern for her and could not be thought of as music at all. There is a portrait of her, full-face, with short hair curling round her features, in which she really looks as though she might be living in the 1980s. Then we turn to a profile sketch and see that behind the short curls, and invisible from the front, there was after all a long tail of hair done up in a knot.

Nevertheless, such reminders are few; usually she can be appreciated simply as a human being, not a human being of the nineteenth century. Her affections were strong and lasting; once she had become a friend, no rebuffs, 'dampings' or other vicissitudes ever permanently chilled her. She spoke her mind (often rather more than her mind, for she enjoyed a bout of hyperbole) but she was equally frank about her own failings—to her pain sometimes, but to the letter-reader's great advantage. 'She had never a breath of posing or "edifying" in her presentation of herself, even when it would have been most desirable,' wrote Florence Nightingale, half in admiration, half in disapproval. 'She was always un-dressed—naked in full view. A little clothing would have been decent.'[13]

Like her attitudes, her language (both French and English) is often curiously modern, or at any rate 'un-period'; on the whole she has little of the formality, the stateliness of vocabulary or syntax, one might expect to find in a woman whose first surviving letters were written only six years after *Persuasion*. But perhaps this is not so curious after all. She was usually writing at top speed, in the heat of her first impressions (so much so that she was often too impatient to punctuate, a habit which makes her letters so baffling to the reader that both her earlier editors and I have taken the liberty of inserting full-stops and commas). Moreover, she was never a 'typical' Georgian or Early Victorian or Late Victorian—or, for that matter, Englishwoman or Frenchwoman. She could, no doubt, have written both 'proper' French and 'proper' English if she had chosen to take care—Tocqueville testified that 'she spoke French with the fluency and accent of a native'[14]—but very often she did *not* choose, and listeners to both of her languages spoke of a certain 'originality' which they put down to her Frenchness or Englishness according to their own native language. In reality she seems to have enjoyed being unconventional in language as much as in behaviour—throwing in colloquialisms in unusual places, resurrecting her grandmother's eighteenth-century oddities to as-tonish her mid-Victorian correspondents, dashing off Englishisms to the sober Fauriel, flourishing Frenchisms when she was being the uninhibited Frenchwoman for the benefit of her English friends. Playing with language was her great delight; she liked to invent words to suit her meaning—'I need to demicroscopize my-self'[15]—and to pounce on vivid images, trenchant, touching, or deliberately incongruous. Nothing gave her greater pleasure than to 'sniff out words as a dog sniffs out a hare';[16] she was quite right to 'like my bad English better than Mr Greg's good,'[17] when her publishers' editor smoothed out the style of her one book. Fortu-nately, her letters remain in her own style, as spontaneous as her personality.

In her early days the spontaneity was, for reasons of both charac-ter and outward circumstances, somewhat cramped, and she kicked against the 'shackles' of daughterhood, womanhood, and the infuri-ating intractability of others with the frustration of a real-life

Marianne Dashwood—but a Marianne more untidily diverse in character than Jane Austen would have tolerated. It was only gradually, as she fought her way through financial difficulties—not to speak of the Revolutions of 1830, 1848, and 1870—that she learned how to do, think, and feel what she wanted, without looking over her shoulder at the expressions on other people's faces. But even in her earliest days—the earliest from which letters survive— her characteristic mixture of warmth, sharpness and resilience is apparent; one is not surprised to find her observing, at sixty-five: 'It seems ridiculous at my years and discretion, to be finding out how to improve; my only comfort is that Michael Angelo wrote at eighty about some discoveries he had just made, and painted himself as a child in a go-cart, as an emblem of his learning-state.'[18]

By the end of her long lifetime she was already considered a valuable first-hand witness of history. By the 1980s, historical perspective having changed, some of the attitudes which struck the younger generation of her later years as most archaic seem less so than the accepted views of the 1880s. The prefect-mentality which overtook Britain at the height of her late-Victorian prosperity was as foreign to her as to us. 'I remember well the movement [the Greek-Turkish conflict] towards 1825 or thereabouts. . . . It never came into anybody's head that we alone were to go to war all across Europe to make the Turks behave themselves well; for that is, I suppose, what these absurd people are aiming at.'[19] Similarly, her vision of female emancipation as a state in which women would, like the generality of men, combine work with personal life, strikes a more modern note than the total dedication of so many admirable—but vulnerable—nurses, teachers, and other professional women of the 1880s generation. There is something curiously modern too about her feeling that material progress has gone too far and spilt over into enervating self-indulgence.

I am shocked to see the absurd luxury of such useful and in fact indispensable operations as weddings. The breakfast . . . would have nourished a whole parish for a week with good wholesome food, instead of kickshaws (taken from the French *quelque chose*); and in the primitive old-fashioned house it looked to me like a respectable old lady dressed *en Vénus* with cupids and doves.[20]

But in the end her relationship to her own period and ours is less absorbing perhaps than her relationship to individuals, including herself—her learning, in her own phrase, 'how to live.'

II

In some respects she was not a nineteenth-century woman at all, despite the fact that she lived through three French revolutions, two English Reform Bills, and the entire careers of Dickens, Thackeray, Balzac and Stendhal. Her roots were firmly established in the previous century. She herself, having been born in 1793, experienced only seven years of it, but her grandmother, to whom she was close throughout her childhood and adolescence, was very much of the eighteenth century, as were the English acquaintances that Mary made through her. The raptures and despairs of the Byronic-Romantic 1820s never sat quite easily on her; she was apt to break out into frivolity at what should have been moments of extreme poignancy. Nor was she entirely at home in the earnest 1840s or the pompous 1860s. In short, she was as *dépaysée* in time as in space.

Her grandmother was a Mrs Hay, the widow (by the time Mary knew her) of a sea-captain. The Hays were an old and distinguished Scottish family. It pleased Mary, when she was in her twenties and a passionate devotee of Scott, to be able to say that her 'ancestral home' was mentioned in *Marmion* and *The Bride of Lammermoor* (the story of one of her connections was said to have given Scott the plot for the novel), and that it was another of her ancestors, the 'wizard' Sir Hugh de Gifford, who had built the Castle of Yester in Tweeddale—'the wildest spot I have ever seen.'[1] Moreover, despite the fact that in later life she liked to think of herself as anything but a flag-wagging patriot—'It is wonderful to me that mankind are such intense fools that they can't or won't declare they will not have a war'[2]—she was always much attached to the sword 'used by my ancestor John Hay of Hope at the Battle of the Boyne', and claimed it back very smartly when it lingered in the hands of another descendant.[3] Its correct resting-place was over Mary's bed.

These attachments were largely sentimental: 'I have the Scotch feeling for relations'[4], she observed. Mrs Hay, on the other hand, was a direct formative influence.

She had spent most of her adult life in Edinburgh in the second half of the eighteenth century, when the city was a strange mixture of New Town elegance and Old Town filth, advanced liberalism and extreme conservatism, bouts of drunken coarseness among even the most educated classes and a flowering of inventive sensitivity which has rarely been surpassed. Mrs Hay, one of the liberals, was able to mingle informally, at gatherings where 'people did not ... meet to eat, but to talk and listen',[5] with the philosopher David Hume (a particular friend of hers), Adam Smith, Robert Adam, Raeburn, Ramsay, Henry Mackenzie—a variety of distinguished innovators. Among her closest friends were the Fletchers, both of them pioneers of social reform. Mrs Fletcher, indeed, was thought by Edinburgh's Tories at the time of the French Revolution to be so extreme that she was keeping a small guillotine and practising beheading rats and mice, 'in order to be expert when French principles and practice should prevail in the land.'[6]

To mix with the best—that is, the most interesting—company it was not necessary to be very wealthy, or to stand on ceremony or one's dignity. Mary's grandfather, for instance, had not been above 'nailing up the lines in the garden for the two maids to hang up the clothes on washing days'[7] or, in the dreadful winter of 1789, 'banging and unfreezing certain legs of mutton, made so awfully hard by that great frost.'[8] She herself, after many years as a celebrity, took a pride in the fact that she could fill in a gap between two servants and enjoy doing it: 'I have been getting up these four days at twenty minutes before seven—hardly light. What for? ... to light the fire. ... The new maid came yesterday afternoon, but nevertheless I got up at half past six this morning to show her how to light a coal fire, which nobody knows how to do here, and I dare say *you* don't know. If I were but stronger, I should be a capital housemaid. ... I fetched the coals downstairs; I did a hundred odd jobs. ...'[9] She was seventy-seven at this time.

To the end of her life her taste in everything, down to interior furnishings, favoured unpretentiousness. She grudged spending time and energy on 'fiddle-faddle'—and this at a period when drawing-room décors were as fussy as manners:

Miss J. Fitton called a few days ago and very kindly (meant) brought me a beautiful wax flower in a beautiful wax vase—so slender that it fell on my nose yesterday and broke all to bits, scratching me into the bargain. I must write to thank her; she is a good creature. But I have a perfect antipathy to all gimcracks. I never have the smallest thing lying about, as they are sure to break, and I feel like a bull in a china shop whenever I am in a room with them, so that my house, when it is not in a state of confusion (which it almost always is) looks like a room packed up for an absence; and that is the state I like—that is my *beau idéal* of a room. The dusting, sorting, arranging, mending of all those abominable things which strew the rooms in England puts my head in a fever.[10]

The Hays left Edinburgh at least twenty years before the turn of the century. That is to say, they regularly visited Britain in the summer months but their permanent place of residence during the rest of the year was Dunkirk. Their daughter Elizabeth (Mary's mother) had proved to be delicate: her chest was 'weak', she coughed up blood at regular intervals and in later life 'lost part of her lungs'.[11] The climate of Britain was thought to be too severe for her, and France had the added advantage of being a good deal cheaper than England; the Hays, despite their connections, were far from wealthy. It was still, of course, the France of the Ancien Régime, in the difficult years leading up to the Revolution of 1789. The Hays, like most of their Whig friends in Edinburgh and elsewhere, sympathized entirely with the 'first principles' of the Revolution and although later excesses sickened them, their sympathy for 'the people' (and the anticlerical, anti-Bourbon parties which seemed to have the people's interests at heart) stood firm. Elizabeth was as ardent on the people's behalf in the 1830 revolution as she had been some forty years earlier, despite subsequent marriage, motherhood and old age. 'I got home at six o'clock,' wrote Mary in 1830, 'weaving my way through the cannons and cannonballs. . . . All the roads . . . were full of working people, armed, who were tearing up the paving stones to use as barricades, over which I scrambled as quick as I could. . . . Everyone was shouting that I would be killed and telling me to go away. . . . When I got in, Mama said: "Tell me the news for Heaven's sake—I have been quaking in my shoes!" I said, "But I told you I would take great care—" "Oh," said she, "it was not you I was worried about; it was the common people!" '[12]

Mrs Clarke 'doted on politics'[13] all her life, and her allegiances never changed substantially. Nothing tormented her more, in her extreme old age, when she was immobilized by arthritis as well as her lung ailment, than to be forced to live where 'nobody sympathized with her politicks and religion.'[14] Fortunately she was by nature less abrasive than her younger daughter and had no doubt learned stoicism over the years. '[Mme Mohl] told me,' Mrs Simpson remembered, 'that her mother had the sweetest temper of any one she had ever known, and that she owed her own unfailing spirits to never having been snubbed by her.'[15] Mary reflected more than once, not very ruefully, that her mother 'spoiled' her.

In 1785 Elizabeth Hay married Charles Clarke, an architect living in Millbank Row, Westminster. About his antecedents little was known even by Mary. She wrote to her mother in 1834: 'The old Duke Doudeauville will have it I am a connexion of his (I wish I were, 'twould be a credit to the family and mighty useful—he is such a grand man too). It seems a cousin of his married General Clarke, the Duc de Feltre. I wish I could find out if the latter was really a relation of ours. . . .'[16] The General was an Irishman—a descendant of one of the many Irish soldiers who had fought for James II and were later allowed, under the Treaty of Limerick, to emigrate to France—which made such a connection possible, for Mary's father too was of Irish blood, although he certainly lived most of his adult life in England. According to Mrs Simpson, who had it from Mary herself, 'her grandfather Andrew Clarke was an Irishman who left wife and family to follow the fortunes of the Stuarts, and was never heard of more; but in recognition of his services the Stuarts accorded a small pension to his son'.[17] Who brought up the young Charles Clarke and how he came to settle in England is not clear. Probably the Stuarts' 'small pension' proved insufficient, for in the first documentary evidence about him[18] he describes himself as a 'plasterer and surveyor', by which he seems to mean the equivalent of the modern architect and builder. (It was not until the 1830s that architects came to specialize in designing and gave up speculative building and contracting to supply materials, as architects of Adam's and Nash's generations had done.) Certainly Mr Clarke's manuscript catalogue of his private library[19] lists many more technical works on architecture and practical building than one would expect to find on the shelves of a gentleman not engaged in some related profession.

Mary never mentions her father's work in any of her surviving correspondence, and indeed mentions her father only rarely; she knew him much less well than her mother and grandmother. In 1791, after two children had been born of the marriage—a daughter Eleanor and a son who died in infancy—Mrs Clarke, with her mother and the five-year-old Eleanor, set off for France again, and gave up the idea of resuming residence only because they found the Revolution still in full swing. In 1793 Mary was born, in

Westminster, and for eight years the family lived together in England. But by 1801 Mrs Clarke had departed again, this time accompanied by Mrs Hay and Mary. After 1808 Mary never again spent a full year in England until she was forced to do so by the events of 1870-1.

What she recalled about her father, from their eight years of living together and the further eight years of summer visits (Mr Clarke died in 1809), suggests that he was a cultivated man of artistic tastes. He 'played on the organ, though he had never been taught,' Mary told Florence Nightingale. When Eleanor was two years old, 'my father . . . played her a tune in a minor key, and she cried—but she sang the tune through after hearing it only once more.'[20] This must have been family legend, since at the time Mary's birth was still five years away, but it is indicative nevertheless, as are the titles of the non-technical books in his collection: there were 103 volumes of 'poetry, plays and novels', fifteen of 'lives, letters and memoirs', twenty-five on 'history, voyages and travel' and 152 on 'natural history, physic and gardens', besides fifteen on law and numerous anthologies of sermons and classical texts.

At first sight it may seem significant that he and the gentle Mrs Clarke chose to split the family, particularly at a time when the two countries of their choice were at war, but there is no evidence to show that they were driven by anything but Mrs Clarke's ill-health and Mr Clarke's need to earn a living. Certainly there is no suggestion of marital incompatibility. When a silly acquaintance attempted to drum up scandal, Mary was merely amused: 'Miss J. Sharp told my mother that my father had a mistress (not true), so that he begged she would not favour him with her company any more. . . . She also told me what an ungrateful puss my sister was, though for what favour I could not make out—unless she was to consider the information about my father as one. She is a curiosity, nevertheless, and more like something in a book than in reality.'[21]

Even if it was not sensational in that way, Mary's childhood was undoubtedly odd. For four or five months of every summer she lived the secure life of a Jane Austen child, first in London, later at her married sister's place in Leicestershire. For the rest of the year she was in France—the south until 1813, afterwards Paris—where war was a matter of everyday concern and memories of the Revolution still fresh. 'As I was sitting by the fire, alone, reading,' she wrote in the revolution of 1848, 'I heard the tocsin down the chimney. No English can understand the horror of that sound. Every great massacre of the great Revolution was ushered in by it, and in my childhood, when tales of the Revolution were in everybody's mouth, the impression made was so black that the very word makes me shudder.'[22] During most of her girlhood the detested Napoleon was in power—to be followed by Louis XVIII and the even more repressive Charles X, 'whose folly,' she observed, 'brought on the Revolution of 1830.'[23] She was a sharp child and learned 'at sixteen' never to 'mention to one conspirator what another has said to me, though they both know that I know it; because if we were in a court of justice and privately questioned, nothing could come of what I had said.'[24]

It was no wonder that she felt, throughout her life, that the English, who for so long had suffered neither invasions nor revolutions, could not fully appreciate Continental feelings—or their own luck. 'Oh English people!' she wrote to a friend a year after the various revolutions of 1848, 'don't shake down the good old house over your heads because it has cobwebs and narrow staircases and old-fashioned rooms. You all little know what it is to have no house at all.'[25]

In France, until well into the Restoration, Mary, her mother and grandmother formed a sort of triple alliance against difficult circumstances. Mrs Clarke's chronic ill-health alone would have debarred them from many projects and pleasures. But there was also the not unnatural coolness of the French people around them towards English nationals. In addition, there was their constant anxiety over money. Captain Hay had died in 1788 leaving his widow poorly provided for. Mr Clarke left his widow and unmarried daughter (Eleanor had married in 1808) a number of houses in Westminster, whose rents gave them only a small, ever-fluctuating income. Later they invested in a 'law journal', from which they 'drew their substance' in the 1840s, but these dividends too were subject to unforeseeable fluctuations; at one period they dwindled so alarmingly that Mary was forced to think of taking a lodger, or even—last of all possible resources—going out as a governess.

Until she was in her fifties she was always pursued by money problems, so that it was fortunate that her upbringing had been frugal. 'I was brought up to breakfast on bread and cheese and a glass of *eau rougie** of the lightest pink. . . . Milk was a luxury I did not get,'[26] she boasted in later years. On the other hand, her youth was mercifully free from both false sentiment and the miserable soul-searchings that tormented many of her contemporaries in England. 'I was not brought up in it, and faith is a habit of mind,'[27] she observed, when eighty-three—half-regretfully then, for she envied those who could draw on the 'efficacy of religion' at times of great affliction. But for most of her life her 'faithlessness' had protected her from much: spiritual doubts, priggishness, the rigours of the English Sunday. . . . As a girl, and all her life, she read constantly, copiously, in French, English and the classical languages; there was no question of limiting her to works 'fit for the young person'. That alone was a considerable gain.

In her early youth her literary idol was, of course, Mme de Staël—'the saint of my childhood and youth'—who had not only, in the first wave of Romanticism, introduced the 'North' and the solitary female intellectual to the French consciousness, but also flouted convention in her loves, deeds, and magnificent rudeness to Napoleon. During one of the Clarkes' summer visits to England, where Mme de Staël was a refugee from Napoleon's displeasure, Mary even made an opportunity to see her. She told Mary Simpson when she was an old lady,

I happened to have a little money in my pocket, so slipped out of the house, called a coach, and ordered the man to drive me to the hotel. . . . I had heard that Mme de Staël was looking out for a governess, and I resolved to offer myself. I was shown in; Mme de Staël was there, and the brattikin (a little boy). She was *très grande dame*, very courteous, asked me to sit down, said I looked very young, and proceeded to ask me my capabilities. I agreed to everything, for I wanted to have a little talk with her. Of course, I couldn't have taught him at all. I could never have been bothered with him. So at last she repeated that I was too young, and bowed me out. This was the only time I saw Mme de Staël, and I never told anybody when I got home.[28]

Obviously she was a high-spirited girl. Indeed she was mischievous enough to be a torment to both mother and grandmother,[29] and was sent for a while to a convent-school in Toulouse, which entirely failed to check her. The redoubtable Mrs Hay recommended her to 'turn her tongue in her mouth seven times before she spoke'[30] and declared that she was 'as impudent as a

* Water with a little wine in it.

highwayman's horse'—which, looking back in 1870, Mary considered 'a valuable historical recollection, because when my grandmother was young, highwaymen were so common on the roads round London that their horses were instructed to stop at the door of the stage-coach, opened by the riders, while the trembling traveller fumbled for his purse, and the horse poked his head into the carriage, not knowing, poor fellow! how ill he was looked upon.'[31]

This volatility was both an asset and a handicap. To the end of her days she could never stop herself flaring up from time to time. 'Want of sense puts me out of patience!'[32] she cried even at sixty-nine, when she had had much opportunity to practise that virtue. And, ruefully: 'A good temper is an admirable gift. . . .'[33] 'I am not gentle,' she recognized; 'I never was.'[34]

But in the end she also recognized that her vivacity had stood her in good stead too, on many occasions. In 1850, for instance, during one of the several lawsuits she plunged into at various times, a dramatic advocate, with upraised hand, accused her of indescribable iniquities. 'I at first was agitated,' she reported, 'and then inclined to laugh.'[35] Even when she was seventy-nine, and the grim events of the Commune had broken her husband's spirit, she acknowledged the strength of her own resources: 'The gift of my habitual animal spirits, which . . . led me into perpetual mischief, though worn down, has enough left now to be of value to him, as when he comes home he has someone to cheer him and make him laugh, instead of going alone into his den like a poor sick lion.'[36] It was no small thing to be able to say, towards the end of a long life, despite all political and personal upheavals: 'I'm ridiculously and basely fond of living.'[37]

In her youth her high spirits were much needed. In France she was free but isolated. In England, on the other hand, when she was with her sister's family, there was no shortage of company or material comfort, but constant restrictions on her freedom to think, or at any rate say, what came naturally to her.

Her sister Eleanor had married into the landed gentry—perhaps the most conservative section of a society which was in general inclined to insular complacency. Mr John Frewen Turner, M.P., who had been captivated by Eleanor when she was living in Westminster, was a man of considerable wealth. He owned not only Brickwall in Sussex, a 'beautiful black-and-white half-timbered

Elizabethan manor house' surrounded by 'old walled gardens, stables, parkland with enormous oaks . . . rich Sussex acres which had belonged to Frewens for three centuries',[38] but also Cold Overton, near the Rutland border of Leicestershire. The latter, where Mary spent most of her stays with the family, was a particularly charming and remote seventeenth-century house surrounded by miles of hunting country; the nearest town, Oakham, was not much larger than *Emma*'s Highbury, and equally inward-looking. Indeed, although the estates in Sussex and Leicester were so extensive and prosperous—it is indicative that some time during the nineteenth century Eleanor was able to lend £60,000 to a 'ne'er-do-well Irish relation' and leave it unclaimed for decades[39]—the minds of the local society were the reverse of broad. Despite moments of intense irritation, Mary never ceased to love Eleanor herself—for her sweetness of temper, her enduring beauty ('it is an incomparable gift and worth every other,'[40] she decided after a lifetime of experience) and simply for the long associations which bound the two sisters together. After twenty years of marriage she could still write: 'Though my husband has a much greater place in my life, though he is my best friend and an incomparable companion, I have an indescribable tenderness for her that I have for no one else, nor ever had except for my mother.'[41]

Eleanor, however, was an exception; the rest of Cold Overton society was hard to bear. It consisted largely of 'very well-bred, old-fashioned and broad-landed country squires. . . . The men talk together; the lady of the house may be addressed once in a way as a duty—but they had all rather talk together, and she is pretty mute if there is no other lady.'[42] It was hardly a congenial ambiance for a girl whose greatest pleasures were intellectual and emotional, and who was used, moreover, to a country where the society of lively-minded women was positively courted. And the one departure from convention at Cold Overton was in a disagreeable direction: Eleanor (and later her daughter and their whole circle) became strongly Evangelical in their views and practices. Like Evangelicalism in general, they did a great deal of good—not merely indirectly, through their anti-slavery sales-of-work and their missionary teas, but with more substantial benefactions such as the village school which Eleanor founded and long supported at neighbouring Knossington; but about all things non-Evangelical they seemed to Mary maddeningly narrow-minded. 'I find,' she said, after many fierce battles, 'that the only way of living in peace is to let the poor Catholics be called all the names in the dictionary. What an odd thing it is that there is not a greater punishment than to hear propositions one disapproves put forth, and not to answer them. . . . Here I have for years been accustomed to keep silence when I hear what I call absurdities set down as axioms, and it is as irksome and irritating to me as ever. What is it to me!—I am no Catholic! My politics are of the blandest, or rather of the most weathercock order!—I am always repeating that to myself, to keep myself quiet, but my own self has nothing to do with the irritated feeling. Neither will it serve the cause, for I know if I were to talk myself hoarse, it would only increase the enmity.'[43]

In 1808, when she was fifteen, she was sent to stay at Cold Overton for a year, to 'improve her conventional manners', and the strain was considerable. There was no agreeing with the Frewen Turners, no possibility of being stimulated by those conversations which did avoid controversy—and no getting away from them either, such being the convention of polite country-house life. 'I was fatigued,' she wrote later, of such experiences, '—but much more with the never being alone than with the going out. It is to me inconceivable, that *vie de famille* you lead in England—sitting four or five people together all day. I must be several hours alone, or I am knocked up! And seeing company at stated hours never fatigues me like that dripping twaddle called, *par abus*, conversation.'[44]

As an adolescent she took refuge, as she was to do many times on later visits, in the countryside and dreams—in the place rather than the people. 'I was glad,' she wrote on another visit, over fifty years later, 'to wander about in the groves and alleys in which I have so often gone dreaming and building castles that never were realized. I suppose I am so fond of it because the total absence of incident leaves me more leisure for my dreamy life than I ever have anywhere else, and as one can crowd more thoughts and images and events into one day of mere mental activity than in ten years one can realize, I may really say I have lived centuries in this place, and only a few years in Paris, or any other.'

In summer, when she and her mother were usually there, the place was often in a state of undress, the family away, the servants making the necessary repairs to be ready for the hunting season in the autumn.

There are but two or three servants, the carpets are up, the curtains down, all the house in curl-papers except two rooms; . . . The paths are almost obliterated—some stray rose will peep out in the midst of bushes and weeds in the shrubberies.—And all this makes it a place more delicious to me than the rambles about Lago Maggiore. All my past life comes before me with a vividness it never has in any other place.[45]

Fortunately, she was not thrown back entirely on dreams during her adolescence. In the first two decades of the century she was introduced, through her grandmother, to a number of English acquaintances who woke her up very effectively.

They were literary people for the most part, with a sprinkling of artists and architects—the circle, in fact, frequented by Hazlitt, Coleridge, Crabbe, the Lambs and Wordsworth, to name the best-remembered of them. These great figures can hardly be called friends of hers—though she certainly met them at social gatherings (the diarist Crabb Robinson mentions, for instance, that he met both her and Wordsworth, among others, at Charles Aikin's on 13 May 1812)—but with other members of the circle, whose names are less known today, she was on intimate terms, as far as a young girl could be on intimate terms with established artists, and the experience gave her a feeling for unpretentious toughness that steadied her throughout the Sturm and Drang of her later life.

The person she knew first and loved best was Elizabeth Benger, a connection of the Ogilvies, who were Scottish friends of the Hays. As a writer, Miss Benger is of small interest today; she was no Jane Austen in her novels, no Macaulay in her historical writings. But as a social phenomenon—and as an individual—she was far from insignificant.

The early years of the century had, of course, seen a great boom in professional writing. With the increased prosperity brought by the Industrial Revolution more people had the leisure (and the ability) to read for pleasure. Book-production had become cheaper, circulating libraries more common, book clubs a necessity of civilized life. To meet the demand there had emerged a largely new class of men who earned their livings entirely by their pens, and—even more significantly perhaps—a class of women who found themselves able to do the same. Not that professional authorship was an easy option; but it was at least a more hopeful one, for those with the mind and spirit to pursue it, than the grim governess-ships and companionships which had previously been the only means of support for those without husbands or inherited wealth.

Miss Benger was such a woman. Born into a family of very modest means (her father had been a purser, and died when she was young), she managed to get herself an education by 'planting herself at the window of the only bookseller's shop in the place, to read the open pages of the new publications there displayed, and to return again, day after day, to examine whether by good fortune a leaf of any of them might have been turned over[46]', until she was allowed to go to a boys' school (the girls' schools of the period offering few opportunities for education as she understood it). Later she made her way to London, bringing her elderly mother with her, published a long poem on the slave trade, a critical essay on Mme de Staël's *De l'Allemagne*, a translation of Klopstock's letters, two novels, and then, 'sensible that she had not yet attained the power of doing justice to the conceptions of her fancy'[47], a number of biographies of historical figures. She never became celebrated; she probably never quite made a living (although she certainly supplemented her mother's meagre income). But her calibre was apparent to all, even if she did not manage to transfer it to paper. The literary London of the period was glad to walk up to her shabby second-floor lodgings in Grafton Street, to be regaled with nothing but a cup of coffee and Miss Benger's mixture of scholarship and vivacity. Mme de Staël said she was the most interesting woman she had met during her stay in England. And to Mary Clarke, in her late adolescence, she came as a revelation: 'Nothing could bring back the newness of that first meeting, or the astonishment I felt, as a very young girl, when for the first time I encountered a fine mind. The first man to hear music or poetry must have experienced the same sensation.'[48]

Miss Benger kindly took Mary under her wing, allowed her—a curious young hybrid, who 'chattered like a magpie, interlarded with French'—to sit enthralled at her eight o'clock tea-drinkings, at which Hazlitt or Mary Lamb was very likely to 'pop in and stay an hour perhaps, to talk'. She trotted her about 'as a curiosity, to many other teas at the same hour'[49] in the Strand or the Temple or outlying villages like Hendon, the home of James Stephen, or Mrs Barbauld's Stoke Newington. Her friends were 'a kind-hearted, natural, simple set'[50], but no less inspiring for that. They included successful writers, such as the Porter sisters (historical novelists), the poetess L.E.L., and the dramatist Joanna Baillie; artists whose professionalism was a good corrective to the amateurishness most girls were brought up on, such as the Royal Academician Robert Smirke, his daughter Mary, who was also a gifted translator, and his two architect sons, who between them designed (among much else) the British Museum, the College of Physicians and the Carlton Club; and social pioneers like Henry Crabb Robinson, who was a prime mover in the foundation of University College, London, the first such institution open to those outside the Church of England.

There were prodigious accomplishments to be admired: John Bowring (later knighted), who was only a year older than Mary, had already, in his home town of Exeter, learned French from a refugee priest, Italian from 'itinerant vendors of mathematical instruments', and Spanish, Portuguese, German, and Dutch from various sources. He later acquired Magyar, Arabic, Chinese, and 'sufficient Swedish, Danish, Russian, Servian, Polish and Bohemian to enable him to translate works in those languages',[51] besides becoming a diplomat and for a time the editor of the *Westminster Review*.

There were also less showy individuals (many of them Unitarians) who were, in a quiet, unsentimental way, revolutionizing England's previously narrow concept of 'civilized society'. Mrs Barbauld, for instance, was primarily a writer; one of her poems inspired Wordsworth to say: 'I am not in the habit of grudging people their good things, but I wish I had written those lines.'[52] But in addition, as early as the 1790s, when her husband went insane and she was forced to keep a school, she had daringly taught girl pupils to construe Horace and make comparative analyses of Pope and Boileau. More daringly still, when she found in the 1800s that the Jewish families in her village of Stoke Newington were being 'treated with great coldness', she straightaway, with complete naturalness, 'persuaded the other members of a Book Society she had lately established to ... admit one or two Jewish ladies, from whose company she ever after derived much pleasure.'[53]

Such intelligent, unsloppy liberality made a deep impression on Mary. When she was first taken to meet Mrs Barbauld, she was 'so emotioned that I cried—no mortal could understand why. It was all at the idea of being with such wonderful people. Children are mysterious creatures; their emotions are so strong that they scarcely know what they feel: admiration becomes pain.'[54]

III

By the 1820s Mary's life in France too was opening up. In 1813 the Allies had entered Paris—an event she had witnessed from the back of a dragoon's horse, having persuaded the rider to let her perch behind him. In the interval Napoleon had been sent to St Helena, Louis XVIII (brother of the Louis who had gone to the guillotine) had ascended the throne, a certain normality had returned to French life, and it was not long before the Clarkes' drawing-room had become an evening meeting-place for the bright young liberals of Restoration Paris.

One may well wonder how this came to pass. The Clarkes, after all, had no great connections in France. Mrs Clarke was already an invalid and, it is clear from all accounts, not the main attraction. Mary herself was no beauty—not even, by the standards of the time, a pretty young woman, with her small, slight figure, turned-up nose and long upper lip. (Stendhal went so far as to declare that she was 'half a hunchback'[1]—but this was after a quarrel; no other 'friends' mention such a deformity.) The best ever said of her outward person was that she had a pink-and-white complexion and a tuneful high quick speaking-voice.

On the other hand, the climate of taste in the France of this period was all in her favour. Anglophilia had been growing since the beginning of the century, and not merely in literature, where the Romantics' well-known discovery of 'Englishness'—landscape, tragicomedy, grotesquery, everything that was unclassical, in fact—was moving towards the climax of infatuation which caused one writer to declare in 1824 that whenever he read anything by Byron his 'soul was marked for life'[2], another to proclaim himself 'in love with all English art and poetry'[3], a third (Balzac) to model his huge *Comédie Humaine* on the Waverley Novels (minus their 'Anglo-Saxon prudery').

Socially and politically too England seemed, to the avant-garde, immensely enviable. The 'gentleman anglais', with his understatement, his informality, his spleen, was probably only ever an intermittent ideal, but his country's constitution, the liberty he enjoyed, were ardently admired. France herself was conscious of enjoying very little liberty under Louis XVIII and Charles X, and this was the more disappointing after all that had been suffered to get rid of the Ancien Régime, and all the upheavals of Napoleon I's reign. The Terror, the Revolution, and the Imperial campaigns seemed to have brought the country nothing but censorship, repression, and ever-increasing secret-police activity.

France was, of course, not alone in its lack of freedom. For example, much of Italy was under Austrian rule, Greece was struggling to emancipate itself from Turkey, Spain from the Bourbons. Britain seemed (from the outside, at least) to be virtually the only country which had got its revolution over more than a century earlier and banished tyranny for good.

Restoration Paris was still a very small city; by 1830 its population had reached only 800,000. It huddled together, a tangle of narrow, winding, ill-lit streets, still surrounded by the toll-wall of the *fermiers-généraux*, with its thirty-two gates still guarded by troops. Indeed its character did not change materially until the Baron Haussmann pulled down many of the little alleys to criss-cross the city with grandiose avenues reflecting Napoleon III's *soi-disant* grandeur. In February 1862 Mrs Gaskell was still half-regretting the old Paris, and in the process gives a good picture of the town Mary was brought up in:

It was a network of narrow tortuous streets; the houses high, irregular, picturesque, historical, dirty and unhealthy. I used to have much difficulty in winding my way to certain parts in the Quartier Latin from the Faubourg St Germain, where I was staying. Now the Hôtel Cluny is enclosed in a neat garden . . . the Sorbonne Church is well exposed to view; and the broad artery of the new Boulevard [Sévastopol] runs up to the Luxembourg gardens, making a clear passage for air and light through the densely populated *quartier*. It is a great gain in all material points; a great loss to memory and to that kind of imagination which loves to repeople places. The street in which our friend lived was old and narrow; the *trottoir* was barely wide enough for one uncrinolined person to walk on; and it was impossible to help being splashed by the passing carriages, which indeed threw dirt upon the walls of the houses till there was a sort of dado of mud all along the street. In the grander streets of former days this narrowness did not signify; the houses were of the kind called *entre cour et jardin* (of which there are specimens in Piccadilly), with the porter's lodge, the offices and stables abutting on the street; the grand court intervening between the noise and bustle and the high dwelling-house of the family, which out-topped the low buildings in front. But in the humbler streets . . . there were few houses *entre cour et jardin*; and I could not help wondering how people bore to live in the perpetual noise and heavy closeness of atmosphere.[4]

In this tight-knit, still small town people of like mind soon became known to each other. In the first instance, Mary's Englishness no doubt made her drawing-room attractive to young liberals who wanted to thrash out their ideas in a sympathetic atmosphere— politicians, such as Thiers, who could take no part in direct political action; writers such as Mérimée, Stendhal, and Hugo, who were struggling to create an audience for their new sort of writing (Hugo's Romantic *Hernani* still provoked outrage at its first performance in 1831); and scholars of a new type, like Augustin Thierry and Claude Fauriel, who, as opponents of the government, had no chance of university posts (indeed even long-established scholars such as Cousin, Guizot, and Villemain found themselves abruptly 'un-chaired' when they offended Charles X).

But in addition Mary was not just any young Englishwoman. She was highly intelligent. She was extremely well-read, both in the French and English classics and in the new authors who were beginning to excite the European Romantics. Walter Scott's work, in particular, had thrilled her since the publication of the *Minstrelsy of the Scottish Border* in 1803—long before he became well-known in France—and she was able, indeed eager, to introduce numerous poets, historians and novelists, equally thrilled by these novelties, to works which had not yet been translated. The Jeune France was hungry for such intellectual adventures. It was as though, as political freedom dwindled, cultural freedom broke out like water from a burst dam. Under Napoleon innovation had been largely discouraged; for centuries before him there had been a tacit assumption that culture meant classical antiquity and classical France, classical rationality and classical order. Now, in the Restoration, there was a cultural revolution to match the political one of 1789: it was not merely England that fired the imaginations of artists and scholars, but everything that had previously been exotic—'strange' periods of history, 'strange' parts of the world, 'strange' classes of society, 'strange' levels of culture, 'strange' facets of human character.

Scott's work was immensely influential for a generation. Here were primitives, in the form of Highlanders and border peasants, exotic locations in remote, unknown Scotland, an intimate approach to history which included the common man as well as kings and generals. Similar interests, whether or not they were directly inspired by Scott, activated many of Mary's habitués as well as Mary herself. Augustin Thierry, for instance, was one of the most outstanding of a new breed of historians who went to original sources and tried to think themselves into the minds of the Normans or the Merovingians or the revolutionaries of 1789—simple minds, as well as those of the influential. Claude Fauriel pioneered the study of primitive cultures, from ancient Provence to Modern Greece. Julius Mohl, who joined the circle in 1826, was passionately interested in cultures even more exotic than Scotland's—those of the East, which preoccupied more and more French scholars of world repute.

All these passions were shared by Mary, as her letters show. Moreover, she had a charm of manner, a directness which somehow did not offend, and a sort of family intimacy uncommon with French young ladies, whose Rousseauesque confessions and raptures (on paper) tended in real life always to come second to discretion. Several of the habitués fell in love with her. Thierry pined after her for several years; Thiers was so assiduous in his attentions that the concierge of the Clarkes' apartment-house eventually refused to sit up to let him out at night, saying that he could cool his ardour in the lobby. Mary's own account of how she came to know so many of the (future) mighty seems more than a little self-deprecating. Her mother, she said,

was very fond of politics—a great liberal. . . . The Jeune France liked an evening haunt of their own opinions, where they found also a lively young lady. Besides, they were not spoiled by fine society, who despised them. And this is the source of my intimacy with so many who are no longer the Jeune France, and some older, such as Benjamin Constant. Lafayette, Thiers, Mignet, Cousin, Scheffer, Augustin Thierry, Carrel, Victor Hugo, Ampère, and others were glad to come, to talk politics with my mother and nonsense with me.[5]

In reality, despite her wilfulness, she was shrewd even when she talked nonsense. And if she seemed a little mad in some respects, no doubt that merely added to her delightful Englishness. It was, if anything, gratifying to find her uninterested in dress—Guizot is said to have remarked that she and his Skye terrier patronized the same coiffeur[6]—and besotted with domestic pets. 'She is madly in love with a horrid little black cat,' wrote Quinet, 'and spends all day in her drawing-room, kissing its mouth and crying "You adorable creature!" '[7]; and the animal motif continued throughout her life, as it did throughout Florence Nightingale's.

Thus she appeared—and, it is clear from her letters, took care to appear—to the habitués of her mother's drawing-room in the early '20s: amusing, enthusiastic, attractive, self-assured. Privately, she was less secure. The chief of her frustrations concerned occupation; this was, of course, a common frustration among ladies of too good family to work for a living and of too great liveliness to be content, as Florence Nightingale said her mother and sister were at a later date, with 'lying on two sofas and telling each other "not to tire by putting flowers into water." '[8] For Mary it was not a question of finding out some suitable pursuit; she had a talent ready to hand—for art (painting and particularly drawing). For as long as she could remember '*recherches* about colour, etc. . . . . have been part of my life and occupation'[9]; even when she was quite a young girl 'old Mr Smirke was very fond of me and used to take a great interest in my efforts'[10], and she had done the portraits of all the people who came to Cold Overton—'very badly, but it was good practice.'[11] In Paris she studied in the ateliers of Jean-Hilaire Belloc (a well-known painter of the day, who incidentally was to become the grandfather of Hilaire Belloc), the Baron Gérard's daughter Clotilde, and other artists. She copied pictures in the Louvre, kept a sketchbook always with her. Like many people who are very sensitive to art, she was convinced for many years that she would equally enjoy creating it, as a full-time occupation—if she were not prevented by piffling domestic duties, or emotional upsets, or lack of application. Indeed at one period, when it seemed that her small income might disappear altogether, she tried to prepare herself for a professional career as a portrait-painter. This would no doubt have been the ideal antidote to the danger of idleness, which she was better able to diagnose than cure: a drifting-away into 'my dreamy life', where proportions only too easily became distorted and she swung uneasily between unreal bliss and unreal despair. But the crisis passed off, and with it her burst of industry.

For many years, too, she saw herself as a scholarly writer—at least from the mid-1820s, when she began to plan her 'history of women', and probably from long before. But 'nothing is easier than to plan', she observed some twenty years later. Writing was an even more solitary act than painting.

She knew only too well that solitude was not good for her, and why. Despite her appearance of devil-may-care *désinvolture*, she needed constantly to test herself and her opinions on people she respected. 'Society is a necessity to me, not a luxury,' she cries again and again in her letters; and, more explicitly: 'We all depend dreadfully on each other. We live in a world of looking-glasses, and it is our mind, not our face, that is given back to us by the reflexions. . . . Our very being seems composed of how we stand in the minds of our fellow-creatures.'[12]

Her other interests, equally strong and genuine, were no better able to solve the problem of companionship. Reading remained a constant necessity to her—'If there were no more books, the best thing would be to be buried as fast as possible'[13]; during the Restoration she was studying 'much metaphysics'[14], including Cousin and the Idéologues, a wide range of Greek and Roman authors, and numerous Oriental (particularly Indian) writings, as well as contemporary publications. Her interest in nature extended beyond the domestic pussies: she revelled in the natural history lectures given at the Jardin des Plantes and the Athénée: 'I enter the lecture-room as my sister enters a church—my soul is filled with a religious passion for nature.'[15] These lectures, and others on philosophy, literature, physiology and much else, were given by scholars as eminent as Cuvier, Benjamin Constant and Geoffroy Saint-Hilaire, and were not only free but open to both men and women—a fact which later caused her to show a certain lack of sympathy with the English movement for higher education for women, separated from men: 'Whenever ladies can go to the same lectures as men, is it not better that they should?'[16]

But even going to lectures was a solitary affair: other women with similar interests were hard to find. She had a few female friends in her twenties, of course. The chief of them was an equally striking character, of a different type—Louise Swanton (also of Irish ancestry), a studio acquaintance who later married Belloc. Where Mary was Scott-ian, Louise, though young for the rôle and of the wrong sex, was Byronic. 'She has a certain severe grace, mingled with youthfulness . . .', noted the diarist Delécluze. 'Unfortunately she is short-sighted, and this compels her to make habitual use of the ignoble eye-glass, which lends the most unassuming people an air of pretentious impertinence.'[17] Stendhal, in one of his scabrous moods, declared that she, 'the one pretty woman in [the Clarkes'] circle . . . was in love with another hunchback, Mlle de Montgolfier, and as a matter of fact I approve of the poor creatures.'[18] Whether or not this was true, Louise was a spirited young woman, one of the first to write on Byron in French, and the maker of many admired translations. For a time she and Mary were very close; then, in the way of strong personalities, they fell out for a matter of twenty years. Adèle de Chalaze and Joséphine Ruotte, two other studio friends, were more enduring; but all of them together, plus the other women friends added in the '20s and '30s, did not provide the sort of regular mental exercise Mary constantly complained of lacking.

Not surprisingly, she fell back on the theatre for escape from the tyranny of the everyday. 'I cannot tell you what pleasure it has given me. . . . I thank God for it, which would astonish many a devout mind.'[19] If she could get Molière, Racine, or, above all, Shakespeare, she was transported; failing them (and Shakespeare was not successfully presented in France until 1827) she could find excitement even in the run-of-the-mill Scribes and Pixérécourts of the day, particularly when they were interpreted by such virtuosi as Talma or Pasta, or later Rachel, Ristori or Sanson. She had none of the Victorian English mistrust of expressiveness which makes Trollope, for example, say of his despicable Lizzie Eustace, establishing her villainy beyond possibility of error: 'She might certainly have made her way as an actress, had fortune called upon her to earn her bread in that fashion.'[20] To Mary expression was life and life expression. 'What a capital actress I should have been!'[21] she told her great-niece in after years, with some complacency.

The stage being denied to her, she had far too little opportunity to express herself in the twenties. The evening gatherings to which the young liberals came were indeed stimulating. During the day her studies, her art and her friends went some way towards occupying her. But there still remained in her a reservoir of energy which demanded to be used in some way.

On her twenty-ninth birthday, 22 February 1822, she happened to go to yet another lecture at the Athénée. There, standing next to a certain Father Julien, a noted Chinese expert, was a man she had 'long desired to know'. He seemed to her to combine all the qualities she most admired. 'When I saw you so near,' she wrote to him a few months later, 'my heart gave such a leap that I almost gasped for breath. . . . But I was so shy that I could not even talk to Father Julien in front of you. Yet to be near you made me so happy! Was it not a presentiment?'[22]

IV

Claude Fauriel was twenty-one years older than Mary and already, within a limited circle, a celebrity. Perhaps his distinguishing quality, among celebrities, was his universal appeal: he was liked by the most disparate judges, from T.A. Trollope, who called him 'delightful', to Sainte-Beuve, and even the difficult Stendhal, for whom he was 'the only writer in France who is not a charlatan.'[1] Even more strikingly perhaps, he was disliked by practically nobody—and this in a tight little society of scholars, artists, and politicians. Moreover, he was a strikingly handsome man, not always a guarantee of popularity among men. His portrait shows a romantic face with large, dark eyes, elegant features, tumbling Byronic hair, a haunting expression. Stendhal said he had been 'the handsomest man in Paris',[2] and he must certainly have been among the leading contenders for that rank.

However, it was generally understood that his vanity (if he had any at all) was directed towards scholarship rather than worldly matters. He was known as a man who would go to any lengths to do his subject justice, pursuing source back to higher source, backing up one language-study with a study of all its (presumed) related languages—in general, being so conscientious in the quest for thoroughness that his publications were few and regrettably tardy. Nevertheless, he was no Mr Casaubon. His intellectual ability was, on the evidence, genuine, and although he was not considered, by the standards of his day, a *coureur de femmes*, he had had a great deal more experience of women than Mr Casaubon ever dreamed of.

His origins were humble. His father was a joiner who in the mid-eighteenth century had migrated from the rural Haute-Loire to the local big town of St-Etienne in search of work. Claude's grandparents, however, continued to live and farm among the wooded mountains of the Cévennes, where he often visited them. Nostalgia was not common with him, but that country brought it out:

I spent the earliest years of my childhood in a country which I have hardly ever revisited since that time, and yet I recall it clearly. . . . It was on the banks of the Loire, near to the mountains where it rises: I can still see in my mind's eye the two gigantic walls of rock between which the stream flows, and the limpid water gliding over the golden rocks it has polished until all the veins can be seen, and the lumps of lava from extinct volcanos that float on its surface like great black sponges. I promise that you would think it very beautiful.[3]

For Fauriel's immediate family in St-Etienne life was always a struggle. His father was a good craftsman, but earned little—out of which he had to support not only Claude (whose mother died at his birth), but the four surviving children of his two later marriages (nine had been born). The poverty of the Fauriel family was clearly of a different order from that of the Hays and the Clarkes.

In certain respects, however, Claude was exceptionally fortunate. First, he had an excellent brain. His father—influenced, according to tradition, by a dying wish of Claude's mother's—gave his son an education fit for a priest, at the Oratorian schools of Tournon and Lyon. There he grasped every educational opportunity the monks offered, and a good many they did not.

Second, he had, to quite an unusual degree, the power of detaching himself from the circumstances that surrounded him. 'You ask me why I tell you so little about myself,' he wrote to Mary, who always had a hundred things that she was bursting to tell. 'My life has been more inward than outward; and it is only from outward events that one can make a narrative that is clear and striking.'[4] An anecdote of Sainte-Beuve's suggests how, living through the Revolution, the Empire and some fairly stormy affairs of his own, Fauriel managed to find his life so empty of incident:

The young Fauriel was completing his studies . . . when the Revolution of 1789 broke out. All France was uplifted by a surge of generous feeling, and he and his schoolfellows, as enthusiastic as the rest, re-enacted a session at the Assemblée nationale. . . . One was Mirabeau, another Barnave, another M. Necker, etc. . . . . One day M. Fauriel mentioned this game to his old friend M. Guizot. 'Ah,' said Guizot, interrupting him, 'I have no doubt what part you played.' 'And what was that?' said Fauriel. 'Why, you handed in your resignation.' This was indeed what Fauriel was always inclined to do . . . to retreat from external life into private, profound unprejudiced study. Again and again, throughout his life, he handed in his resignation.[5]

He left the Oratorians with a first-class understanding of the classical languages and literatures, and (which was much more unusual) some knowledge of English and Italian. The few surviving early letters[6] show him to be fascinated by Ossian, as so many were in the 1790s, and delighted to be given the job of arranging the library of a wealthy resident of St-Etienne. Already at twenty-one he had embarked on a small research project: 'If you have any spare time, I would be obliged if you would go to the Oratory library and ask for . . . *The History of the Quakers* by Father Catrou and *Préservatif contre le Quakérisme*, translated from the English. . . . I would be grateful if you would make detailed notes on these, principally on those passages concerning the sufferings and persecutions of the sect. . . . What I am chiefly interested in is the dates. . . .'[7]

The meticulousness and the genuine feeling for the oppressed, particularly if they were not too close to him, were entirely characteristic.

In 1793 orders came through to St-Etienne, as to every part of the provinces, that a large proportion of the male population between eighteen and forty was to be conscripted. Between that year and 1799 Fauriel made various unenthusiastic contributions to the 'war' effort. For a few months he was sub-lieutenant of a battalion in the Pyrenees; later he was a 'municipal officer' during the period when the Lyons rebels were being punished (sixty executions one day, two hundred and nine the next, seventy-three three days later, etc.) and when famine, due to bad harvests and the depradations of the revolutionary armies, was ravaging the area. Later still he was a member of a deputation from St-Etienne to Paris, where he was able to pursue the kind of activities which came naturally to him. Then, returning to St-Etienne, he found the place once again in disorder and himself and his friends 'proscribed', suspected of some complicity in setting free eleven prisoners who were massacred in the open street one night. For a period he took refuge with the army in the Alps, but by 1876 was back in St-Etienne, fulfilling yet another tedious administrative function.

It is not difficult to imagine why in later life security, financial and other, might have been important to him—why, since he could not ward off all life's blows, he might have done his best to make himself invulnerable to them.

In 1799, when Napoleon became First Consul, Fauriel at last

managed to move to Paris for good. At first he supported himself by working in the Ministry of Public Security, whose head was the notorious Fouché. Sainte-Beuve, in his *Portrait*, repeats the story that Fauriel became Fouché's private secretary and surreptitiously saved many an innocent from the guillotine, but there is no proof of this, except what may perhaps be inferred from the fact that from the '20s to the '40s he did his best to help oppressed refugees from Greece and Italy.

What he certainly did in the early years of the century was resume his studies with redoubled energy. During his six months at the École Normale he had become friendly with the pioneer physiologist Cabanis, whose lectures on hygiene he attended. Cabanis was a member of the Société d'Auteuil—not a formal society, but the circle of thinkers who foregathered at the house in Auteuil of Mme Helvétius, the philosopher's widow. They included the philosophers Destutt de Tracy, Daunou, Guinguené, and de Gérando; they were on familiar terms with most of the other intellectuals in Paris.

Their common philosophy, Idéologie, was poised delicately (like Fauriel himself) between the eighteenth and nineteenth centuries. The Idéologues liked to think of themselves as scientists, like so many thinkers and artists of the early nineteenth century, from Balzac, classifying all the human species in the *Comédie Humaine*, to Bentham, 'scientifically' determining the nature of ethics, in the name of Utilitarianism. They saw Idéologie as 'that branch of zoology which is devoted to the science of ideas'.[8] It was no longer enough to enumerate fixed principles according to which the mind was said to work and knowledge be acquired: philosophers, like the more recent scientists and medical men, needed to study actual cases, real symptoms, and derive their theories from what they observed. It was a philosophical position which stressed the importance of environment, conditioning—and, as a practical policy, education. Nothing could have been more encouraging to a natural educator (and Republican) such as Fauriel. He remained a rationalist—a non-believer, an opponent of mindless fervour—to the end of his life. And yet—and this was his peculiar attraction—he was able to be thoroughly sympathetic to the young Romantics of his acquaintance, reading their experiments with pleasure, advising them generously, and applauding their successes, even if they were not at all in his own line.

When he was still under thirty and had published nothing but a handful of reviews, he had already made a strikingly favourable impression on the established intellectual world. Benjamin Constant said he was the only Frenchman who had understood the spirit of German tragedy, and so the only one able to judge his translation of *Wallenstein*.[9] In 1800 Mme de Staël, writing to thank him for a review of her *De la littérature*, deferred to him as to a master and volunteered to make various changes in the second edition on the basis of his criticisms. Destutt de Tracy begged for his opinion on an economic treatise he was writing. Cabanis publicly addressed to him a *Letter on Primary Causes* which exuded respect for his views.

He was very young and might well have been spoiled, but he seems to have remained surprisingly level-headed. Even the adulation of Mary's idol Mme de Staël—'Every time I see you I feel more profoundly that no character has ever captivated me more than yours'[10]—failed to throw him off balance. Women clearly found him very attractive. As to his own susceptibilities one can only speculate; prudently, he kept his own counsel. Even his liaison, which lasted for twenty years, with the great Mme de Condorcet is not unambiguous: she was very lovable, but she also provided him with a roof over his head and an even more secure footing in intellectual society.

But perhaps the last two facts played no part in Fauriel's motivation: Mme de Condorcet was by all accounts a prize in her own right. She too had known insecurity, though she came from the opposite end of society to Fauriel's. In 1793 her husband, the great philosopher (whom she had greatly loved, and with whom she had studied, debated and entertained the most revolutionary thinkers of the later eighteenth century, including Hume, Adam Smith, Grimm, Alfieri, Franklin, Jefferson and Paine), had been 'judged' by the Revolutionary authorities to be a traitor to the Revolution and condemned to death. He had left Paris, eventually committing suicide, and his property had been forfeited to the State. Mme de Condorcet, then twenty-nine, had been left almost without means, and with three dependants to support. Up to then she had been accustomed, of course, to a life made easy by many servants. Now she used the very small sum of money she still possessed to buy a linen shop at 352 Rue Saint-Honoré, put a manager into it, and herself lived over it, supplementing its meagre takings by painting miniatures, cameos and other pictures—often of *proscrits* who knew they would soon be dead and had no other mementoes to leave to their families.

By 1801, the emergency having passed, she had left the Rue Saint-Honoré and recovered some of her funds, but still lived a retired life. For twenty-one years from that date she (the aristocratic sister of the Maréchal de Grouchy) and Fauriel (son of the St-Etienne joiner) lived together quietly either in her Paris house or her country residence La Maisonnette at Meulan, some twenty-five miles from the capital—an unmarried but generally acknowledged couple, in a curiously suburban setting, as Guizot described it:

Placed halfway up a hill, it looked out over the little town of Meulan, with its two churches—one still in use, the other somewhat dilapidated and used as a store. To the right of the town one saw l'Ile-Belle, its broad green fields surrounded by huge poplars. Opposite there was the old bridge, and beyond . . . the vast fertile valley of the Seine. The house . . . was modest. . . . Behind it there was a garden, designed by no great artist, but pleasantly criss-crossed by flower-edged paths climbing up the hill. At the top there was a little pavilion, where one could happily read in solitude or converse *à deux*. Beyond the garden, further up the hill, there were other country houses and gardens. . . . Nothing especially beautiful, nothing especially rare. . . . [11]

Thus Fauriel had, in a sense, 'settled down' twenty years before Mary had even found her opportunity to break out. Although he and Mme de Condorcet still mixed with the cream of France's intellectuals, of all generations, he was of course excluded, as a liberal, from any public post and forced to devote himself to private study and writing; but to the discerning few who knew him personally he was already a great man.

He had, however, still published very little, for reasons which illustrate his curiously mixed nature. In the early 1800s, for example, he had embarked on a large-scale *History of Stoicism*. It was generally agreed that this would be a major work, when finished. But just at this time he met the young Manzoni (brought by his mother to visit her friend Mme de Condorcet), recognized a talent which must not be wasted, and devoted himself to encouraging the young man to write. He introduced him to new literature (including *Ivanhoe*, which, Manzoni declared, set him on the road towards *I Promessi Sposi*), bolstered his confidence, acted as his agent in Paris when Manzoni had returned to Milan, found publishers for him. The *History of Stoicism*, meanwhile, languished, and similar episodes occurred again and again.

Manzoni, who came to understand Fauriel as well as anybody, was constantly repeating his thanks, his dependence on Fauriel's judgment, his impatience to see Fauriel complete something. 'You, with so much to do, have copied the rhapsody for me? I am overwhelmed. . . . Now I am more eager than ever to see you bring your work on the Stoics to fruition!' (6 September 1809.) 'And your excellent project for a book on Dante? . . . When completed, it will be of the greatest interest, I am sure.' (February 1811.) 'I am delighted to hear of your plan for a history of the renaissance of literature in Europe . . . though I dare not hope to read it in the near future.' (20 April 1812.) 'Tell me if you have finished the Dante. . . . It would be such a sadness to me if a mind and heart like yours were to remain unknown to all but your personal acquaintance.' (13 July 1814.) 'And your wretched book on Provence? Here we are at the date when you had promised to make your first delivery to the printer: have you kept your word?' (10 September 1826.)[12]

Fauriel's projects change; Manzoni's theme remains the same. The Stoics book was never published; the life of Dante only reached the public in 1834, at least twenty-three years after he had begun it; and the work on Provençal civilization was never fully completed, although parts of it were published later in his life. However, when one grasps the scope of this last project as he envisaged it, one is amazed that he ever managed to commit anything to paper: in order to support his picture of Provence as the cradle of western civilization, he found it necessary to make himself expert in all the literatures and languages of the Mediterranean basin, from Modern Greek to Basque (and then, for comparison, Celtic). He studied Arabic under de Sacy and Sanskrit under Sir William Hamilton (he had now tracked back to the Indo-European origin of western culture). Small wonder that Manzoni urged him to be less perfectionist.

In the meantime he published a few less all-embracing works, unconnected with each other or the grand plan. In 1810 he had translated into French a long poem, *Parthenaïs*, written by the Danish writer Jens Baggesen; Fauriel's introduction to it is said to constitute the 'literary manifesto of the Idéologues'. In the period just before he met Mary he was working on his translations of Manzoni's two tragedies, which were published in 1823, as was his free translation of the poem *The Refugees of Parga* by the Italian refugee patriot Giovanni Berchet. In the same year he began to collect (from the many political refugees he befriended) modern Greek folk songs for a translated collection, with lengthy introduction, which he published in 1824–5. This was one of the first, and certainly one of the best, introductions to a subject which hardly existed for the rest of Europe before Fauriel wrote on it.

If he had been single-minded, his name might have been as well known today as Carlyle's or Michelet's. But equally, if he had been single-minded, he would not have been so helpful to exiled writers like Berchet, or the Greeks Mustoxidi, Triantaphyllos, and Basili, or such a father-figure to younger French pioneers like J.J. Ampère and Thierry. The last wrote gratefully in 1835:

As has often been remarked, every true passion demands a confidant. I had one to whom almost every evening I gave an account of my discoveries during the day. . . . This friend and counsellor, whose advice was always both honest and valuable, was Monsieur Fauriel. . . . In any case of doubt I was ruled by his advice, and the sympathy with which he followed my work stimulated me to press on. . . . After thirteen years I still remember our evening walks along great stretches of the outer boulevards, during which I told him, in the minutest detail, about the chronicles and legends . . . of the eleventh century.[13]

One can hardly despise a man with the humility to put his own, much admired, work second in such a case.

Mary was entranced by his looks, his ideas, his fatherliness, his magnanimity, and above all his apparent omniscience. When he declared his love, she waved away the twenty years' difference in their ages as being of no importance, and took it for granted that Fauriel could keep up, indefinitely, the pace of the passion she had aroused in him. Fauriel, for his part, took it for granted that she knew of his liaison with Mme de Condorcet.

Some time after their first meeting Mary had written him a diffident note, asking if she could paint a small portrait of him to give as a memento to Thierry. A week later they had met at the Théâtre des Bouffons, to which Mary had gone with her friend Joséphine Ruotte to see Rossini's *Tancredi*, and Fauriel had found her conversation 'greatly to my taste, though I had no suspicion

then how much more it would come to enchant me.'[14] They met
constantly in Paris that spring, and grew ever more intimate,
although their opportunities of being alone together were limited
to chance corners of crowded salons, or alleys in public gardens,
which presented themselves only too rarely. In private rooms, such
as Mrs Clarke's, where Fauriel soon became a regular visitor, a
third party must always be present. By the summer of 1822 they
were exchanging letters whenever they were apart. Fauriel, bowled
over by the novelty of this relationship, which included thoroughly
disrespectful teasing, breathtaking outspokenness and warm devotion, was confessing that he could not keep his mind off Mary,
and trying to adopt her tastes—even phrases from her Anglo-Saxon
language. Mary was basking in Fauriel's protestations (with all
their eighteenth-century floweriness), his real kindness, and his
obvious good sense. 'Pray do not mark your envelopes with so
many asterisks,' he begged mildly, after they had been correspond-
ing for a while. (He had arranged to collect her letters to him from
Joséphine Ruotte's house—a suggestive device which, however,
suggested nothing to Mary.) 'It could attract the attention of our
inquisitive police, who might imagine we were stupid enough to
tell each other what might interest them. A very small cross at the
corner of the address will be enough to indicate. . . . In an extreme
emergency you may write to me directly; but I am more and more
convinced that my letters do not reach me as they should, if they
are from abroad, and that I am rarely the first to read those which
do come to hand. . .'.[15] But the secret police and their activities
interested her less than his dreams of future travels together, his
inability to 'think of anything else but her'. For the first few days
at Cold Overton she had been content to 'lie on the grass and think
of you. . . . But now I desire more. . . . Oh, if only I could feel your
arms about me, I think I should be satisfied for ever so long! I try
not to think of it, I desire it too much. I feel as dry as a plant that
has not been watered. . . .'[16]

Letters

I

1822–1823
The beginning of a passion

Fauriel to Mary Paris, 15 July 1822

My dearest dear*, I rise fresh from my bed to write to you—or rather, to continue the conversation I have been holding with you throughout the night. Yesterday I was so vexed by chance callers at the time when I had hoped to begin this letter that I was unable to take up my pen and could only re-read your dear letter twice over. But if you only let me know where you are, as you travel, I shall send you volumes, whole journals of my days, my minutes, my thoughts. They will probably be very dull. But that will not be my fault, my dearest life: *I* am not travelling about . . . meeting new acquaintances and receiving new impressions every day. I am alone here . . . sad, stationary, waiting for you to return. . . . From tomorrow I shall begin to write down my thoughts and feelings every day. . . .[1]

Mary to Fauriel Edinburgh, 27 July 1822

. . . My darling, how can you let yourself be eaten up by promiscuous callers! You fritter away your life with shameful prodigality. It's true that M. Thierry goes to the other extreme; he's wrong to turn himself into a machine with only one purpose. But I'm not sure that you are not *more* wrong to have no purpose at all, or, if you have one, to waste so much effort *en route*—to go down so many side tracks that your goal becomes a mere plaything for your imagination. If the side tracks made you so happy that you had no need of the other dream, I would say amen with all my heart! Happiness is the greatest success in life. But it is not true that you are happy. At least, it has seemed to me that you are not without ambition, even if it is stifled by pride, reason, laziness, and

* In English.

of course good nature. . . . I _need_ you to work,—not because my love depends on your success, but because I am full of energy. If _I_ had been a man, I would have been only too ambitious. Not being one, I invest my energy in you, and if it an't used to the purpose, it will torment you: think of that!

. . . For my sake you will, I know, forgive this tedious sermon. Besides, I write from Edinburgh, of all cities in Britain the one where sermons are the most popular, and consequently the most numerous. On Sundays every one scampers off to church, as in Paris they scamper to a new play. . . . In the salons they discuss the merits of the various preachers, as Parisians discuss Mademoiselle Mars and Talma. I don't mean only the devout. Every one is the same—men of letters, unbelievers even—for church is a temple of the muses. Mr Alison, reading the prayers, is more charming than Talma declaiming Racine, and obviously far more cultivated. His style is delicious—I was quite cast down when his sermons came to an end. . . .

And then, to go to Melrose, only two miles from Scott's house! I can't describe my feelings! Everything speaks of him—the countryside he has so often described, the ruins of the abbey . . . the memories of the battles of the borderers, the tombs of the warriors—it's _all_ Scott, for it was the source of all his first and best ideas. . . .

28 July

. . . The Scotch are the Scotch—so far all my impressions are favourable. Their language is charmingly natural—the only thing that vexes me is that it is gradually disappearing and will soon be gone altogether. It is already considered to be only a dialect, although to my taste it is preferable to ordinary English. But perhaps that has merely lost its freshness for me, because it has been used by so many writers.

I brought with me a letter of introduction to the Fletchers, who please me above all things. I like the daughter very much. . . . But she is so complete in herself that I don't know what good I can do her, which depresses me a little. Now you, whom I like better than any human creature I have ever known, are blessedly endowed with defects, and they match my own pretty well. . . .

Dear me, when shall I see you again!

3 August

... I have been to see the ruins of a castle built by a wizard—one of my ancestors, by the way. (And I wish he'd bequeathed me some of his power, that I might waft you here, if only for an hour a day.) It was the wildest spot I ever saw in my life—Heavens, I was transported! ... climbing almost on all fours and leaping from stone to stone in the middle of the mountain stream ... so roofed in by trees that I could not see the sky. ... I could have stayed there for days.

I fear there are no legends of wizards or fairies in your Provence, my love, with its three successive civilizations. I don't care for civilization, my dearest—don't care for it at all, find it utterly repulsive. Once folk understand everything, goodbye fairies, goodbye ghosts, goodbye talismans—goodbye all strong feelings too, all energy, even new ideas—except chemistry and such kitchen-work. ... Science kills and poetry gives life. How can you expect me to care for those centuries when the intellect dominated! And you see that I am right, for nowadays all the writers of talent are going back to the simple, feeling peoples of the Middle Ages, or those who still live in the same way, like the Scottish highlanders. (And by the bye, I saw some of the last-named dancing the other day, and the composers of Opéra ballets would do well to study them and learn true grace and vivacity.)

You must read all the works of Scott, my dearest, but not until I return, because I adore them ... as I do the whole Scotch nation. ...

They *talk* much more than the English.

4 August

... But there is no one here who is completely in sympathy with me, as you are. I am often quite tired from having to hold back my thoughts, or hearing them contradicted, or being the only one to realise that people are talking twaddle. How did you learn to be so gracious, my love? Where did you spend your childhood? I want to know, above all things. But I have a thousand questions to ask you when we meet again. You have but one fault, which is that you don't tell me everything about yourself—all your thoughts and feelings—unless I ask. I don't know if that comes from a habit of being silent for lack of an understanding listener, or from a lack of animal spirits (for you do lack them), or whether it is because you

have lived too long among people preoccupied with themselves—
I have noticed that that too makes a person unforthcoming. . . .[2]

Mary to Fauriel   Edinburgh, 11 August 1822

. . . This winter I mean to learn the Scotch dialect, instead of
whatever you intended to teach me, so that I can read what remains
of the poetry, for nothing pleases me more than old ballads. The
Scotch and Gaelic ones are so delicious that all my spare time is
passed in reading those I can get. I have just received a letter from
Amédée, telling me that M. Beyle is to write a book on old ballads.*
I beg you, dearest, if you have the smallest regard for what I love to
read, do not direct him to a single line or stanza. I am revolted at the
thought of his odious paws being laid on such a subject. He is like the
harpies: he has the gift of spoiling all he touches—to the end of my
days I should never want to read a ballad he had spoken of. And you
are a man he loves to exploit—please, I beg you, *do not see him till
I return*; he will squeeze all sorts of good things out of you. . . .[3]

M. Beyle was, of course, Stendhal, who was then thirty-nine and had
not yet published any of the works for which he is now best known. He
was making ends meet as best he could in Paris, frequenting a number of
salons (including Mary's until they quarrelled for good), and cultivating
a reputation for Byronic immorality. 'In fact, I amazed or shocked all my
acquaintance at that time,' he recalled later. 'I was either a monster or a
god. To this day all Miss Clarke's circle firmly believes that I am a
monster—above all, a monster of immorality. The reader knows how little
true this is: I had only once been to a prostitute, and the reader will
remember how I fared with her.'[4]

It was not his conduct with prostitutes that annoyed Mary, if she knew
about it, which is unlikely. She thought him affected, and was the last
person to tolerate his intolerance, which irritated even milder personalities, such as Delécluze, who gives a sample of his conversation at this time:

Reynier: But if the democratic decision . . .
Beyle: Oh, Cicero's consensus omnium gentium is nonsense—
          accepted in its day, but indefensible now.
Cerclet: You know very well that there are men—and clever men
          too—who not only accept it, but base their politics on it.
Beyle: Oh, they are all knaves, if they are not fools.[5]

Not surprisingly, he was not universally popular. 'I think he is beginning
to find us all stupid,' said Delécluze in 1824, 'and I am glad of it.'[6]

** Amédée Thierry, Augustin's brother: the book was *De l'Amour*.*

Stendhal, for his part, was not attracted by Mary's sharpness. Fauriel, with his kindness, malleability and 'civilized' restraint, was much more to his taste, and he viewed his friend's new passion with a jaundiced eye:

M. Fauriel is the only French writer known to me—apart from M. Mérimée and myself—who is not a charlatan. Consequently M. Fauriel has acquired no fame. . . . He was often to be seen at the house of little Miss Clarke—a shrew, half a hunchback. She was an Englishwoman— sharp-witted, I must admit, but with a wit like a chamois' horns: dry, hard and twisted. M. Fauriel, who thought highly of my talents at that time, soon took me to Miss Clarke's. . . .[7]

It is not hard to see why Mary and Stendhal did not take to each other. However, her plea to Fauriel came too late: on 7 July Stendhal had already written to thank Fauriel for his help. It was almost certainly Fauriel who directed him to all the material for chapters LI to LIII of *De l'Amour*— on love in Provence and Arabia—and translated their Provençal and Arabic anecdotes for him. 'If I were not so old,' Stendhal wrote in appreciation, 'I should learn Arabic, so delighted am I to find something, at last, which is not a mere academic copy of the ancients.'[8]

Mary to Fauriel   Edinburgh, 13 August 1822

Every day I feel my faculties and my energy returning and am so happy to owe it all to you. I'm more grateful to you than you will ever know for not wanting me to faddle about dress. . . . I can't describe what I suffered on that account during my wretched affair with M. Thierry, and how humiliated I felt to be always worrying about what I should do to please him and knowing always that it was largely a question of what buttons I had on. . . .

Now *you* love me as a free creature, as nature made me, and any woman who can say that should be passionately grateful—it's so rare! To increase the distance between the sexes, men's usual device is to humble women, instead of trying to raise themselves—and no doubt that's the easiest way. It reminds me of the wag who wagered he could make six pairs of shoes in a quarter of an hour, and did it—by cutting the tops off six pairs of boots.—There! a moment ago I was weeping with gratitude, and now I am laughing. Some-times . . . I am afraid you will not take me seriously enough, when a joke can turn me so easily from tears to laughter. . . .

18 August

. . . I have just been running like a hare to get a sight of Walter Scott . . . and think I caught a glimpse of his profile. Unfortunately, the people we know here who move in literary circles are Whigs and my adored Scott is a Tory and will have nothing to do with Whigs, which makes me blush for him, particularly as I suspect it has much to do with the 1500 louis' worth of official posts he holds. He is the greatest genius of the century—but alas, genius and nobility of soul do not always go together. . . .

I feel closer to the history of Scotland than to that of any other country . . . but shall try to reconcile myself to Provence, for I want to have no affections, no thoughts, no tastes, no habits and no occupations but what I share with you. I want to live so much *in partnership** with you, that we will be but one huge soul in two bodies. But that's already true. . . .[9]

Fauriel to Mary   Paris, 15 August 1822

My dearest love, in my last letter I promised to write a few lines every day and send you the whole when it amounted to a few pages . . . . But I have not written, my dearest; indeed, I was determined not to write, for I would either have hidden my feelings from you (which I cannot conceive of doing) or saddened and worried you, which I did not want. The truth is that I have just spent one of the saddest months of my life. Mme de Condorcet has been gravely ill—ill enough to disquieten her family and friends, and me more than any . . . . The memory of you, and the hope of a letter, were my only consolations. . . .

You must not imagine that I am without ambition . . . but in these days ambition of any kind has so many obstacles to overcome, and so few prizes to gain, that it is hardly worth having. One should at least endeavour to have no ambitions but those one can entertain with a little pride, a little nobility of spirit, in the hope of doing some service, little or great, to mankind. The ambition to be Greek or Spanish† seems to me almost the only one worth voicing . . . . I cannot promise that you will be as captivated by the traditions, memories and poetic feeling of the South of France as you are by those of Scotland. They are there . . . but they are older and buried

---

* In English.
† I.e. to win independence for those countries.

deeper. Few but scholars know anything about the poetry and originality of its past life and they, not being noted for their emotions, have aroused little emotion on the subject. Give the region its Walter Scott: then you will see!

Yes, my dearest, I will read all Walter Scott, if I may read and discuss him with you. But I may tell you now that we shall have some fine quarrels—not exactly about Walter Scott, nor even about your enthusiasm for fairies, wizards and legends; I love every kind of life, and the ages of ignorance and barbarism interest me as much as any man. But I wish your enthusiasm for them were not so exclusive and absolute . . . . One should understand the past and love it, but not at the expense of the present or the future. . . .

I take up my letter, broken off this morning. I have just returned from my evening walk, which I always take alone . . . because it is only then that I can think about you at my ease . . . . There is only one thought, one feeling which dominates my mind . . . that of being loved by you. I am only afraid that you are not sufficiently convinced of all you are to me. . . . What can I do to prove that my heart has never been captured as you have captured it? . . .[10]

Mary to Fauriel   Keswick, 8 September 1822

Who is this Mme de Condorcet? I did not know that there was any lady whose illness was capable of making you ill! Who is this lady, whose illness afflicts you more than her own family, and prevents you from writing to me! . . . Imagine your own state of mind if I wrote to you thus, of a man whose name you had never heard me mention. Pray reply immediately and answer all my questions. And be grateful that I ask them!—I must love you very tenderly indeed, for twenty times in these past three days I have sworn never to write to you again, only to weep and weaken. . . . Oh, I can hardly express how I feel! I seem to have shrunk into myself. . . .

Before your letter I had so much pleasure in thinking of all I had to tell you, but now that *all* is only a heap of uninteresting scraps. The joy is quite gone out of it. . . .[11]

Mary to Fauriel   22 September 1822

. . . But my poor dear, if I were only free, I would hurry to your side. What good are words written on paper! A few caresses would do far more . . . although I must love you very much to share your grief for someone you were so fond of and yet never mentioned. (I still cannot understand that.) Forgive my last letter—I had not yet realised how unhappy you must be. . . . I can't bear you to be suffering and far away from me, with no one to pet you. It's not right for you to suffer. . . . Pain has done *me* good on occasion—I needed it to become anything at all, and had enough energy and animal spirits and to spare—I could lose half and still be lively. But you, my darling, are so melancholy, so tender, that you need happiness, to put life into you. . . . I can't explain why, but you have always struck me as a man who was resigned rather than happy. But perhaps I am wrong. . . .

Adieu. I love you with all my heart.[12]

Fauriel to Mary   Paris, September 1822

My dear loving friend, when I wrote of the misfortune threatening me, it was already certain; now it has happened. Afterwards I was taken into the country; now I have returned . . .

Do not scold me, I beg you, or wonder that I had not spoken to you of a person who meant so much to me. I do not know why, but I had taken it into my head that you already knew of it, at least vaguely—at least as much as you could need, or want, to know.

But the truth is that it was because I had too *many* fond hopes and plans that I postponed—only postponed—telling you of someone who meant too much to me to mean nothing to you . . . and you would have known all this long ago if you had remained in Paris. . . .

Ah, in losing this friend, I have lost the one person in the world to whom I could have spoken of you and been understood. What I wanted above all else in the world was to unite our three lives— or rather, our four lives.* But there's an end of my dream, and it is as though not I alone, but *we* have suffered this loss. . . . .[13]

Mme de Condorcet had died on 8 September. With her Fauriel lost not only the homes he had been used to for twenty years but his peace of mind for some time to come, for her relations (particularly her son-in-law General O'Connor, who disliked him both as a man and a legatee) took the occasion to declare publicly that he was far too easily consoled—had indeed provided himself with consolation beforehand in the shape of

---

* His own, Mme de Condorcet's, Mary's and her mother's.

Mary Clarke. Many believed this. Even those who, like Stendhal, did not, took an equally bleak view of the relationship:

> Fauriel had been the handsomest man in Paris. Mme de Condor-cet... a great connoisseur, took possession of him, the bourgeois Fauriel was simpleton enough to love her, and when she died . . . she left him 1200 francs a year, as if he had been a servant. He was profoundly humiliated. I told him . . . 'When one has to do with a princess or a woman who is too rich, one should beat her, or love fades away.' This remark horrified him. He repeated it, no doubt, to little Miss Clarke . . . and shortly afterwards she sent a booby of a friend of hers* to admonish me—after which I dropped her acquaintance.[14]

Meanwhile Fauriel, in a daze, allowed himself to be led away by Mme de Condorcet's daughter to her house at Bignon, where, however, her husband's hostility soon became intolerable. Then he drifted for a while to the house of Mme de Condorcet's sister, Mme Cabanis. Finally, he migrated to Victor Cousin's apartment, where his old friend Guizot eventually found him out.

When he again wrote to Mary, on 3 November, it was to reiterate his exclusive love for her and say that the only way of avoiding their present sadness in the future was 'never to part again—do you agree, my dar-ling?'[15] Yet through the autumn and winter, long after Mary's return to Paris and Fauriel's recovery, their marriage plans hung fire. It was all a mystery to Mary. Only by being married could they be together alone, travel together (Fauriel was already making tentative plans to pay a long visit to Manzoni in Milan), deliver Fauriel from his depression and his dreary lodgings. The solution to all their problems was so obvious; and yet Fauriel continued to leave himself vaguely uncommitted. His doubts seemed to be mainly concerned with money: he professed himself unable to subject her to the privations of a life on such an income as his.

Mary to Fauriel Spring 1823

My love, it took all my reason to stop myself from asking you to come to us today, as you did last year on just such a balmy day. . . . But perhaps even if you had come I should not have had the courage to say what I want to say, for it makes me appear so bold, though I am not, I assure you. . . .

Mama objects to the imprudence of travelling with you, staying in the same towns, returning at the same time, and positively courting gossip. . . . She says (to speak horribly plainly) that we *must* be married, at least before returning, if not before going. . . .

* Probably Thierry.

I'm sure that with the aid of tears I can make her do what I want. But where is the sense, dearest, in our running the risk of ruining my reputation, for the sake of your absurd scruples? Is it fair to me and my family? A Frenchman can have no idea of how the slightest breath of scandal would harm my family in England, particularly my niece who is just coming out. You don't know how it would grieve my sister, even if she and all the world knew there was not a word of truth in it. . . . I was ready to wait or to do whatever you liked, but if that [money] is the reason, I call it absurd! What if we are not rich!—we can both live! What I have will be more than enough for me, so you will be no worse off than you would have been if I had not existed.

You say you do not wish to until, etc.* But if we continue apart, you will continue sad and feeble. Far from hastening our union, a separation will delay it. One would think, to hear you talk, that our being together would hamper your work, whereas peace and harmony are just what you need for the purpose. Besides, even if you don't succeed, do you think I will love you one whit less!

But even if marriage were sure to be a distraction, and your scruples continued, what would be the result? Why, we should still be exactly as we are now: constantly racking our brains to find ways of being together, constantly being vexed when a third party is present, constantly wishing the summer away because it separates us, constantly being on our guard or out of spirits. . . . You would still be perpetually disturbed when you try to work in your lodgings, still have to snatch a few hours with me, still have to return at night, sad and alone. My love, I cannot bear to see you sad. It is because I see so clearly the life you lead that I have found the courage to write you this unwomanly letter. . . .

Dearest, believe me: you exaggerate the difficulties of life. In particular, you are unjust to both of us in thinking that either needs more money or more fame. Heavens! those gewgaws, that men set so much store by, matter very little when people are as happy together as we are! We have enough. It is almost indelicate of you to want more for me—as though I loved you so little. And after all the proofs I have given you . . . including a letter such as this! . . .

Adieu, my love.

Mary

* Until Fauriel had made himself financially secure by finishing his book.

And such a beautiful day, too! How can we torment ourselves so, with the sky so blue and the birds so cheerful! Is it not madness to separate, when our great regret is that we did not meet earlier. . . ?[16]

II

1823-1824
Travels

In the end Fauriel's motives were left unclarified, and Mary set off to travel in Switzerland with her mother and her old studio friend Adèle de Chalaze, now married to a Monsieur Cornillot. The Clarkes' plan was to drop down into Italy later and there join Fauriel, who might reasonably be expected to have done enough work on his Greek ballad collection (his current task) to allow himself the projected visit to Manzoni. But everything remained irksomely vague.

Mary to Fauriel   Berne, 8 September 1823

Switzerland bores me. . . . The mountains are just large white lumps, the lakes large deserts of water . . . and everything here is so cultivated—there is nothing wild or solitary. The whole country looks like a gentleman's park, and the people are as stupid as geese. . . .[1]

Mary to Fauriel   Zwei Lutchinen, 18 September 1823

. . . At nine in the morning we arrived at Thun, from which there is a superb view of the Alps, and I began to feel that my love of nature was not gone for ever. The lake is very fine—not quite as fine as the Scottish lochs, but near them. From Neuhaus we walked to Interlaken—to a wretched little inn which would only hire us an unsprung cart for the journey to Lauterbrun (three hours), and wanted us to pay nine francs for it! I was so indignant that I said we would rather walk. It was splendid weather—so, engaging a boy to carry our bags, off we went. And all along the way thanked our lucky stars for the unsprung cart—the valley was so beautiful! . . .

A charming girl came to meet us on the bridge at Osteig—she was the only one in the village who spoke French—to tell us that the innkeeper was moving house that day . . . but that she could give us eggs, milk, honey and fruit, if we could be content with that. . . . I was only too happy to dine in a cottage, instead of a rascally inn. . . . She keeps a school for forty-two little girls, and that day they were all out on the mountain-side, singing perfectly in tune—and in parts, too. Those who have the means pay thirty sous a month, those who do not (more than half) pay nothing. She teaches them French, needlework, reading and refinement. She will end by civilizing her village. . . .

At four we left her and came here to Zwei Lutchinen, where we shall spend the night—a good fifteen miles' walk in one day. But the scenery was so delightful that I was hardly tired at all. . . .

We were planning to sketch near the house and rest a little, but hardly had we been here half an hour than it settled to rain hard. Luckily, with the rain there came a wedding-party and a fiddle. We asked to see the dancing, and as they are very courteous here, they not only let us in but pressed us to join them. . . . I took some forget-me-nots off my hat to give the bride and so won her over that she half-coaxed, half-dragged me off to waltz with her. And I assure you, we acquitted ourselves very well! . . . Later the host and hostess joined us and executed a sort of pas de deux—with amazing grace and lightness, considering that they were both six feet tall and five feet round—a magnificent couple. They gave me great pleasure. . . .[2]

Fauriel to Mary   [September] 1823

. . . What can I tell you about myself? I am much lowered, now that you are away. . . . I think of going into the country for a few days, if only to get away from these Greek songs, which rain down on my head from the unlikeliest quarters. Piccolo . . . has sent me four, two reached me yesterday from Wallachia. . . . They will be coming at me from China, if I do not get matters in hand. . . .[3]

Greece's struggle to free herself from Turkish domination was capturing the imagination of all western Europe at this time: Byron was about to join the Greek insurgents, Delacroix was to paint the Massacre at Scio in 1824, and 139 books of verse on Greek themes were published in France in six years; 1829 was, according to Delécluze, dominated by the Greek question. Fauriel was among the first to write on the subject and, despite the fact that he resented the task as an intrusion into his 'real' work on Provence, he did it well. In the 1860s Victor Cousin wrote to Sainte-Beuve: 'I feel a kind of remorse at not having insisted more urgently, in the 1820s, on Fauriel's abandoning his great historical work,

to which he was but ill suited, and devoting himself with his whole heart
to the primitive, spontaneous, popular poetry of all ages and countries.
There lay his genius, his taste, his true vocation.'⁴ His book was followed
by a spate of ballad-collections from other outlandish regions—and
eventually pastiches. It is ironic that Mérimée's cod 'Illyrian ballads', *La
Guzla* (1827), are probably the only relic of this whole movement still
known to non-specialists.

Fauriel to Mary   Paris, 10 September 1823

   . . . Yesterday I received a letter from Schlegel telling me of
another publication similar to mine, which is about to appear in
Germany. Its author is a baron—a friend of Schlegel's and a man
with a fine mind. He has asked Schlegel to offer me some verses in
exchange for some of mine that he needs. I want nothing to do with
the business; it will delay me still further. This wretched German
is yet another thorn in my flesh, and I have no one here now to pull
out my thorns and replace them with balm and flowers. . . .⁵

Mary to Fauriel   20 September 1823

   . . . For my part, I don't think your German *is* a thorn in the
flesh. He writes in German, you in French. He has certain songs,
you others. All these people occupying themselves with Greek
songs only go to prove that the subject is arousing interest, and far
from harming each other's causes, they will help them, in my
opinion. I have heard a London bookseller say that was usually the
case: the more that was written on a subject (especially when it was
fresh), the greater the public's appetite for it. But the first writings
are always the best, so finish your book as quickly as possible, and
don't on any account enter on exchanges with German barons.⁶

She ordered him to write his introduction 'on the road, in inns, on
mountains, anywhere'⁷, and leave the proofs to be corrected by his
publishers, otherwise 'we may say goodbye to our visit, for you will be
sure to correct the text too, and will take three months over it.'⁸ Nearly
every letter contained trenchant advice on routes, times, passports. Re-
garding the last, he must not be put off by any difficulties made by the
police, she wrote (knowing that they were probably reading the words),
for they were 'pigs, and not worth changing any of one's plans for.' 'I
hope they *do* open this letter,' she wrote at them, 'because eavesdroppers
never hear any good of themselves, and they will of course send it on to

1. Self-portrait of Mary Clarke in 1831

2. Claude Fauriel as a young man

you in any case, because they will feel in honour bound to show that they are a little less scoundrelly than I think.'[9]

Mary to Fauriel   Vevey, 24 September 1823

. . . You were right: Switzerland *is* very beautiful . . . and I should not judge from first impressions. . . . But dear me, if I don't, I forget, or cool down so much that everything is dead as a doornail. I suppose one should never speak out at all—that's the only way of never saying anything one don't mean. I suppose that's why you are so silent. . . .[10]

Mary to Fauriel   Geneva, 15 October 1823

. . . You are a bold man to ask what you can do for me. First: go to Chalopin's, at no. 7 Rue Vivienne, and buy me a pair of black velvet slippers, lined. Choose a pretty lining. I enclose a paper sole—choose them too long rather than too short, but as near as possible. They should cost between twelve and fifteen francs. Then go to our apartment, ask Louise for a trunk which is in my bedroom—the key is inside, the rope on top—shut and rope the trunk yourself, and bring it with you, taking care not to lose the key. . . .

If you had not been deprived of my company for two months you would grumble like an old soldier at having to do all this, but as you know you will be repaid with kisses, you will bear it patiently—even enjoy it. . . .[10]

On 19 October, before setting off for Italy, Fauriel made his will, appointing Mary his executrix and making her responsible for handling all his unpublished papers. But in the end he did not get to the Manzonis until January 1824, and Mary, who arrived with her mother in Milan at the same time, found her stay something less than the paradise to which she had been looking forward. It was not the fault of the Manzonis, who took to her at once and became lifelong friends. 'We spent most of our time there playing blind-man's buff with Pietro and Giulietta and Madame Manzoni,' she later told a biographer[12] of Manzoni, who had been hoping for more dignified memories. 'Madame Manzoni, having married at sixteen, was almost a playmate of her older children. Manzoni enjoyed these games as much as we did, but did not join in; he talked with M. Fauriel and my mother.'[13]

But there was still very little opportunity of being alone with Fauriel, and there was—now that she had an opportunity of observing him regularly at close quarters—a gallantry in his manner to other ladies that maddened her, particularly as he professed himself unaware of it. 'You will never understand why I was so unhappy, or believe that you could have prevented it,' she protested. 'You are like Mama, like everybody—for almost everybody means to be kind, but they will try to make others happy after *their* fashion and not their own.'[14] Again and again, during the Clarkes' subsequent tour of the rest of Italy, she struggled with disappointment with herself, her restlessness, her discontent with a life spent haggling with shopkeepers and innkeepers for her mother's benefit, the absence of an 'engrossing occupation' to take her mind off her miseries and suspicions. It took an effort of will to keep up her ebullience. Despite all, she set herself the task of learning Italian.

Mary to Fauriel   Florence, 23 May 1824

... I had a lucky find in the stage coach—an admirer who knew no French but made me a declaration, and ogled me, and passed me a *billet doux*, and who knows what besides. Unfortunately, he had to leave two days after we arrived here, but he hopes to come to Rome to see me. ... You may well believe that I was anything but severe with him. I shall welcome all *soupirants* who know no French, be they bandy, hunchbacked or one-eyed. But, as a matter of fact, this one was very handsome and clever, and (for an Italian) well-read. He's very fond of Manzoni. ... But his head is as full of *le donne* as a Spaniard's is of fleas. He told me that he had had nineteen love affairs—and he is only twenty-two! And that he had found no one capable of fixing him before me. Nineteen women, dear heaven! and the man has the impertinence to tell me about them and picture me as the twentieth! ... But he was very honest and amiable ... I read him a good sermon, in well-chosen Italian, on having nothing more to do with *le donne*, not even myself. But it is to be hoped my sermonizing will have the usual success of such endeavours, and we shall meet again. ...

Goodbye, dear Dicky.* Twice since we parted I have been on the point of returning to Paris—nearer it than I have ever been before. I cannot live without companionship—it's a misfortune and a cruel dependency. I could if I had an occupation which I liked and which tired me out at the same time. But how can I, when half my energy is used up in haggling with innkeepers! The sad fact is that I am more restless, irritable and fidgety than truly energetic. Before this wretched journey I thought better of myself than I

---

* Her nickname for Fauriel.

deserved—that's my sad discovery. But it's not Italy's fault—I don't hate Italy, only myself. . . .[14a]

Mary to Fauriel   Rome, 4 June 1824

. . . There were many letters waiting for me here. Adèle tells me that M. Thierry is correcting your proofs, but that he's hurt at the lack of letters from you. She says too that you have not written to Cousin and others who have sent you many letters. No doubt they are now curl-papers for some lady in Brusuglio, for all the genius of their writers. . . .

We are lodging with two excellent ladies—not very clean, but fond of me. It's as though we've known each other these ten years. They speak not a word of French, and I make them chat from morning to night. . . . The truth is, I like Catholics better than Protestants—much better. These two good ladies go to Mass every morning and confession once a week and are as happy as sandboys. Heavens! If faith were to be bought, I'd sell my last shift for it. These ladies are neither young, nor beautiful, nor witty, nor learned, nor rich, nor loved (by lovers), and yet they are ten times happier than I, who am charming and could have a dozen lovers if I wished—and ten times better too. . . .[15]

Mary to Fauriel   Rome, 17 June 1824

. . . Today I saw His Holiness and a whole procession of all the monks imaginable, and was much entertained. All were clean and washed—which is not always the case. If they sold their fine laces and bought some soap, it would be no bad thing. After them came the finest horses and riders in the world—the horses tossing their heads, champing their bits and pawing the ground. . . . All Rome was there, and the cannons rang out—it was superb! I love ceremonies, they are much more amusing than Martin Luther. . . .

Oh, Rome is delightful! Italy only begins at Florence, say I. That's where the air becomes bright as silver and everyone starts spending all their time in the street and you begin to see pine-trees like parasols and evergreen oaks with beautiful shapes, just as Claude Lorrain painted them. Oh, the landscapes in Tuscany and near Rome! The Tuscan ones are just as I picture Arcadia, and the Roman ones so majestic! And the Coliseum—all covered with greenery and birds, with a nest of nightingales in every hole that some Vandal once made! And they speak ill of the Vandals! And yet thousands of creatures now live peacefully in a place once used only for killing—black-beetles, moles, all sorts of things. I think the Coliseum is what I like best in this beautiful city; it is so peaceful, only peasants come by. . . .

St Peter's is the worst piece of architecture in Rome, if you think of its expense. . . . It should make ten times the effect it does, particularly the interior—from inside the dome looks no bigger than any other. All in all, it's a failure . . . or at least a very flawed masterpiece. . . .

But there's a temple—which they use as a customs house, the monsters!—which is quite another matter. I gasped and stared when I saw such a superb building as we approached Rome. Then I came up close to it and saw it was—a customs house! I was so vexed that when they wished us a good journey after examining our boxes, I said there would be no good journeys till all the customs men were dead and buried. But they did not mind—they are used to insults. . . .[17]

Mary to Fauriel   Rome, 30 June (?) 1824

. . . My Prussian admirer makes me laugh fit to burst (I don't show it). He is convinced that women are poor little things to be kept in leading-reins, and I lead him by the nose and let him say all his follies. At first I felt some remorse at my arrant coquetry, but since I have made out his creed I have grown more callous than I ever thought I could be. I have been hard on one or two men in my lifetime, to pay them back for their impertinence on this subject. . . . It's my religion, my politics, my 1789, the passion of my life. . . .[18]

Mary to Fauriel   Naples, 21 July 1824

. . . One day, when I was walking in the Monte Pincio gardens in Rome, I met an artist I knew in Paris, who joined us like an old friend. . . . How singular it is that French and Italian painters are stupid and uncultivated, while German and English ones are clever and companionable—and produce daubs. But not all of them, perhaps. I have made acquaintance with another who is full of talent. . . . We were looking at the Raphael rooms in the Vatican, where he was copying the pictures. He answered in English when I asked him something in Italian, and in a moment we were conversing like old friends. I told him how vexed I was not to be able to work in the Vatican, and he said: 'Nothing easier! Come tomorrow—let's go and ask permission of the Majordomo together.' I went, got permission—and there I was, perched fifteen feet up in the air, perfectly happy. . . .[19]

Mary to Fauriel   Naples, 17 August 1824

. . . Oh, the other day, I brought out a capital piece of eloquence, in Italian too, to get a baby unswaddled somewhere near Naples. Poor creature, it was crying fit to deafen you, and was only a fortnight old, and the heat was terrific. We adults could hardly bear our loose clothes—and there the baby lay,—bound, wound, imprisoned. As soon as he was unswaddled he was all smiles and happiness. My young English painter, whom I adore, tells me he has done the same thing for at least a hundred babies in the three years he has been in Italy. . . .[20]

Fauriel, still in pursuit of Greek ballads, had made a visit to Trieste, where his friend, the refugee Mustoxidi, helped him to look for possible sources. It was not easy: 'Respectable Greeks know no ballads—Heaven forbid!—while the poor devils who do know any are refugees tucked away in miserable corners where they are not easy to find. Moreover, they are hard at work all day. It is not easy, either, to convince them that one is not making fun of them by asking to hear their folk songs.'[21] Altogether he was disenchanted: 'In future I shall only devote time to such work when I have nothing more serious to do, by way of relaxation.'[22]

Despite his trials, however, he was still expressing ardent love for Mary. In Venice he returned to the inn where he and the Clarkes had stayed, and wandered the corridors 'choking and inexpressibly conscious of your absence.'[23] On his return to Brusuglio he could not stop himself from being 'indiscreet' to the Manzonis, so strong were his feelings; 'They had suspected what I feel for you, and now they know all, clearly and distinctly. I told them that I love you, with all my heart. I told them of our plans for the future—without hiding my doubts as to whether I have the capacity to make you happy, which I desire more than to be happy myself. They were not shocked by these confidences, nor did they seem to make much of my doubts—you might have primed them on the subject!'[24]

His financial problems were indeed pressing, the more so since in March 1824 General O'Connor actually accused him of tampering with

Mme de Condorcet's estate, and threatened him with a lawsuit which might end in his losing her legacy. So far from considering that legacy a 'profound humiliation', as Stendhal had airily asserted, he looked on it as a 'sacred right', and indeed needed it badly, but had no stomach for a fight. 'If I followed my own inclinations, all would be easily dealt with: I would simply let the low, sordid pettifogger have what he claims, and consider it a small price to pay for removing his deeds from my consciousness.' Moreover, his instincts told him he would lose in any such fight, 'having a delicate conscience, rights which are moral rather than legal, and an adversary bent on the grossest, most odious chicanery. . . . But it will in no way affect my plans or happiness. Nor will it make me love you any the less. . . . It will only mean, perhaps, that I need to work rather harder and faster, and there is no harm in that—it may even be good for me. . . . I have always been too ready, perhaps, to submit to the charms of independence and a kind of proud laziness—to be scornful of worldly goods, which are not to be altogether despised.'[25]

Whether there was any truth, technical or moral, in O'Connor's allegation was never established. At all events, he never pursued the affair.

As if all this were not enough, Fauriel's health too was giving cause for concern. For some time Mary had been urging him, with her usual matter-of-factness, to seek treatment for a nasal polyp: 'I am not as foolish as you—*I* do not suffer for months without at least trying to get rid of the pain.'[26] In September 1824 he at last agreed to undergo the operation, no small matter for a man of fifty-two in a period long before the introduction of effective anaesthesia. 'I have kept my word to you,' he wrote afterwards, 'and made the effort to get rid of the ugly excrescence you pointed out. . . . Now I have only to take certain precautions against its reappearance. . . . If you still hope to spend the winter in Florence . . . and if I may flatter myself that I still mean anything to you, I shall set off to join you and be happy.'[27]

Mary to Fauriel   Saturday, I don't know the date, 1824

. . . My dearest, how can you say 'If I may flatter myself that I still mean anything to you!' Who governs all my actions, if not you? Who is the beginning, middle and end of everything for me? I know I wrote that I loved you less now, but *primo* I am not at all sure that it's true: it is when I am vexed with you that I think so— and then I have a sort of devilish satisfaction in hurting you. . . . I know that's wicked; henceforth I mean to keep my mind always occupied, so as to have no time to torment you. For if I don't, I can't promise not to torment you again—I know myself too well. . . .

My dear love, that horrible growth would have become impossible for you to bear in a few years. Think how much it had grown in a year! It hurts me that you can believe I would have you suffer so much out of a mere whim about your appearance. . . .[28]

Mary to Fauriel   Tivoli, 26 August 1824

. . . We have been here for eight or nine days and it has rained on every one of them since the second, so that I could not finish the picture I had started, which vexes me greatly, for I had rather draw landscapes than be Prime Minister. . . .

My dear, your Greek ballads will soon be finished, and you are the only man in Europe who has taken up your pen on their behalf—at least the only one who has done it on a grand scale. They are so interesting, pray believe me, that if I could help them on by sewing (my only marketable skill), I would do it!—and I hate sewing. . . .

Luckily Mama has made the acquaintance of a painter's wife who is as bored here as she is, and they keep each other company. If she had not, I could see that we might have to leave, and was cursing my fate and the miserable prison in which it has pleased God to shut me up. For tell me: if I were a man, would it be necessary for Mama and me to be always shackled together? I tell you: if I were asked 'Would you rather be a woman or a galley-slave?', wouldn't I volunteer for the galleys! . . .[29]

Mary to Fauriel   28 September 1824

Dear love, I am extremely anxious about you. This is the twelfth day without a letter, and I am tormented beyond words by the fear that there has been some dreadful consequence of your operation. . . .

The Italians are right to drown their sensibility in libertinage (if it's true that they do). What is the use of having feelings so strong that they make you suffer, and others too! The Italians hurt no one. They are the kindest people in the world, as I can see with my own eyes.

We are lodging with a doctor of laws, in a very fine house. He has a wife, as kind as can be, who—to my great joy—has a *cavaliere servente*. I see no harm in it!—although if I were the *signora*, I would prefer my husband to the *cavaliere*. There is also a Sicilian count . . . not very talkative; in fact, he never opens his mouth, so as to look deep. In addition there's a Spaniard, round as a ball, very fond of his dinner, very good natured. . . .

There! in writing I have forgotten my fears. . . . But it takes only four days for a letter to reach Milan—why have I received no reply, though I begged you to write, or get someone to write for you? If you are *not* ill, you are the greatest wretch in the world. . . .[30]

Fauriel remained as dilatory as he was with all his correspondents. In the deepest of her depressions—when he revealed that he would not even be returning to Paris on the date he had planned, but must first travel in Provence for the sake of his book ('the great affair of my life'), which would take another year—she allowed her feelings to drown her judgment altogether, and wildly accused him of caring nothing for her feelings and concealing his intentions from her. 'Tell me: if you had to give up either literature or me for ever, what would you do? If you would choose literature, there is no point in your joining us—I would rather never see you again. God knows how I would bear that. But I would rather be chopped into pieces than come second to anything in the world.'[31]

Fauriel to Mary   25 October 1824

 . . . I hardly know how to set about . . explaining what you used to understand and even approve. It is true that I attach the greatest importance to my work on the History of Provençal Poetry. For some fifteen years I have devoted myself to it, dreamed of it, promised my friends—all those who wished me well and have a better idea of my capacity than it may deserve—to bring it to a successful conclusion. . . .

But since you force me to write it, fame is by no means the only motive for my determination to continue. There is the small matter of earning my living. . . . I see no other way of doing that than by publishing at least a part of the work as soon as possible. I should have been only too happy to need only the glory, and offer it all to you. . . .

My dearest one, despite all your unjust accusations and constant anger—which make *me* angry, in spite of myself—allow me to make my very last attempt to justify myself. I have loved you since I first met you, and without ever reflecting whether, in all my circumstances, it was wise or foolish to do so. . . . Your lively mind and warm heart aroused in me a feeling that I have never experienced for anyone else and did not think I was capable of feeling. . . . But now the mistrust of myself, and the fear aroused by your accusations and your confession that you have changed towards me, leave me no illusions. . . .[32]

Despite these emotional crises, however, their real, underlying intimacy was never threatened: in this very month, when Mary was pushing emotional explanations towards the brink of disaster, Fauriel was still amiably interested, and informative, about her intellectual projects.

. . . So now you are taking up political economy! I am heartily glad of it, if it interests you. If you continue with it, you will soon know all the objections which have been raised since time immemorial, and which are still being raised, against machines. And you will realise that not one of those arguments holds water or deserves the slightest attention. As for steam engines, I have not calculated how much wood they consume; but without calculating, I can assure you that a steam engine consumes far less *space* and far fewer *agricultural products* than would the men needed to produce the same quantity of work. Moreover steam pumps are run on materials dug out of the earth, not produced on its surface; and they will soon be run on gas, as they already are in England. . . .[33]

Mary, for her part, never allowed the dramatic side of the relationship to obscure for long the reality of her affection. However wild her occasional outbursts, she always knew that she was intimate enough with Fauriel to scold him (as she did on 17 August 1824) about his taste in dress and convince him that he would never really be abandoned by her.

. . . I hope you have left your execrable peaked cap in Trieste, for when I picture you in it I am quite disenchanted and can't believe you are the same man I met three years ago. I know it's wicked of me to care so much about your appearance, and I have tried as hard as I could to change myself. But there! I cannot do it. I would rather you wrote a book that was stupid than wore that cap.—Perhaps it is because I am so convinced that you are the cleverest, most able man in France that I have no worries on that score—you cannot be angry with me for that.[34]

III

1825–1826
Frustration

Late in 1824 the Clarkes returned to Paris, leaving Fauriel still at work in Italy. The following summer they made their customary visit to England.

Mary to Fauriel   11 June 1825

. . . Some very interesting things are happening here, my dear. The working people have invented some institutes [the Mechanics' Institutes] where they attend evening lectures on the sciences, such as chemistry, mechanics and mathematics. They pay for these out of their own money, although they were helped a little at the beginning. It all started in Glasgow in 1800—it is only in the last three years that other towns have followed. There was a poor working man in Edinburgh who walked ten miles to every evening lecture—and remember, they work all day. . . .

I have read part of M. Thierry's book.* The introduction is very good, but he is too much committed to a single idea—the three volumes are all full of it. I like more variety. And I like to see the whole fabric of history, not a single thread, however strong. He is a man of talent, but his book does not engross me: I know in advance that every fact will be there to prove a certain proposition—not to show a mass of people living a life quite different from my own. That is what I look for in books—to be introduced to lives quite different from my own—mine bores me to distraction. Is that wrong? Tell me, Dicky dear, you who are wise above all men, and always right—*nearly* always right—except where women are concerned. . . .[1]

In her previous letter she had complained, not for the first time, of her sister's earnestness. The Evangelicals at Cold Overton, like others of similar mind throughout Britain, were now abjuring white sugar, as a gesture against slavery in the West Indies.

---

* His *History of the Norman Conquest* (1825), in the preparation of which Fauriel had played such a sympathetic part.

Fauriel to Mary 24 June 1825

. . . So you are condemned to Demerara sugar, my dear. You seem to think that very heroic, and I will gladly agree with you, if that will give you any comfort. But for my part I cannot think of anything more like sugar than Demerara. . . .[2]

Mary to Fauriel Cold Overton, 7 September 1825

. . . Don't, on any account, cut short your visit so as to return to me sooner. A fortnight, or three weeks, or even four, are not much after six or seven months, whereas they may be important to your book. I have just received your letter—only the third after five months of separation, but you see I have not blamed you once; I was sure you had written. . . .

I am so sorry you are low-spirited, my dearest. But reflect that nearly half our separation is now over—that even if your work is difficult it will come to an end at some time—and that nothing in the world is achieved without effort, not even a hat or a dinner. . . .

But Heavens! if it's money you need, take mine! Joséphine has a thousand francs of mine lying absolutely idle in her bureau—I have so little need of it that I told her to keep it the day before we left Paris. I lent five hundred francs to M. Thierry, who must have paid it back since then. . . . That's fifteen hundred francs that I don't need in the slightest. Do write straight away, so as to lose no time, either to me or to Joséphine. . . .

I hardly know how time passes here. I have my tasks. I am painting a full-length portrait of my sister. I have translated a little of your Greek book—and *added three pages of my own*!—the whole to be put in a little magazine concerned with the slavery question. Heaven knows what a jumble I have made of your work, but as no one will know of it but my family, and you will never see it, I don't care. I only tell you so that you shall not lose all hope of ever seeing me in print.

In addition I read, study, teach French to the children. Altogether I am calm for the present and full of hope for the future. . . .[3]

A month later Fauriel, delayed by shortage of funds, was still at Brusuglio. He still hoped to be able to finish his travels in the Midi by the end of November, but on the way he would have to visit Hyères, where

Thierry, who was suffering from syphilis, was taking sea-baths in an attempt to stave off his increasing blindness and paralysis.

Mary to Fauriel   Cold Overton, 19 October 1825

... I am not surprised that your letter comes from Milan. I know you by now. When you mention a date of departure, I always add on a good long stretch. ...

As to M. Thierry, he has got no benefit from his travels because he would not listen to my advice—he's a fool, and don't know good advice when he hears it. ...

And whenever you don't follow my advice, *you* will regret it too, and I hope you will suffer for it. And what is more, I shall not have the smallest sympathy. ...

I have bought you a charming umbrella, mounted in ivory. It is as light as a feather and will stop you ever catching cold, for you will never go out without it. ...

Adieu, my dear love. I love you in spite of all your follies. I love you, my dearest, I love you.[4]

By November, when the Clarkes returned to Paris, Fauriel had still not completed his researches in the south of France. Suddenly, whether out of pique, frustration, or pride, Mary lost her balance completely. Forty years later she gave Mary Simpson an airily insouciant account of her youthful affairs: 'I was always an arrant coquette, whether in France or England, and am sorry to say the only wise thing is to be a coquette in youth, because it is the only means of self-defence. I think those that are *not* are much gooder, but if I was born an animal and consulted before-hand, I should choose not to be a lamb but a cat, with good claws to defend myself. I have had some pretty sharp practice all my life in England, France, Germany and Italy, and know more of the men folk than most women. I had five admirers at a time once, and could compare, besides seeing more men than women all my youth. I have a strong sense of justice on the subject and much tenderness for my own poor sex.'[5]

In the '20s, without benefit of hindsight, she was considerably less in command of the situation.

The man she fixed on in 1825 was Fauriel's old friend Cousin, who had recently (from October 1824 to March 1825) been in a Dresden jail, accused of conspiracy against the reactionary government there; he had only been released after strenuous efforts by his fellow-philosopher Hegel. Perhaps this dramatic episode influenced her; Cousin was not, by several accounts, the obvious candidate for a bout of therapeutic coquetry.

Delécluze, for example, found him 'the most disagreeable over-actor of my acquaintance. . . . He has acquired the habit of talking always as though to an audience hanging on his lightest words'[6]; Delacroix and Grant Duff both found him insufferable; even Mérimée, who in later life enjoyed his company, had to admit that he was pompous.[7]

'Remember,' Mary later adjured Fauriel, 'that it was after Venice, after Mme B—, after you had been absent for nine months, for four of which I had been waiting for you in Paris—and imagine how my blood was up, how much I hated you.—And remember too that I loved you so much that I told you everything afterwards, regardless of the cost. . . .'[8] At the time her motives were painfully unclear.

Mary's journal   Paris, 29 December 1825

. . . How can I control my imagination? I pray—but without faith, work—but without interest. What will become of me when I am old? . . .

Two days more and the year will be ended—what shall I be in a year's time? More reasonable? I pray that it may be so. All my sufferings come from my wild passions and imaginings. God give me grace to control them.

I see only one way of changing myself for good—if I were to renounce all vanity and sentimental complications, retire to the country, and devote myself to nothing but work. How well I understand the Carthusians, Trappists and Carmelites! If I were married, perhaps I should be happier. But I fear not—my imagination is insatiable. I have almost everything I could desire, and yet a few little wants make me dissatisfied! . . .

Cousin looks as though he could love . . . but is it right to turn to Cousin? Am I not committed elsewhere? . . .

Perhaps the theatre will distract me this evening. I *must* drive these horrible speculations from my mind. . . .[9]

31 December 1825

. . . Today I forced myself to go to the Louvre and work with more application than I have shown since I left Cold Overton, and felt a little better. . . . Joséphine came back with me to dinner. With a great effort I managed to speak to the porter, but it was not worth it and I was exhausted for the whole evening. . . .

Why can I not live entirely in books and ideas? . . .[10]

2 January 1826

... I draw, I read—but beneath all there is always a deep
melancholy.... I deserve some dreadful punishment....

Mme Belloc came yesterday evening.... It is curious how
nobody notices that I am ill with melancholy. I don't speak of it,
but I know very well that it's true....[11]

4 January 1826

... Why do I like Cousin so much? He lacks Manzoni's beautiful
candour and Fauriel's elegance and reasonableness.... Indeed he
makes a rather mannered effect—but no, that cannot be right. Last
night we came near to quarrelling. According to him, affection is a
purely nervous thing.... I did not collect myself quickly enough
to say that the nerves are only the instruments of the mind....[12]

Before January was out she had decided that she was, after all, passionately in love with Cousin, and he with her. When Fauriel finally returned
to Paris, after yet another delay, caused this time by floods in Provence,
he found her poised for attack. He was cold, he was cruel, he contradicted
her in public, he had no sympathy with her sufferings, whereas she had
rushed to France to be at his side after Mme de Condorcet's death. In
short, he had never loved her and she only wished he would declare it
candidly and put an end to her illusions.

Fauriel, for his part, had problems of a more practical nature to cope
with. His work continued to be demanding, and in addition he had to
find somewhere to live and could afford only a very modest rent. At first
he moved into an *hôtel garni* in the Rue Croix des Petits Champs, then,
when even this proved too expensive, into cramped quarters suitable for
a student, at 47 Rue de Verneuil.[13] For a distinguished man of fifty-four
his lot was not easy. The only 'home' now available to him was the
Clarkes' apartment, and for the rest of his life he continued to spend some
part of nearly every evening there throughout the winter and spring; the
correspondence was now confined to the summers and autumns, when
Mary was usually in England and Fauriel often in Provence or at some
watering-place. It was a curious situation. In some ways Mary and Fauriel
were very nearly as intimate as a married couple; they saw each other
almost as regularly, knew each other's minds on almost every subject,
bullied each other—or rather, in Fauriel's case, accepted bullying—on
matters of dress, health and irritating mannerisms. On the other hand,
they still rarely saw each other alone and in private. Mary could not, of
course, go to his rooms, and the usual difficulties about meeting in public
still obtained. Fauriel's feelings remain obscure. Mary was still always

ostensibly the vivacious hostess to the friends who gathered at 13 Quai Malaquais, where the Clarkes now lived, but privately she continued to seethe and suffer, particularly in this dark period of 1825–6.

The only book that suited her was *Werther*. For a time Cousin seemed to love her—'embraced her tenderly, sat with her head resting on his shoulder . . . repeating her name over and over again, as if simply saying it were an unspeakable pleasure.'[14] Then once again she lost her self-control. He refused an invitation of hers because of a previous engagement; she begged him to come and accused him of all kinds of treacheries, and none of her later apologies could restore the romance to life.

Whan next they met, by chance, in the Jardin du Luxembourg, they 'spoke of Fauriel. He said he was very fond of him, even if he did not think like him on every question. Fauriel, he said, was very fond of me— much fonder than he, Cousin, could be of anyone. . . . When I told him that Fauriel had loved me for three years *sans passion*, he seemed to envy him. "Yes," said he, "Fauriel has waited long to find someone who could arouse such feelings in him. I shall never find anyone."'[15]

After more humiliating quarrels, she turned back to Fauriel for comfort.

Mary's journal   23 April 1826

. . . 'The trouble is,' I told him, 'that I have a perpetual need for pleasure.' He said that I did not know what pleasure was . . . that I only understood intellectual pleasures, that I was a stick (but the dearest stick in the world), that kisses only mattered to me because they expressed affection.

I was astonished to be called a stick. If I am one, it's a stick which is on fire. 'That's true,' he said, 'but you are a mass of contradictions.' I tried to prove to him that it is the *excess* of passion in my nature that turns me into what he calls a stick; but he did not understand. 'And it's pride which makes me despise the sensual side of love. But I am no more a stick than any other woman.' But he maintained that it was constitutional with me—my pride, etc. merely helped. . . .

I left him at noon, spent the rest of the day painting in the Louvre, and sank into the deepest depression. . . .[16]

Mary's journal   5 May 1826

. . . On Wednesday I went to Mme Belloc's, resigned to an evening of *ennui*. After half an hour Cousin came in . . . and sat down next to me. We chatted for a little, and for a moment I was at peace. But he is not the same. I know it is my fault: it is I who have ruined our intimacy, with my headstrong folly. After an hour he left, under the pretext of seeing Fauriel at Mme de Broglie's, but really to avoid seeing me home. . . .

And yet he *did* love me. I cannot have imagined all he said . . . or those times when he could hardly suffer me to cross the room because I would be away for a moment. And even if I may have exaggerated these things, Jacques said it was so . . . and Cousin's best friend said he was madly in love with me. . . . The truth is that it is his sense of duty that has changed him. Even at the time when he cared most about me he said once: 'Mary, our fate is written on marble, on bronze: we cannot abandon Fauriel—it would be the basest ingratitude.' That's true; I could not deny it. . . .

But oh, I did not preserve my dignity with him—I said too clearly how much I loved him, I was too carried away, I asked him too often if he loved me. . . .

One must control oneself. This morning I suddenly caught a glimpse of Cousin's conduct and mine, as it were from a distance and by surprise. He never loved me passionately (but he did love me, I'm sure). . . . He saw that I was not able to be the friend he wanted, and so broke everything off. . . . If I had not written those dreadful letters, all could be as at first. I cannot express what I feel when I think of that. Oh, I'm convulsed with pain. . . . If pain could only kill, I would be glad of it.[17]

Fortunately, in this year she had also made another new acquaintance, of a post-Wertherian generation and wholly un-Wertherian temperament. This was Julius Mohl, then twenty-six, an Orientalist from Würtemberg, who had come to Paris in 1823 with his two brothers to pursue his studies at the Collège de France, which then had the only school of advanced oriental studies in Europe. The two brothers—Robert, who became a distinguished jurist and politician, and Moritz, who distinguished himself equally in economics—eventually went back to Germany. Julius, however, stayed in Paris, and gradually made himself the first expert on Persian in France—possibly in the whole of Europe. When he was only twenty-six the French government, in the grip of the passion for scholarship which has been mentioned above, entrusted him with the first European edition and translation of the *Shah Nameh*, the famous epic poem of Firdusi[18].

He was a quiet man, who made a point, in the febrile society in which he found himself, of being undramatic, unemotional. Where others threw themselves into complicated attitudes to express their ecstasy at music, he claimed to dislike it. Where J. J. Ampère, with whom he shared bachelor lodgings for sixteen years, was 'passionate, impulsive, demonstrative and restless'[19], he was 'quiet and self-contained' and, as Mary Simpson says, without sexual intention, 'played the part, in their ménage, of the careful housewife.' Clever, reliable, and dryly amusing, he was a welcome addition to the Clarkes' circle, and, like Fauriel, spent almost every evening at their home, from 1826 onwards.

IV

1826–1829

'*I'm going to read a great deal and work at everything*'

After the crisis of 1825–6 Mary sank back into the old routine of her life. There were no more journeys to Italy or Scotland, and the prospect of enjoying complete happiness while travelling with Fauriel—or even of travelling with him at all—must now have seemed remote. Her winters and springs in Paris were interesting and amusing; her circle of friends and her reputation as a witty personality grew constantly, and in the next three years she was able to read, as they came out, the early works of such literary revolutionaries as Vigny, Hugo, Mérimée, Balzac, and Stendhal (if she could bring herself to read anything by the last-named). In her Paris life she also had the almost daily pleasure of conversations with Fauriel. But during the summer months she was annually forced back on her own resources and such small diversions as could be made to brighten life at Cold Overton. In her letters the summers of 1826, 1827, 1828 and 1829 follow each other like beads on a string—each little different from the one before, none offering any greater hope of a radical change in Mary's situation. She clutched at scholarship, to save herself from this frustrating sameness, but even scholarship had its frustrations.

On the 1826 journey from Paris to Leicestershire she was accompanied by her sister, who had been travelling in Europe.

Mary to Fauriel   Abbeville, 7 June 1826

. . . We spent all Sunday here, because it is of course a *crime* to travel on Sunday. On Saturday evening my sister ferreted out some English people whom she did not know from Adam or Eve, in her anxiety to find out if there were a Protestant church. For my part, I was perfectly easy on the subject. Then it turned out that these very people were in the habit of holding a service, complete with sermon, in their dining-room. In our great haste to profit from such a magnificent opportunity, my cat was lost. When I came back and discovered the loss, I burst first into tears and then into a rage.

My sister said the maids at the inn had let her out on purpose, I turned everything upside down, the whole house was in an uproar as we miaowed our way upstairs and downstairs. In the end the maids were told that if the cat was not found, they would not get a sou, and despair reigned in every breast. And at about six in walked Pussy from I know not where, and my shrieks subsided. . . .

I am reading M. Quatremère's *Essay on nature, the aim and means of imitation in the fine arts.* There are some good things in it, and others less good attacking the Romantics. It has already given me the embryos of several ideas which I can feel growing in my head, and which will have been born and left home before I see you again. . . . If I can lay my hand on some paper at a suitable moment, I shall pin them down for posterity and you. . . .

The supporters of Classicism are strange folk. You would think, to hear them, that there had been no one but Greeks in the world, and that everything that is different from them is nonsense. This is what I read yesterday morning: 'What, then, is the style known as Classical? Quite simply, the style which has dominated the world for the last two or three millennia, which has been the model for all the peoples of modern Europe, and in which every admired work has been created.' Now that shows gross ignorance!—grosser ignorance even than mine, for I have at least heard of Sanskrit and Arabic. Secondly, even if it were true, it is only one instance, which does not prove a principle, and as he started by basing his argument on immutable principles of the human mind, what business has he to fall back on a trifle of three thousand years to prove what should only be proved by the nature of things! . . .

I am going to read a great deal and work at everything. I'm already better in mind than when I was in Paris, where there was far too much excitement for me. . . .[1]

Mary to Fauriel   Cold Overton, 23 June 1826

. . . I was to leave here on Wednesday morning, but learned on Tuesday that they were still polling at two places in London and was so eager to see it that I told my sister to leave without me—I would follow in the stage-coach on Thursday. And off I went to the Guildhall, where they were electing the city member. I was half-killed but did not care a fig, I was so excited and entertained. Only, I wished more than ever that I were a man. How delicious it would be to live in the public eye, and work for the public good, and have a busy life, instead of sitting by the fireside imagining. . . .[2]

Fauriel to Mary   Paris, 28 June 1826

. . . Your letter puzzles me. . . . It seems to be a mixture of affection and passion—the affection for me . . . and the passion for the polling, the joys of 'living in the public eye, working for the public good', etc. I cannot tell, of course, but I imagine that a woman must be very discontented with her lot—must feel very little affection, or perhaps be unfortunate in her love—to form such a strong desire in connection with an *election*. Would you have written in such terms three years ago? I think not. I suppose I must resign myself to these new ideas. . . .[3]

Mary to Fauriel   Cold Overton, 7 August 1826

. . . Apart from rides, I have been only to the Bible Society at Oakham, which was packed. The great topic was that Tsar Nicholas has forbidden the distribution of any more Bibles in Russia, which greatly shocks our little world. For the Evangelicals in England really are a world apart, with their own books, bookshops, magazines, journals, opinions, news, etc.—as separate from the rest of England as if they were in America. Unfortunately I know it all like the back of my hand, and it never changes. Give me entomology! It's strange that people who believe in Adam and Eve and all that never bother their heads about whether the inhabitants of the other stars have been saved or damned. You would think, to hear them, that God took no interest in anyone but us . . . and yet this sphere is but a tiny speck in the universe. Whenever I try to believe in what they tell me, the vast universe keeps popping into my head, and dear me! Christian humility seems nothing but a bad joke. . . .[4]

In 1827 there was a small diversion: a visit to Oxford, where she attended a degree ceremony.

Mary to Fauriel   Cold Overton, 1 July 1827

. . . We have just been to Oxford. . . . The town itself is most beautiful—charming gardens everywhere. Nearly all of its twenty-three colleges are built in a fine Gothic style, so that you might fancy yourself in the fifteenth century. . . . But the students—! It's the most pedantic place in the world, and the most aristocratic.

Three poems in Latin were recited—cruelly long—and two or three orations ditto—and then various persons were summoned to be created doctors, still all in Latin. . . . Then someone made a speech in English on 'Whether the Crusades were beneficial or not' and, after giving voice to much folly and ignorance, decided that they were. . . . All the students were in the gallery and Mr Peel being present down below, they started to cheer at the tops of their voices. Then someone pronounced Canning's name, and the hissing cracked my eardrums. Every time a Tory's name was mentioned they applauded and shouted so loud I thought I should be deafened.

The next morning I was breakfasting with a party of Tories. We were twenty-two around the table. [The hostess] turned to me, when politics was spoken of, and said: 'And you, Miss Clarke—are you not interested in the politics of your country?' 'Oh yes,' I said: 'very.' 'And are you not in despair at this new Whiggish ministry?' 'Not at all: I am rather pleased,' I said—so sweetly, in such an affectionate tone, that butter would not have melted in my mouth. It was so droll—they were all so heated, and I so calm. . . .

Tell me all the Paris news and scandal. How is the collection for the Greeks progressing?

My news is that Mrs [Elizabeth] Fry has left for Ireland, with a mission from the government to visit all the prisons, make a report, and do absolutely everything she desires. What do you think of that! *There*'s an advance in civilization! *There*'s the beginning of women's rise to power and government—not through love and men's ridiculous passions, but by sheer moral force and intelligence. I would be obliged if you would get it mentioned in the *Globe*. . . .[5]

Any news was welcome in the remote dulness of Cold Overton, even (perhaps particularly, given Mary's zoological enthusiasm) the information that the zoos of London and Paris had each acquired its first giraffe.

Mary to Fauriel   Cold Overton, 1827

. . . What is the news? I know that . . . the giraffe has arrived. When Major Denham was travelling in Africa, he saw five out walking together one morning, and a herd of a hundred and fifty elephants. Imagine it! His book is the most entertaining in the world.

I am also reading Thucydides. It is not a quarter as nice as Herodotus—he tells of almost nothing but battles. When I have read all the Greeks, I shall go and visit their country, I have quite made up my mind. . . .

Please ask Cousin if he still wants an amanuensis who knows Greek—you will greatly oblige me. The candidate I have in mind is intelligent and honest—and is starving to death, so he will come very cheap. Moreover, he is very ugly—a great misfortune, which should arouse the sympathy of every right-thinking person. But don't tell Cousin that *I* am recommending the young man; he's so absurd that he might reject him for that very reason. . . . He's like the Yogis . . . who believe one must hurt those who love one. . . . When it comes to philosophy, the Indians beat us hollow, especially the sect which spends its nights in drunkenness and libertinage, expressly to practise stoicism, . . . vice being such a penance. . . .

Tell me what historian I should read after Thucydides, and where I can find an account of Greek manners, customs, religions, etc.—and above all, the condition of their women. I intend to write a history of women. But don't tell anyone, or they will steal my idea. . . .[6]

Mary to Fauriel   Cold Overton, 28 July 1827

. . . I'm striving to extend my intelligence as much as possible, but sometimes fear my head is like rubber—stretching while one pulls, but in the end no bigger than at the beginning. . . .

I've just read a book on India—written by a fool, however. (I wish I could find out the truth, from someone more intelligent.) He's a missionary . . . and gives accounts of their books, poovanas, poems, etc. (and writes like a pig); his name is Ward.

One thing seems certain: that the condition of women in India is wretched, which is no trifle to me. He says their religion is the cause of it. . . .

Indian poetry is as amphigorical as I am. If I allowed myself, I would speak exactly like that. I was going to give you a sample just now, but stopped in time. . . . I think just as they write—all in huge red images. . . . If only I could learn Sanskrit!—but my memory is so wretched. . . .

I want my book to include India. What was the name which that

German, Huber, gave to the study of man?—something like an-thropophagy, only it was not about eating. My book will be gynae-pophagy. . . .[7]

Fauriel to Mary   August 1827

. . . As for Sanskrit, is it really so difficult? Not more so than Latin or Greek, and one finds young ladies everywhere, even in France, who know one or other of those languages. There are no difficult works in Sanskrit except those not worth reading . . .[8]

Mary to Fauriel   Cold Overton, 2 August 1827

. . . Yesterday I was at a *missionary meeting*, where they made speeches and took a collection for missionaries going out to convert Africa and the Indies. I had hoped to learn a few facts about India, but no—although they prattled on from three to half past six. But the extraordinary thing is that they collected £45—in a little village a hundred miles from London! . . . Last year £43,000 was collected in Britain as a whole!—Well, I have nothing against it: Christianity is supposed to put men and women on an equal footing, and if it did nothing else, it would be a great step forward in civilization. . . .

Selina* and I go butterfly-hunting every evening; it's very amus-ing. Of all the females I know, now that my dear Miss Benger is dead, Selina is the one I like best. If only I could find some ladies in Paris of equal energy, I should be so happy. . . .[9]

While in Leicestershire Mary was reduced to butterfly-hunting and mis-sionary meetings, in Paris there was real excitement afoot. A second attempt was being made to introduce the exoticisms of English theatre to French audiences. It was still a risky experiment; a previous one, in 1822, had been received with boos and catcalls, and the troupe had soon retired defeated.

Fauriel to Mary   Paris, September 1827

. . . You have no doubt heard that we are being visited by a company of English actors, who have already given us two comedies by Sheridan and three or four of Shakespeare's great plays. They have been received with a kindness, courtesy and satisfaction I was pleased to see; *Hamlet*, *Romeo and Juliet* and *Othello* have all been enthusiastically applauded, without any notable complaints from

* Her niece.

the traditionalists. Apparently they were taken off guard at first, but they are said to have recovered themselves and to be planning some sort of anti-Shakespearean explosion. So I do not know how the affair will end. At worst it will have proved, I think, that Shakespeare can succeed with the public, even if it shocks a clique. I saw only *The Rivals* and *Othello*, in which Kemble seemed to me to have some fine moments. But there were many things in his acting and delivery which I could not understand; they did not make sense. Altogether the piece made only half the effect it should. Iago should be played as a highly intelligent man, with something in his appearance to indicate the devilish impulse driving him from within. But this Iago was a great strapping fellow, as good-humoured as you like, so that Othello (who, with his soot-coloured face, looked a little devilish himself), seemed to be being bamboozled by a harmless fool of a peasant.—Messrs Foote and Kean are said to be coming, if the anti-Romantics fail to cause a commotion. . . .[10]

They did come, with success, in the following year.

Mary to Fauriel   Cold Overton, 18 September 1827

. . . I have not yet finished Xenophon's *Memoirs of Socrates*, but am beginning to feel much more at home with the Greeks. The translations I have strike me as poor, but *faute de mieux* I must put up with them. I have three of Sophocles' works, and am borrowing right and left. . . . The *Iphigenia in Aulis* is extremely beautiful—perhaps I shall read the *Bacchae* next. . . . Socrates seems a little bourgeois—there is nothing so bourgeois as moral advice, so it is a good thing that all religions tend towards fatalism, otherwise the human race would decline into irredeemable vulgarity, moralizing being so close to self-interest, which is always dangerous. But fatalism is profoundly unjust and does away with the importance of the individual—

God knows if you will be able to understand what I mean!—by dint of speaking to no one about my ideas and thoughts, I am growing to express myself in a language of my own—as a matter of fact, every one is so stupid that it's a pity one must talk at all. . . .

Now that I am throwing myself into study, I despair at my ignorance—and the irrecoverable past I have wasted, as though I were a creature of no intelligence. But regretting is yet another waste of time, so I am trying not to.

Have you read Jean-Paul Richter? He's said to be very original and full of imagination. Have his books been translated? Do you know if an antiquary called Potter (English) is good? He wrote *Antiquities of Greece*—is it worth reading? . . .[11]

Mary to Fauriel   Cold Overton, 3 August 1828

. . . Everything here continues just the same . . . except for one upheaval a week ago. Have I ever spoken to you of a German called Ernst, who was my first admirer, a very long time ago? . . . At that time he begged me to marry him, but . . . we were always quarrelling when we were together . . . and I had the good sense to refuse. But so as not to hurt his feelings, I made up all sorts of excuses, such as that my health was too bad and I could never keep house (I thought that an inspiration, for he liked women to be good housekeepers above all else). But lo! he said he did not mind—he would rather be uncomfortable with me than comfortable with anyone else. . . .

That was ten years ago, and since then I have heard nothing of him. . . .

Then, a week ago, the servant brought in his card, on which he had scribbled 'Monsieur G. desires to enquire after Mrs and Miss Clarke' . . . and in no time he was with us.

As soon as he was alone with me, he said: 'Will you permit me to speak of the past?' and I said I had treated him ill, and he said: 'No, it was he, and he loved me as much as ever,' and goodness knows what else. . . . To continue loving me, after ten years' separation!—only a German could do it. . . .

He said, by the by, that I had not changed at all; on the contrary, I was prettier. Which shows that his eyesight is not of the best. . . .

En passant, I have received a letter from M. Mohl . . . in which he says he sees you sometimes. . . . Do cultivate him, to please me. In my opinion he's a better man, and more worthy of you, than any other of your intimates in Paris. Altogether, he is one of the *completest* men to be seen anywhere. . . .[12]

Fauriel to Mary   Paris, 22 August 1828

. . . Mohl is the person I see most often. He comes to me nearly every evening; we dine together and then walk abroad. I like him more and more, and see ever more kindness, wit and humour in him. I gave him a few opportunities of speaking about you . . . when we were walking in the Tuileries gardens, but it seemed to embarrass him, so I have since refrained. He does not realise that his silence and the few indirect remarks he has let fall speak louder than many a long speech. . . .[13]

Mary to Fauriel   Cold Overton, 22 September 1828

. . . As to M. Mohl's remarks . . . I'm sure you are imagining hidden meanings that don't exist. . . . I would stake my life on it that what he said to you in the Tuileries gardens had as much to do with me as with the Emperor of China. Probably less—for he thinks much more about the Chinese, Tibetans, Tartars, Mongols, Persians and Singhalese than about my humble self. And so he should! He's better able to live through his intelligence than any person I have ever known, and all his energy is so much devoted to it that I believe him incapable of passion. He's as pure as an angel and as simple as a child. . . .

We have just had yet another collection, this time for the conversion of the Jews. . . . This whole miserable country is eaten up by tiny little virtues and tiny little duties, and people's feelings are so frittered away on them that not an impulse remains for anything noble or grandiose. It is like the English towns: great masses of houses, all very clean and tidy, and not a single grand building to inspire you. If the English continue so, constantly scratching away at themselves to be sure of being nice and clean, nice and tidy, they will end by having souls like pygmies'. Even their piety, instead of ennobling, cuts God down to their size. My niece spends all her time making little embroidered bags . . . to be sold for the Anti-Slavery Society . . . which would be all very well if, instead of turning seamstress to gain some £10 a year, she put some *poor* woman in the way of the work. Oh, if only I could travel to the Himalayas, or the Ganges, or the ocean, to demicroscopize myself! . . . I'm burning to return to France, where I can speak freely. To tell the truth, I would go to live in a robbers' cave, I am so tired of virtue. . . .

I'm reading Mill's *History of India*. . . . He strikes me as a good advocate—an anti-metaphysician, of the school of Gibbon and Voltaire, but good-hearted, liberal, and not an inveterate Englishman. But he has as much idea of sympathizing with other cultures as a broomstick—not a good character for a historian. . . . When shall we see a historian who rises high above his own country? . . .[14]

It was at this time that, still casting about for an 'engrossing occupation', she hit on a new idea.

Mary to Fauriel   Cold Overton, 11 or 12 October 1828

. . . Would you be so kind as to ask Cathérine* to get our beds ready for the 27th and put up the truckle-bed in the closet behind my alcove? . . . I am bringing with me a little girl whom I intend to educate to know everything (if she prove clever enough). Goodness knows how I shall win Mama over, but a fig for the consequences! I *will* have my own way, for once in my life, and have full confidence in my skill. . . . Whenever I feel a doubt, I read over the letter from her mother thanking me for taking charge of the girl. Poor woman, she is delighted! She has ten children, and her husband went bankrupt two years ago; they can hardly make ends meet. I shall bring up Nancy to be able to earn her living. If she's clever enough, you shall show her how to write books, and if she's stupid she can always be a governess . . . since she will know French. She's not pretty, but looks as if she were quick. . . .

I keep telling myself not to count on the affair too much. And I did tell the mother that I would only take Nancy on trial for this winter (because one must beware of one's enthusiasms) . . .

I shall allow you to give advice, so long as you are very humble, for I consider myself rather a genius where education is concerned. . . .[15]

It was not until much later that her pride allowed her to probe deeper into the motives for this venture: 'Do you really believe, my dear, that I did not feel all the desires, all the affections natural to my sex?—all that need for family affections which is an instinct, and which engulfed me? Did I not suppress all these, for your sake? I even adopted a little girl for a while, to try to satisfy those instincts—did not that suggest anything to you?'[16]

In 1828-9 her hopes of happiness with Fauriel were at a low ebb. Despite his protestations, he seemed to turn as often to others as to her— particularly to Mme Arconati, one of the exiled Italian aristocrats. At the Castle of Gaesbeck, about nine miles from Brussels, she and her husband

* The Clarkes' maid.

'presided over a little court of the most distinguished of the Italian refugees, in which Arrivabene was the Prime Minister and Berchet, Scalvini and Collegno were the principal courtiers.'[17] Mary sympathized with their cause, admired their steadfastness, even liked Mme Arconati herself; but Fauriel's behaviour was clearly hard to bear.

Mary to Fauriel (*at Gaesbeck*)   Paris, 17 June 1829

... Mérimée has just left us. He has made the acquaintance of an old Basque woman, a charwoman, who delights him. She is as bright as a button, and cleans for one of his friends, and they have written down a whole collection of her sayings. ... She told him, for instance, that the devil had lived seven years in the Basque country to learn their language, at the end of which time he had only mastered 'yes' and 'no', and left in a passion, declaring that they were greater devils than he. ...

Mme Arconati tells me in her letter that you have the gout. ... Drink very little wine, or it will get worse. And walk a great deal when you can. Gout is a very respectable, aristocratic malady— proof, the English say, of one of those good old-fashioned constitutions which are fast going out because of the softness of our present-day habits. ... So you should be pleased! But if you drink too much, it will get worse. ...

I have been three times to M. Audouin's lectures on entomology—they are extremely interesting. ... Mme Arconati writes that she will try to interest herself in plants and insects, as I urged. Do interest her in them, as you can if you try, and talk to her about geology and the globe and fossil animals, and perhaps she will acquire a taste for them. ...[18]

Fauriel had just been offered the Chair of Literature at Geneva. He himself was reluctant to accept it, clinging to the hope that one day he would be appointed to the Sorbonne, but Mary decided instantly that he should clinch the matter, and forthwith offered advice on the technique of lecturing:

Mary to Fauriel   Paris, 14 July 1829

... Take care not to say 'as it were' too often: that's a habit of yours. But otherwise I think you have a remarkable talent for lecturing. Your roundabout style is capital for explanations, but pray don't overdo it. M. Audouin, instead of circling round his idea from a distance, working up to it and then pouncing on it like a falcon, simply bangs away at it, like a bad workman hammering in a nail. Sometimes he hits the spot, sometimes he is miles off, but simply by hammering one is bound to hit something, which is the aim, after all. . . .

I have done many foolish things in my life, and suffered for them, but none so foolish as taking on Nancy, who has been an inexpressible torment for the whole of the past eight months. At least, thank God! I'm not married to her. How a man must rage when he finds that he has been fool enough to marry some idiot for her face . . . and discovers that he has tied a millstone round his neck and must toil and moil for the creature, without even letting his distaste show, for fear of hurting her feelings. . . . I hardly dare believe that I shall be rid of my millstone tomorrow. . . . She is so stupid,—so *stupid*! . . .

Have you read M. Constant's new book?* If so, who is Julie? In the book the author gives his thoughts on love through her mouth, making her say 'that it is only when women have accepted their defeats that they begin to have a clear goal: to keep the lover for whom they have made what seems to them a great sacrifice. Whereas men, at this point, cease to have a goal; their erstwhile goal becomes a tie. It is no wonder that two individuals placed in such unequal relations soon find themselves unable to agree, etc.' So, according to him, love is a game of chess, and when one of the parties has lost her best pieces she has nothing to do but stave off the checkmate as long as she can! . . . So women are to believe *they* must always remain constant! *I* say they should—but it would take too long to tell you; you must read it in my book.[19]

Fauriel to Mary   July 1829

. . . Julie was the first wife of Talma, the actor, and one of the women of those days who had the greatest reputation for amiability and wit. I knew her well: she always called me 'the Savage'. . . . She can hardly have had any very elevated ideas about love: she herself started as a dancer at the Opéra and then became the mistress of several aristocratic fops, including the Vicomte de Ségur, who wrote three volumes of twaddle about women—none of which, I am thankful to say, I have ever read. However, Julie was an amiable person—better than her doctrines, and a very good friend. Indeed

---

* *Mélanges de littérature et de politique*, 1829.

she was a good friend to Benjamin Constant, who would have done better, in my view, not to repeat opinions . . . only given as *jeux d'esprit* and meant to live no longer than the conversations they arose in. . . . [20]

Mary to Fauriel   Cold Overton, 28 August 1829

. . . Faugh! Here is a topic more to my taste. The doctor at Oakham . . . was crossing the road and saw a weasel carrying something in its mouth which he took to be a mouse.. He came forward—the weasel seemed to be having difficulty, and, having reached the grass by the opposite roadside, dropped her burden and was off into the hedge. Coming up, he saw that it was not a mouse but her baby, which was so fat and heavy she could hardly carry it. He saw the mother watching him anxiously from a few paces off; when she thought he had gone she came back to pick up the precious bundle again. . . .

I am reading a book called White's *History of Selborne*. . . . It is not as full of facts as I would like, but it is the only book of its kind that I know, and I wish there were more. . . .

M. Mohl . . . thinks that M. Saint-Martin has played a horrible trick on him and made him waste all this time on Firdousi without having any intention of getting the Bibliothèque Royale to print it; they are all out-and-out blackguards, those Institut scholars. That is why I asked you how the University of Paris works—because I would like to know why and how a parcel of stupid geese can be so knowledgeable and so superior to me, when I know I have more intelligence—and what they do to gain their positions, and the whole French system of education, and what it means to be a lecturer. . . . It pleases you to say you cannot understand why I should wish to read a book on the subject, but that's because you know it all already. It's not just a whim of mine—it's a necessity. I'm so ignorant about all such things that sometimes I could drown myself from vexation. . . . [21]

This summer, after five years of insensitivity to public opinion, Charles X crowned his follies by forming a government composed of his eccentric favourite, Polignac, and a selection of ministers who between them managed to be unpopular with almost every section of the population. Ampère, who had just been appointed Professor of Literature at the Collège de France, feared for his Chair, Mohl for the printing of his *Shah Nameh*.

Mary to Fauriel   Cold Overton, 3 October 1829

. . . Since this new ministry I pant after the political news like the most ardent politician—and my only resource is a twice-weekly Methodistical journal, containing a sermon, all sorts of news about the conversion of the heathen, and—at very long intervals—a handful of lines on the French government. But M. Mohl writes that it is tottering and dares do nothing. . . .

The news here is that everybody is dying of hunger, because meat is too cheap, and clothes too. I meditate day and night on this, and ask everyone why it should be so, but always receive the same reply: poverty is rampant because there's a glut of food and clothes. . . . Meat is cluttering up the markets and selling at eight sous a pound—and if it continues, it will be the ruin of the country. Political economy is a wonderful thing, as wonderful as religion, since it renders every one perfectly satisfied with this explanation. . . .

My sister tells me that one Ellis* has achieved a great feat. Before his conversions, the mothers on his islands were so unkind that if their babies only whimpered . . . they killed them out of hand— simply dug a hole in the floor of their huts and one-two-three! buried them! Whereas now they are tenderness itself—tenderer than European mothers. And if I were to hint that this might not be true, she would go red in the face with anger, as she did last year, when I ventured the remark that Buddhists were not atheists! . . .[22]

Fauriel to Mary   Gaesbeck, 4 October 1829

. . . Did you know that the new Ministry of Education is seriously threatening to suspend or suppress all the courses given by Guizot, Villemain and Cousin? I do not yet know what will be decided, but it all makes the creation of my famous Chair seem increasingly unlikely. . . .

At times I feel a passionate interest in my book, when I think what it could be—at times I am disheartened, when I think how much remains to be done. . . . As to the book *you* intend to write . . . I look forward to it, not only for the pleasure I shall derive

---

*William Ellis, the missionary who worked in Tahiti and other South Sea Islands.

from seeing your thoughts expressed, but because writing it will give you a little sympathy with my struggles. . . .

The Arconatis have taken a momentous decision with regard to their little son Carletto; he is to be sent to boarding school at Brussels. . . .[23]

Mary to Fauriel   10 November 1829

. . . I'm sorry for it. . . . I have nothing but contempt for our present system of education, which is the disgrace of modern civilization. In order to drum a little bad Latin and Greek into a child we cut him off from all his deepest affections, his parents. . . . I'm sure that in antiquity and the far-off countries we have the impertinence to call primitive we would be considered the most unnatural creatures in the world. And we find infanticide incomprehensible! It is more sensible to stifle little animals at birth, when their bodies are only half formed, and it's done to save them from having a miserable life, than to deprive them of life when they are already thinking creatures. . . .[24]

In France the political unrest was growing. It seemed as though everybody was opposing Charles' government at once: the students, Lafayette's supporters, the Orleanists, and above all the crowds of citizens who found themselves unemployed because of the slump. Elections had to be held in the summer of 1830, and the opposition was swept to power. The King and Polignac, losing their heads entirely, refused to accept the result and on 26 July issued the Four Ordinances, which tightened the censorship to an intolerable degree and further reduced the franchise. On the same day Thiers published his protest against them. By 28 July there was rioting in the streets of Paris.

3. Julius Mohl by Hilary Bonham Carter

4. Mary Clarke, after 1831, by Hilary Bonham Carter

V

1830-1838
Public and private revolutions

Mary to Mohl   Paris, 5 August 1830

. . . I arrived here just in time for the excitement—that is, on the evening of Monday 26 July—destroyed with the heat and fatigue. Everybody was in the streets, but it did not look like a revolution.

On the Tuesday, at four o'clock, I went out and took an omnibus. The whole of the Rue St-Honoré was packed with common people, angry but not armed—nearly all the shops were shut—and I heard some firing at five. At six I went home, having twice passed through the Rue St-Honoré, which began to look very sinister. Everyone was now grim—they were talking together in little groups, and, to judge from those running past, there was already rioting near the end of the Rue St-Denis. Finally, at half past six, we heard repeated firing at intervals for an hour, and then separate shots, which stopped at about eight and began again a little before half past nine.

I was very anxious about the working people, and walked to the Pont des Arts with M. Fauriel at about ten. On it there were clusters of respectably dressed young men, speaking low. M. Fauriel had great difficulty in forcing his way to Guizot's house in the Rue du Faubourg St-Honoré. The best of it is that the said Guizot had declared that this rioting was nothing, and that people should simply remain calm. And that is what all the bigwigs of the Opposition did all through Tuesday and until midnight on Wednesday—while the common people were fighting like tigers all Wednesday, with no weapons but old pikes, halberds and sticks—whatever they could lay their hands on. I nearly went out to join them with your boar-hunting sword.

On Wednesday the air was full of the sound of the tocsin, and cannons, and gunshots. In the end I was so excited, so longing to go and fight, that off I sped to Joséphine's house, which was in the thick of the worst fighting, to see what was happening. You have never heard anything as terrifying as the Notre Dame tocsin.

Joséphine's house was in a state of alarm. Everyone was at the windows, and troops were arriving in quantities in the Place Victoires and shooting—after which the windows were quickly shut. Before they arrived the people had been running towards the Place, spoiling for a fight . . . there was general enthusiasm. But then when the shooting began in the Place, I saw many of them come running back, and began to lose heart. Joséphine kept saying: 'Oh, we shan't see *these* people throwing themselves on the cannons, like the rebels in the Vendée!' In the end things were so bad—at least it appeared so—that I was obliged to stay the night with her.

At six or seven I had made an attempt to go home, despite everybody's advice—for we were all out in the courtyard keeping each other company. But in the streets all the people were armed and I was pursued by shouts of 'Go home! Go away! Look out! etc.' And rifle shots were ringing out in the courtyard of the Louvre, where the Swiss Guards had entrenched themselves, as though in a fortress. I was so eager to get through that I kept on walking, despite what the people said. But then three very rough-looking men came up to me, and when I asked them if it was possible to get through to the Faubourg St-Germain they said 'No, not by the Pont Neuf', but they were going to try to get through by the Pont des Tuileries and would take care of me if I liked. But in fact I was in less danger than they! for although the soldiers were shooting at everybody, they were trying harder to hit the common people than anyone else.—I went a little way with my escorts, but seeing that there was a whole army beyond the Palais Royal, and noticing a corpse lying on the ground (covered, but with its bloody leg sticking out), I decided that on the whole it would be better to go back to Joséphine's.

On Thursday, I got home at six o'clock in the morning, via the Pont Neuf, weaving my way through the cannons and cannonballs of the Swiss Guards, who had made a clean sweep of the Quais. There was not so much as a cat to be seen. All the roads, apart from the Quais where I was walking, were full of working people, armed, who were tearing up the paving stones to use as barricades, over which I scrambled as quick as I could. I ran like a hare, I can tell you.

Everyone was shouting that I would be killed, and telling me to go away; but to their great credit they all shouted advice and made way for me despite their own excitement. . . . The oddest thing about the whole rising is that there were no consultations, arrangements, or calculations. They all merely snatched up weapons and paving stones and formed themselves into squads to guard the gates instinctively, as if they had been doing it all their lives.

When I came in, Mama said: 'Tell me the news, for Heaven's sake—I have been quaking in my shoes!' I said: 'But I told you that I would take great care.' 'Oh,' said she: 'it was not you I was worried about: it was the common people.'

I had no good news to tell her, except that we (the liberal side) held all the Faubourg St-Germain, and that on the previous day the students had taken, and then lost, the Hôtel de Ville, and that we had no leaders. I was really in despair.

Then I sent to M. Fauriel's lodgings to know if he had been out looking for me the night before—our servant Cathérine said he had, Mama said not. And as everybody was saying there would be a famine, and Joséphine's maid could not go out to shop, I went myself to buy flour and bacon and started to hide all our money in different places. At nine o'clock the cannon-fire and gunfire and tocsins were truly terrifying, and one could not find out what was happening—all the house-doors were shut up tight. In the end I called from a window to a man in our garden, who said that we were finally taking the Hôtel de Ville. The din went on until midday or one o'clock when M. Fauriel came.

Like me, he had spent the night away from St-Germain. He had gone to look for me at Joséphine's, but was out of luck and encountered only gunshots, which did not come too near him, however. But the people would not let him through. At nine or ten he met Cousin and two others on the Carrousel and, there being no chance of returning, they all spent the night at an hôtel.

I should never end if I tried to tell you all the ridiculous things which have happened: how Cousin made fun of the rebels and called them 'a vulgar rabble'—until Thursday evening;* how Villemain and Cousin and all the bigwigs turned heroes on Thursday evening, and on Friday morning appointed themselves mayors and Guizot minister—! No, I must be fair: as early as Monday evening La Fayette had sent to Guizot to say that he was ready to declare

---

* When it was clear that they were winning.

himself and asked what was to be done. He was the only one—he
and his son—who were prepared to commit themselves to the
revolution without calculating the consequences.

Adieu. We are well pleased with the turn affairs have taken. The
writers on the *Globe* are attacking the new government, but the
common people have more sense than all of them put together, and
have settled down to work again. . . .

Oh—they used omnibuses for the barricades, too! They looked
magnificent, lying stretched out on their great flanks.[1]

The events of 1830 were mild, as revolutions go. The blasé Mérimée
complained to Stendhal that it was 'flat and stupid—not a drop of blood
was shed'.[2] But it acted as a tonic on Mary. In many ways there was
promise of a new start, at a time when she was past expecting new starts,
for she was now thirty-seven. Most immediately, Fauriel's worst financial
troubles eventually came to an end. Two months after Guizot became
Minister of Education he created a chair of foreign literature at the
Sorbonne, and immediately appointed Fauriel to it, so that the Geneva
chair could be finally declined. More generally, the repressive atmosphere
of the Bourbon régime cleared away—at least from some areas of French
life. During this decade and the next the aspiring young writers of the
'20s began to come into their own: the literary scene was transformed by
Hugo, Mérimée, Stendhal, Balzac, Sainte-Beuve, George Sand. In
addition, many more foreigners came to Paris. As the '30s and '40s
progressed, Mary's circle came to include not only her old friends but
such newcomers as Sainte-Beuve, the philosopher Tocqueville, and Ivan
Turgenev.

In Britain too there was a change of mood—less abrupt, perhaps, but
equally conducive to a feeling that life still had exciting new possibilities
to offer. The '30s saw not only the passing of the first Reform Bill, the
opening of railways which soon spread all over Britain, and the abolition
of slavery in the British Empire, but the accession of Victoria and the
introduction of the penny post—all of which affected Mary's life in ways
she could not have dreamed of a few years before. It was equally refreshing
to see a change in the mood of English writers—the social concern of
Dickens, Mrs Trollope, Harriet Martineau and later Mrs Gaskell, the
new interest in middle-class life (as opposed to the penchant for 'aristocratic' themes of the Silver Fork school), and by 1847 Charlotte Brontë's
passionate plea for women's emotional independence in *Jane Eyre*. In
general women were making their very varied voices increasingly heard:
not only writers of fiction but social pioneers such as Mrs Reid, whom
Mary came to know well in the '30s and who went on to found Bedford
College in 1849, and even the more extreme feminist-socialists, such as

Flora Tristan, who were outside Mary's sphere of interest but contributed to the general change of mood.

As early as 1830-1 these fresh breezes could be felt in the air. Invigorated, Mary took what may at first appear a step backwards but was in fact *reculer pour mieux sauter*.

For years she and her mother had been constantly changing lodgings, 'plagued by landlords' cheating; one had taken away the staircase, and for three weeks people could only see us by coming up a ladder. (I was edified at Cousin's agility; he was thirty-five years younger then than now—so was I, even I.) I could not manage landlords in those days, so I said to my mother: "Let us try to lodge in a convent; perhaps we shall be less plagued." Two or three gentlemen who came often to see us in the evening were also habitués of Mme Récamier's . . . and had told her about us . . .'[3] and Mme Récamier, intrigued by what she heard, sublet them an apartment she owned in the Abbaye-au-Bois.

This curious institution was indeed a convent, but let out part of its premises to select tenants. 'It was a large old building in the Rue de Sèvres, with a courtyard enclosed on the street by a high iron gate, surmounted by a cross of the same metal. Through this gate you saw the square court, and opposite to it the entrance-door of the chapel, and another small one leading to the *parloir* of the convent. Various staircases ascended from this yard, conducting to apartments inhabited by retired ladies.'[4] No men were allowed to live there—although many came to visit the 'retired ladies'—and by the time the Clarkes moved in the apartments were not easy to let. 'The Abbaye had been all the fashion from 1815 to 1830. The fine ladies with *écorné* [tarnished] reputations went to it, to mend them; the ex-beauties retired to it, like Mme de Sablé—suddenly become "spiritual". But in 1830 all priests, convents, devotion fell a hundred per cent. . . .'[5] Mme Récamier had lived there since 1817.

By 1831 her salon was a rather elderly affair. It was dominated by the sixty-three-year-old Chateaubriand, a survival from the first wave of Romanticism, very Catholic, very Bourbonist, very conscious of the failure of his political career under both Louis XVIII and Charles X, and subject to oppressive fits of ennui, out of which, it was said, only *la jeune Anglaise* could jolt him. Nevertheless being, as Mary soon became, a favourite at this salon, offered her undoubted advantages. The first—an ignoble one, but, as she shamefacedly admitted, not to be despised—was that it increased her standing in French society, and also introduced her to many notable figures outside the liberal connection, whom she would not otherwise have met.

The second advantage was psychological. Mme Récamier, despite her age, was still devotedly loved—not only by the eminent Chateaubriand, but by the writer Ballanche, who had been 'her property' since 1813—a 'simple, perhaps a little uncouth' man, whose face had been 'disfigured by an operation'.[6] According to Mary, he 'never asked, never thought of, a return for his intense devotion; the pleasure of looking and listening was enough', which may or may not have been the case. But the hopelessly Platonic attachment of another of Mme Récamier's lovers was certainly a fact: Mohl's co-lodger J.J. Ampère, some twenty-five years her junior, was besotted with her until her death, much to the disgust of Mérimée, who had known him since their schooldays: 'He came into the world with the most virile temperament, and was castrated by an old coquette.'[7] Faintly ridiculous as these enduring passions may now appear, they seem to have encouraged Mary in a feeling that, although 'such charms as she had once had were faded'[8], she need not necessarily consider her emotional life closed.

But the real stimulus of Mme Récamier's company came from the salon itself. Salons were an old tradition in France, dating back to the seventeenth century and beyond, but it was the first time that Mary had regularly watched one in operation—and chaired by such a distinguished and tactful person (her own evenings in the '20s had been much more informal affairs). 'No one ever understood more thoroughly how to show off others to the best advantage: if she was able to fathom their minds, she would always endeavour to draw up what was valuable . . . and as the spirits of the speaker were raised by his success, he became really more animated, and his ideas and words flowed on more rapidly. . . . Another characteristic was the keeping seriously to one subject . . . and the habit of the same persons meeting often at the same house, where they knew they would be understood. . . .'[9] It must be remembered that few such opportunities were then available to women in England, at any level of society. Between the decline of such salons as had existed in the eighteenth century and the advent of women's colleges and women's entry to the professions, intellectual activity, where it existed, was generally a solitary affair—reading, thinking, perhaps writing, but of necessity mostly alone, or at best within the family. The strongest, like Jane Austen, flourished; others, like Florence Nightingale at certain periods of her life, gave way to neurasthenia or simply lost their quickness of thought from lack of practice.

In short, Mme Récamier's salon gave Mary the equivalent of a university education of the best sort, and the *salonnière*'s personality was a good corrective to the wilder excesses to which Mary well knew she was subject. 'Mme Récamier dreaded exaggeration. Speaking of a person who had fine qualities, but from the violence of her feelings and the vivacity of her fancy kept those she loved in constant agitation, she said: "Il n'y a que la raison qui ne fatigue pas à la longue." [Reasonableness is the only quality which does not grow wearisome in the end.] 'This,' Mary commented, from what must surely be first-hand experience, 'is so profound a truth that it becomes an axiom to those who have once heard it.'[10]

Of course, she did not change overnight, and her old frustrations—over Fauriel, money, the objectionableness of Cold Overton and all it stood for—did not change much for many a long year; but she faced them with increased resilience. In the summer of 1831 she went to the Pyrenees, which certainly offered more excitement and less virtue than Cold Overton.

Mary to Fauriel   Bagnères, 24 August 1831

. . . We couldn't see four paces in front of us, and our guide laughed like a lunatic whenever we mentioned the mist . . . he said afterwards that the route was so precipitous that we would never have undertaken it if we could have seen. . . . The rain was streaming down, and as we rode through it for two and a half hours we were as wet as if we'd been in a bath by the time we arrived at the hospice. . . .

I've made friends with some people from Montpellier—very nice people—one of them is what's called a 'card'. . . . They chat, laugh, have no ideas or emotions . . . and don't write a single word—which is a great virtue. . . .

The waters have worked a great cure on Mama—she is not the same person! All her pains went after the second bath—although she has spat blood and suffered with her chest since then. . . .

How dare you complain of solitude and boredom at Dieppe,—and to me too, who am obliged to endure twice as much, and have no all-absorbing work, and can never drop into a café and engage the first-comer in conversation, as you so easily can! A man need never be alone unless he wants to be, and—what is even better—he can be alone when he does want to be. Women never can. . . .[11]

Mary's journal   Paris, 26 January 1832

. . . At last I have asked M. Fauriel whether his feelings have changed. He said—and his look was indescribable—that he no longer loved me as he once had, although he was still very fond of me, perhaps fonder than ever. I felt a sort of dull pain all over my body; my blood seemed to stop flowing. . . . But at last I continued and asked, through my tears, if he now considered me free. 'Yes,' he said, without hesitation. . . . I said, with a sort of calm, that I had been devoted to him for ten years, that he had been the pivot

of all my actions, and that it was very hard to change, but it must
be done.

He wept bitterly, buried his head in my lap, and begged me not
to exclude him altogether from my life. Again and again I said: 'But
you don't want me! Do you want me?'

'No. I *cannot*.'[12]

After this tardy and painful confession the relationship between Mary
and Fauriel, of necessity, changed—though less than might have been
predicted. She could no longer deceive herself into thinking that one day
Fauriel would turn into another and more marrying man, but she still
treated him as an intimate—a kind of unmarried husband, now gradually
taking on aspects of an elderly father. However, the number of her
surviving letters to him from this period onwards dwindles greatly, and
it seems likely that fewer were written. Happily, letters to other correspondents now begin to supplement the material and give some idea of the
non-Fauriel elements in her life, which she clearly entered into with her
usual gusto. That at least is the impression she gives in her letters to Mrs
Clarke, Mrs Reid and others. It was only to Fauriel that she confessed
from time to time that she was far from happy. Emotional troubles were
not to be mentioned to other correspondents, and least of all to her
mother, who was now becoming more and more chair-bound and by the
end of the '30s had settled permanently in England.

Mary to Mrs Clarke (*at Cold Overton*)   Paris, 14 July 1833

. . . I have made acquaintance with an English sea captain. . . .
We were the greatest friends imaginable in half an hour. He had
been two years at Constantinople—admiral of the Turkish fleet
against the Russians. He talked with great glee about it—he is very
funny—told me he was sure 'I was a good fellow the moment I
spoke to him, and not stiff.' I invited him to come to tea, especially
as he was very curious to see Mme Récamier, whose picture he used
to kiss when he was a boy of seventeen or eighteen and 'began to
look about him'. The very evening he was to come Mme Récamier
had made a party to go to the observatory to see Saturn, whose ring
is just across him. I was in a great fuss for fear of missing my
captain if I went. However, I left word with Joséphine to tell him to
come with his son to see Saturn, and so he did, like a sensible man.
I believe his esteem for me greatly increased when he saw that I
came in the Duc de Laval's party. . . .

Mrs Trollope* is going to Germany to write a book. . . . She has written one or two novels already, but I fear she will write herself out in no time. It really is like sucking the juice out of people—they sell themselves to the booksellers to be boiled dry. . . .[13]

Mary to Mrs Clarke   Paris, 26 July 1833

. . . I like M. Sainte-Beuve very much. I had M. Fauriel and M. Mohl to meet him—it was very agreeable, but the dinner was too much done because I let Joséphine have her own way, which I always repent of. But I am very well pleased with her on the whole, if I look sharp after my prerogatives.

Great preparations are making for the fêtes of July. . . . It will cost thirteen millions of francs. . . . It is Thiers' contrivance, who thinks himself a second Bonaparte. What delights him and the town most is a sham vessel . . . just like a man of war with gilt statues. It is to be illuminated and attacked in sham fight by illuminated boats. The Duc de Noailles offered his terrace, which is nearly opposite to the vessel, to Mme Récamier, so I shall see it very well. My captain, whom I delight in, is so funny. He bothered me to go and dine with him—I assured him I could not, or I should lose my character. Well, says he, bring Joséphine, and he would take us to see the sights. I told him I was engaged to see it from the terrace, so, says he, can't you take me too? I asked Mme Récamier, who was very agreeable. I was glad to do anything to please him, he is such a good-tempered comical creature—with a very red nose, yet he assured me he never drank but one bottle of 20-louis wine a day. M. Mohl declares he can't believe that. . . .[14]

Mary to Mrs Clarke   Paris, 12 August 1833

. . . The vessel was attacked by the boats. It defended itself, and there was such a cannonading, smoke and flashing, and we were so near—only being separated by the breadth of the bridge—that I can fancy what a battle is. All the ladies scampered in except me—I felt a peculiar sensation in the spine of my back, which quite electrified me, and longed to rush into the fight. . . . It was perfectly intoxicating! I dare say it is what the war-horse feels at the sound

* Anthony's mother. Between 1832, when she was fifty-two, and 1856 Mrs Trollope produced a hundred and fourteen volumes.

of the trumpet—for about twenty minutes I was quite lost. . . . The Captain said the whole was very fair and put him in mind of old times. Oh, says he, sniffing the powder, what a nice smell! M. Fauriel, whom I had had great trouble to dragoon into coming, actually forgot his dignity so far as to climb on a chair to peep. . . .

The cat has just accouché'd, after mewing about the house for three days and plaguing me so that I asked Dr Roulin this morning what I was to do. Joséphine wanted to put her in a warm bath. He said it could do her no harm. Then the washerwoman advised making her swallow some oil, so she did. And it turned out well, for in less than twenty minutes it (the kitten) came out and all was over . . . I hope Mrs Tom will get through her affair as safely as Pussy and not be so long bothering poor Eleanor as Pussy did me. What a jobation! . . .[15]

Her nephew Tom had married in the previous year. By a curious coincidence, his bride was the daughter of the Revd. Mr Carus Wilson who later figured as Mr Brocklehurst in *Jane Eyre*. Mary detested her more from year to year, and considered her influence on Tom wholly pernicious. Her domestic troubles were increased at this time by the action she felt obliged to take against a lawyer, M. Sirey, who had 'betrayed their intimate confidence'[16] and lost them a large sum of money.

Mary to Mrs Clarke   Paris, 12 May 1834

. . . It appears that at least a part of the Sirey money is gone for good. Our London houses too appear to me to be very uncertain property. Don't fret about all this. I have delayed telling it, because it is so disagreeable, but it is better you should know it and understand why I am so very saving than suppose it is useless niggardliness that makes me begrudge £20 to go and see you. . . . Unless I sold out I could not do it, and in the present state of our affairs it would be the height of folly. It is very painful to me to leave you alone with Tom and his wife all that time, but Selina advises me *not* to go to Brickwall. She understands her brother's temper and his wife's better than I do. Besides it would be very disagreeable to me, after having been all my life accustomed to grant my company as a favour, to intrude upon my nephew knowing he would prefer my absence, and receiving me upon duty. . . .[17]

Mary to Fauriel Cold Overton, 22 June 1834

... I arrived here about eighteen days ago, and my mother was so glad to see me that I was amply repaid for the 'over-exertion' of the journey. ...

I had heard so much talk of a Dr Jephson at Leamington ... that I consulted him for my stomach pains. ... He ordered me to eat only meat and bread, nothing else whatever. ... After two days my pains began again ... so I abandoned the meat diet and took to eating vegetables, and was soon better. Four days later the good doctor came to see me, and I told him all. He said I should have gone on suffering. 'As to that,' said I, 'I would rather behave badly and not suffer!' Then we went to it hammer and tongs and he told me he would not treat me any more, that I would do him no credit, and that he did not care a fig for patients who did not do him credit. ... In short, he was as cross as if I had admitted to eating babies instead of vegetables, and would not take his guinea when I offered it to him. ...

I have no new books here and have started to read Gibbon again. Every time I read a historian I am more than ever struck by the excellence of the portion of your history which you once showed me. ... If you applied yourself to them seriously, your works would be the most durable of our times, I am convinced. One of the things which most sadden me about the change in your feelings for me is that I have lost my influence over you in this matter. You used to think I did not appreciate you, but I was so convinced that your work would be a monument of scholarship that again and again I gave up the pleasure of seeing you, saying to myself: 'It's for his work' ...

My heart bleeds when I think that, with your great gifts, you could die tomorrow and leave behind nothing that is truly worthy of you. Not that I don't value what you have published so far, but I have such a high idea of what you *could* do. ...[18]

Mary to Mrs Clarke Travelling in Germany, 18 July 1834

... On the Rhine boat the bugs bit us most cruelly. Each of us imagined the other had not suffered, so said nothing. I thought Eleanor was sitting bolt upright that she might not trouble her gown, but next morning we each confided to the other how we had been murdered. . . . They walked over Eleanor's face—poor Eleanor, who is so particular! . . .[19]

Mary to Fauriel   Godesberg, 20 July 1834

. . . The Prussian government is insupportable—it meddles in everything. . . . If you engage a servant, it allows you a fortnight's trial, forsooth!—but after that you must keep him six months, whether it suits either of you or not. That's how it is in Berlin—not here, though. The English are furious because Brougham wants to introduce the Prussian system of education into England. *I* have never known anyone who was unable to read! It's absurd, say I, to put everyone in a bad humour, in order to force them to do what they do already! . . .[20]

Mary to Mrs Clarke   Zurich, 10 August 1834

. . . If I had done the least thing to persuade them [the Frewen Turners] to come here, I should be fretted to death, but it was all their own planning. If you could hear the incessant complaining you would fancy yourself in purgatory—the heat! the fleas! the bugs! the dirt! the smells! the Catholics spending their Sundays so wickedly! . . . Eleanor is sitting on a chair and groaning aloud like a wounded creature, Selina is as cross as two sticks, Mr Moor,* stupid every day, is stupid *and* cross on Sundays. . . . That is the present state of society.[21]

She and the Cold Overton party had visited the Manzonis, whom they found in great affliction; Giulietta Manzoni had just died after refusing for two years to eat anything but potatoes, because she thought herself too fat.

Mary to Fauriel   Milan, 12 October 1834

. . . If you could bring yourself to write to Manzoni, I am sure it would do him good—just a few lines. . . .

He has hardly aged at all, except that his hair has gone grey, and was almost gay the two days we were there, but 'twas not insensibility, as Mme Arconati believes, but his tenderness, which is too great for him to support pain for too long a time. . . . He still takes an interest in everything, seemed to be much entertained by what

---

* John Frewen Turner's tutor.

I told him of Paris, and understands the people there as well as if he had just spent six months in the place. . . . He is devoting himself passionately to agriculture and about to make experiments on his vines, because he thinks they may benefit his peasants.

My sister went with me on the second day, and while I was in another room, he embarked on the trifling task of converting her to Catholicism, she all the while defending her dogmas in astonishing French. Donna Giulia* whispered to me: 'My son is quite in love with your sister!' . . .[22]

It appeared that Eleanor was now silently withdrawing the contribution she had been making to the Clarkes' living expenses in Paris.

Mary to Mrs Clarke Paris, 19 April 1835

. . . It is useless for you to enter into any details about our money or income with her. She must know we were never very rich—how should we have got so? However, methodistical people cut off all their sympathies mighty conveniently. I am convinced it makes them selfish to be always thinking of their own souls—they get a habit of caring very little for other folk's bodies. And they call that religion! . . .[23]

Whenever possible, she took care to forestall the Frewen Turners' reluctant invitations by being engaged to her new friend, Mrs Reid— 'Mrs Reid and I suit to a T'. Mrs Reid was part of the old Unitarian connection, a close friend of Henry Crabb Robinson and Julia Smith, Florence Nightingale's aunt. She was also very intimate with Harriet Martineau, whose novels of middle-class 'everyday life' Mary admired as much as her more serious writings on economics. In April 1834 Mrs Reid sent various American visitors to call on Mary at the Abbaye.

Mary to Mrs Clarke Paris, 19 April 1834

. . . I held a party of twenty-five or thirty for them—out of worldly wisdom. If I get acquainted with Mrs Trollope, who is here, I shall do the same, from the same exalted motives and by no means for my amusement, for it is an intense bore; but I find it wise to keep up and increase my acquaintance. Even my own family, who ought to know and value me for my good qualities, value me much more for what I may appear to the world, for except Eleanor they are all as worldly-minded as possible. . . .[24]

* Manzoni's mother.

Mary to Mrs Clarke   Paris, 1835

. . . My new maid is such a comfort to me that I am afraid it
won't last. I believe she is perfectly honest, and moreover is an
excellent servant. The only drawback is her little boy. The sight of
him makes me miserable—he is a perfect cripple and has been so tormented with pain and doctors for two years that he gives me the idea
of Caspar Hauser, only without his intelligence. He sits moping and
saying nothing all day, never complains—and to mend the matter,
the Methodist school they put him to told him he would go to Hell,
which he tells his mother with a melancholy, resigned tone. . . .[25]

The doctor coming to see me one day, the little boy opened the
door, in consequence of which he examined him and said he
thought his thigh might be set to rights. . . . If it is so, I shall
advance whatever money is necessary, as thigh bones are invaluable, and she may work it out in time. And if she never could pay
me, I should think money well bestowed that would prevent a child
from being a cripple for life. If I can get Emily's arm and his leg
mended, I shall have well employed my headpiece this spring, for
it requires a little headpiece. . . .

We shall not get above a third of our lawsuit money, but I should
be heartily glad if we could get that. . . .[26]

She was not, as can be seen, quite as 'worldly' as she liked to boast—or
quite the imperturbable eccentric that Quinet described at this period.
Nor was she the thoroughgoing intellectual that the American littérateur
Ticknor thought he discerned when he was taken to see her during his
European tour.

Edgar Quinet to his mother   c. December 1837

. . . As for 'my dear Miss', as you call her, I must confess that
she made a strange appearance [at the Princess Belgiojoso's soirée],
although she was very animated and highly esteemed by persons of
discrimination. To the best of my memory she was wearing a brown
silk dress and her hair hung in tangled curls in its usual way.*
Fortunately she has no idea of the impression she makes—trips
along, pauses, exposes herself among all the charming ladies—as
easy in her mind, as imperturbably self-assured, as if she were
Venus in person. I could hardly bear to look at her; but she, thank
God, noticed nothing. . . .[27]

* The more conventional wore their hair parted in the middle and smoothly
brushed down on each side of the head.

Journal of George Ticknor
(*Professor of Belles-lettres at Harvard*)   January 1838

. . . We went last evening to Miss Clarke's, where there was rather more of a party than usual, collected by formal invitation. Fauriel was there, of course, and Mohl; but there was also a number of ladies, among whom were Mme Tastu, the well-known authoress; the Princess Belgiojoso, the well-known lady of fashion, and one of the most striking and *distinguées* persons in Parisian society, etc. I met too several men of note, whom I was glad to talk with: Baron d'Eckstein, the opponent of Lammennais; Mérimée, the author of *Clara Gazul* and now employed by the government to collect whatever relates to the ancient monuments of French art; Mignet, the historian; Élie de Beaumont, the great geologist; the two Tourguénieffs, etc. It was as intellectual a party as I have been with since we came to Paris, except at Jomard's: and I enjoyed it very much. . . .[28]

During Mary's visit to England this summer she witnessed, with a certain lack of solemnity, the solemn occasion of Victoria's coronation.

Mary to Mohl   29 June 1838

. . . I was in Westminster Abbey yesterday from five in the morning to half past four in the afternoon. I saw the queen—who has a charming countenance—and all the dukes and peers and bishops and archbishops and crowned heads. . . . When I saw Wellington, I wept like a calf from tender emotion. The queen had a train twelve yards long . . . the eight ladies-in-waiting pale blue trains . . . the peeresses long red trains. In short, trains played the principal part in the ceremony. . . .[29]

Fauriel to Mary   Paris, 17 September 1838

. . . The only novelty in my life is that I have been setting examinations and awarding degrees. I could not get out of it and know now what it is like: more tedious than my wildest imaginings. Moreover, throughout my new functions I was besieged by a host of supplicants—fathers, mothers, grandmothers, begging my indulgence for their offspring. . . . Among the young men to whom I awarded degrees there were many foreigners—Irishmen, Americans, Brazilians, etc. Among the last there was one curiosity. His features and complexion were more Indian than European, his

French a sort of incomprehensible Portuguese . . . The poor fellow
was so charmed by my grace in making him learned in history that
he came to see me the next day, to thank me. With a great struggle,
he managed to say and I to understand, at last, that he was a
portrait-painter in Rio de Janeiro, that he thought he was a very
good portrait-painter, and would be an even better one now that he
had a degree. He asked if he could paint my portrait, gratis, as a
token of his gratitude; and I tried to look as if I were refusing out
of pure modesty. . . .[30]

VI
1838–1847
The career begins

Late in 1838 the Clarkes left the Abbaye-au-Bois and took up residence at 112 (later 120) Rue du Bac. And now, after seven years' observation of Mme Récamier's methods, Mary at last committed herself to a regular career as a salonnière.

The word 'career' is not inappropriate; she approached the matter professionally in every sense except the financial one. Suitable guests were carefully brought together, likely topics 'researched', debate skilfully stimulated, those at the start of their careers introduced to established figures, the famous of one country put in touch with the famous of another. On Saturdays (later Fridays) she was At Home to all her acquaintances, who simply dropped in without invitation; during the week she held more select dinner- or breakfast-parties, where more detailed discussions took place. In short, she simultaneously fulfilled the functions of agent, club, and stage-manager. Indeed the skills she needed, and found she had in abundance, were very much like those needed by the present-day producer of radio or television discussion programmes, except that her audiences were limited to those in her two large intercommunicating drawing-rooms.

Mrs Gaskell, who came to know both Mary and her salon very well, used some of her views—unattributed, but Mary's style is unmistakable—in an essay on entertaining published in *Household Words* on 20 May 1854:

'[The salonnière] should never be prominent in anything; she should keep silence as long as anyone else will talk; but when conversation flags, she should throw herself into the breach. . . . I prefer catching my friends after they have left the grander balls or receptions. One hears then the remarks, the wit, the reason and the satire which they had been storing up during their evening of imposed silence. . . .

Bah! Celebrities! . . . *As* celebrities, they are simply bores. Because a man has discovered a planet, it does not follow that he can converse agreeably, even on his own subjects. . . . The writer of books, for instance, cannot afford to talk twenty pages for nothing, so he is either profoundly silent, or else he gives you the mere rinsings of his mind. I am speaking of him now as a mere celebrity . . .

I believe that you English spoil the perfection of conversation by having your rooms brilliantly lighted for an evening. . . . I would never have a room affect people as being dark on their first entrance into it; but there is a kind of moonlight as compared to sunlight, in which people talk more freely and naturally; where shy people will enter upon conversation without a dread of every change of colour or involuntary movement being seen—just as we are more confidential over a fire than anywhere else—as women talk most openly in the dimly-lighted bedroom at curling-time. . . .'

Among the foreign visitors of 1838–9 there was one, the eighteen-year-old Florence Nightingale, who was in urgent need of someone to confide in—someone who could understand the scope of her aspirations (as Cecil Woodham-Smith relates so graphically in her biography, she felt she had been entrusted with a God-given mission, but had not yet identified it as a mission to nurse) and yet was bracing enough to counter-act her morbid self-doubts. Mary's independence of thought and action—the ease and efficiency with which she controlled her 'performers', without losing either caste or the affections of those who surrounded her—these were invaluable as an example to Florence, and a stick with which to beat the more conventional females of her family. Perhaps Mary's sympathy with Florence's spiritual hopes and fears was equally valuable; for all her pose of worldliness—'I find it wise to increase my acquaintance'—she was still as youthfully receptive to large ideas, of a kind scoffed at by the majority, as she had been throughout her relationship with Fauriel. Mrs Nightingale and the elder daughter, Parthenope, chiefly valued Mary for her introductions to the 'best' French society, although they also liked her as a person; to Florence she was a vitally important liberator. For the first time, after the Nightingales' return to England, she found the confidence to defy her mother and throw herself into a study of mathematics, then into practical nursing of the sick poor who lived near the Nightingales, then into a positive determination to make hospitals her life, then into a systematic study of hospital reports and Blue Books on public health (in Britain, France and Germany) such as few, if any, single individuals had ever undertaken.

Parthenope Nightingale to Mary Simpson On the winter of 1838–9

. . . She . . . was exceedingly kind to Florence and me, two young girls, full of all kinds of interests, which she took the greatest pains to help. She made us acquainted with all her friends, many and notable, among them Mme Récamier. I know now, better than then, what her influence must have been thus to introduce an English family (two of them girls who, if French, would not have appeared in society) into that jealously guarded sanctuary, the most exclusive aristocratic and literary salon in Paris. We were asked, even, to the reading by Chateaubriand of his *Mémoires d'Outre-Tombe*, which he could not wait to put forth, as he had intended when writing them, until after his death—desiring, it was said, to anticipate the plaudits he expected but hardly received. This hearing was a favour eagerly sought for by the cream of Paris society at that time. . . .

When Mme Récamier desired the large apartment for herself, the Clarkes moved to an 'hôtel' in the Rue du Bac, in which they took very cheerful rooms, looking over the gardens of the *Missions étrangères* to the Dôme des Invalides. The rooms below were inhabited by Chateaubriand and his wife, with whom Miss Clarke was always on most friendly terms. Here it was that we found her and her mother, and met in their salon the best political, literary and scientific society of the day, including a dash of fine ladies and men of the world. . . .

All the Italian refugees—Princess Belgiojoso, Count Arrivabene, Ferrari, General Collegno—frequented her salon; but the intimates were MM. Fauriel and Mohl. . . . These two spent every evening regularly with the Clarkes, and, as we found, assisted in doing the honours of the house. I remember how they used to help in boiling the kettle over the wood fire and the brass dogs to make the tea. . . .

After we returned to England, Miss Clarke . . . came to see us every year and generally stayed three weeks or a month with us . . . interested in everything; reading all the new books . . . or if there were none she fancied, burying herself in Montaigne, Horace Walpole, etc. I can see her now, lying curled up in a great armchair, or in a corner of the sofa, with a large quarto on her knees. . . .[1]

Mary to Mrs Reid   Paris, 12 March 1839

. . . I hope you will be indulgent to the accommodations in our small ménage, as I am a grievously bad manager. Last year we had a room more, but as no one would come, I have made an aviary of it. Therefore, the best bedroom being full of birds' nests, the human beings can't have it. But I will make myself as agreeable as I can, to make up. . . .[2]

Mary to Mrs Reid   Cold Overton, 28 September 1839

. . . I was charmed with *Deerbrook** and have praised it so much
that Mme Tastu is to translate it. Indeed I advised her to do so, as
I think it will have great success in France, barring a few longueurs
at the beginning, which I like, but the French public is impatient.
I think what stamps it as a first-rate work is the originality of the
whole, the having found out how to paint heroism in the very
wash-house. I delight in that. I detest lords and ladies and all the
vulgar cant about them. . . .

My poor mother is very so-so. I wish she would go back to
France . . . but she is quite determined not. My only comfort is
that I can come from Paris to London in thirty-six hours and in
twelve more can get here. . . .

I have read another very nice book by a woman education
progressive. I think you would be delighted with it—by Mme
Necker de Saussure.[3]†

Mary to Mrs Reid   Paris, 23 November 1839

. . . I left Boulogne the day after I wrote to you and was obliged
to come the whole journey at one stretch. . . .

I was going on in a beautiful serene state of mind, till I had a
message from the man who is the treasurer and manager of that
unhappy affair . . . in which our money is engaged, or rather sunk—
telling me that our dividends will be reduced just one half next
January. This is so serious a slice out of my income, especially as
my mother, not being here, does not help to pay the rent—that I
am obliged to try and let (ready furnished) two rooms, or else I
shall not be able to make both ends meet. . . . M. Fauriel and M.
Mohl both offer me all they can spare, but I had rather not take
it—not from delicacy, as I have not the slightest, but I had rather
they should keep it for their own wants, especially M. Mohl, who
has not much more than the needful. You may be astonished at my
being so unscrupulous with them, but as I would willingly give
them whatever I could do without, and think nothing about it, I
am very easy when the case is reversed. Money has its value, but in
comparison with a friendship . . . it is so very small that it is not

---

* Harriet Martineau's novel of middle-class life.

† A cousin and friend of Mme de Staël; her *Education progressive, étude du cours
de la vie* had been published in 1828-32.

worth mentioning. . . . If M. Fauriel were rich, I should just worry him for money as children do their Papa, and he might refuse in the same way, without any other feeling being excited. But he an't rich, and he has a good many wants. I shall nevertheless be obliged to take some money from him, but the less the better.

Could you help me to a lodger? He must be a gentleman and not a smoker of cigars—those are two conditions sine qua non. I'll have no lady who would treat me with her company every evening. . . .

I was the more stunned with this blow because, M. Mohl having been treated with such injustice,* I had means of repairing it to a certain degree if he would have accepted it. . . .

And there is no reason why these dividends which will be reduced by half should not be reduced to nothing, and the whole annihilated—in which case I must go out as a Companion or Governess, or live with my sister (which is worse than all)—unless M. Mohl has the place here which he was cheated out of, or unless he makes up his mind to leave Paris for Germany—and I should leave M. Fauriel and settle with him in Germany, which gives me the horrors. (I mean the leaving M. Fauriel.)

If I could get one or two young girls of twelve or fourteen who would pay a handsome sum (much more than it's worth) to be finished off at Paris, I might sacrifice some of my time and independent habits, but I know of none such. India people would be the thing. . . .

I wish I had room to tell you in detail that two gentlemen (French) the other night both said of their own accord that Mme Dudevant† was the first French writer of the age (not the first female writer!) and had a better right to be a member of the Academy than any man! . . .[4]

The emergency was such that she dropped nearly all her salon activities.

Mary to Mrs Reid   Paris, 16 February 1840

. . . I rise at half past eight, swallow my breakfast, and manage to be by nine at Mlle Gérard's, where I draw till three or four. I go calling or about whatever business I may have till near six, my dinner hour. I am generally so tired that I can't help sleeping

---

* The post of Professor of Persian at the Collège de France, for which he was the obvious candidate, had been given to a peer of France, for political reasons.
† George Sand

nearly three-quarters of an hour after it, in spite of the presence of M. Fauriel and M. Mohl, single or both, and their conversation always nourishing to me beyond all others. They remain on an average till ten. I then read or write indispensable notes. On Tuesdays I return home at one to see callers and settle all the accounts and the business that has accumulated in the week. On Sundays I stay at home to see sundry poor people, read a little, write to my mother, etc. . . . You will ask, why draw with such immoderate assiduity and neglect reading and other improvements? Because when I thought I saw ruin staring me in the face, I made up my mind that if I came to be dependent on friends, it should not be without a good hard struggle. And the thing I can do best is taking likenesses, and by working hard I may improve the faculty. It is no use waiting till I want it. Besides to say the truth, it is no great effort, for I am so fond of the occupation that on the Sunday night I think with delight that the only day in which I don't draw is over. . . .

I receive once a fortnight a quantity of children who play and dance here. My first motive was being useful to my little namesake, poor Adèle's daughter. I forget if I told you that she was an early friend, who died eighteen months ago. Her husband died in a madhouse two years before. The orphan is eleven years old; Joséphine [Ruotte] looks after her entirely. She has no relations but two absurd grandmothers. My business is to give her such acquaintance as I can, and by inviting them here I can judge of those she picks up herself. . . . I had intended this all last summer, but on seeing the turn of my affairs I also calculate that if I am obliged to live by portrait-drawing, the more people I know the better. . . .

My winter has passed particularly agreeably to me. Perhaps the constant occupation, and specially the regularity of it, has greatly contributed to that. . . .[5]

Mary to Mrs Reid   Paris, 5 July 1840

. . . I had rather stay with you (if you will have me) . . . in the autumn. Cold Overton is more agreeable in summer than then. I *must* spend some time there, and I would rather choose the brightest days, for it is anything but a merry place. I'm sure I'm growing old—I feel such an aversion to everything dismal. Melancholy is a luxury to the young, like walking to those who have a carriage. They use it and leave it when they like. Not so with the old. . . .

I have enjoyed life this winter particularly. My drawing is delightful to me, and as I have suffered plentifully in my day, I am resolved to make the best and most of what remains, and be as serene as I can for the remainder. . . .[6]

Mary to Mrs Reid   Paris, 23 December 1840

. . . I arrived at Boulogne in the dark on Thursday evening, and crawled along through a mile of quagmire (mud is too good a name for it) from the customs house to my boarding house, after having one of my cloaks taken from me by rascally customs-house men. I slept in the cabin, making my carpet-bag (containing the tea-kettle) a pillow, and the spout kept getting always in the wrong place, twist the bag as I would. However, tea-kettle-spout, quagmire, customs house and martyrising diligence did me no harm, and I was very well when I got here—when I got a vile toothache and swelled face. . . .

It was well I kept to my determination of getting here by the fifth, for the very next morning came the chief manager of our law paper from which I draw my substance to tell me a mixture of good and bad news, and to ask my decision about a resolution which was to be taken the following week. The bad news was that next year we should receive no dividend whatever; that was bad enough. The good was that our paper, or rather our directory, is going on very well—our subscribers being rather on the increase, in spite of the bad times. That may seem odd to reconcile with no dividend, but the reason is that we are obliged to remodel the whole work and destroy the old editions, because we have rivals who have written theirs on a more modern plan, and we must do the same. In 1842 I shall get half the dividend we used to have, and in 1843 [it will be] as high as ever, unless some extraordinary event should occur. Meantime I must live. . . .

I returned to my atelier with great delight, and my friends in the evening. . . . But what miserable weather for a body with no dividend, who wants to save fuel! The cold absolutely screws my soul out of me, and saving fuel is out of the question. I must sell out or do anything—screw my debtors or go out as companion to a lady—provided she be as chilly as me. I'll be no companion to any of your puffing, open-door-and-window ladies, partisans of the wholesome, who give you your death of cold to make the rooms healthy, as my sister does.

Napoleon I's body had just been brought back from St Helena to be interred at the Invalides. The Napoleonic Legend was beginning to elaborate itself—a fact which Mary, having lived under the emperor, found impossible to believe.

I saw from a window Bonaparte's great Juggernaut-looking coach go forward in the Champs Élysées—never saw so many people, but as for enthusiasm, I saw none. There was a hedge of National Guard five or six thick opposite. They were very cold, having stood there two or three hours, so they just danced a country dance—a very merry funeral, was it not! There was some bawling of *Vive l'empereur*! when the Juggernaut-thing went by. It was an absurd immense car forty feet high, gilded all over—the whole business very like a carnival. The spectators were only curious—the newspapers are the greatest liars that ever existed. From where M. Mohl was standing he heard no bawling at all, except from ragamuffins saying to each other: 'Look at those old codgers from the *grande armée*—don't they look funny, with their little short coats!' The papers said that 200,000 people had bellowed 'À bas les traitres, à bas les Guizot, etc.' We heard nothing of it. . . .

So far the attempts of Napoleon I's nephew Louis to promote the legend, and himself, consisted of two attempted risings, at Strasburg in 1836 and Boulogne in 1840, and a book *Les idées napoléoniennes* published in 1839. The Orleanists in power, and Mary who supported them, considered him a figure of fun.

Mary to Mrs Reid   Cold Overton, 11 December 1841

. . . I think my mother is better, but my sister, always looking at the dark side, makes me . . . distrust myself. For we are so constituted that if a human creature alongside us said all day long 'black is white' we should soon have doubts upon the subject. . . . If we do not *love* our neighbour better than ourselves, we at least believe him better. . . .[8]

Mrs Reid's great friend Harriet Martineau, now forty, had always been both delicate and profoundly deaf. Despite this, she had invented an education for herself and become celebrated as the author of *Illustrations of Political Economy*, 1832, *Poor Law and Paupers Illustrated*, 1833, *Illustrations of Taxation*, 1834, and *Society in America*, 1837, as well as her novel *Deerbook* and her very original stories for children in *The Playfellow*, 1841. In the next year, however, she succumbed to yet another ailment, almost unmentionable at the time, and said to be untreatable. Mary, however, had no inhibitions about mentioning it, and indeed set about getting it treated. Unfortunately, she was not successful, since Miss Martineau (understandably, given the uncertainty of surgical treatment at the time) shied away from the operation Mary urged on her and for the rest of her life struggled on with a growth inside her abdomen—producing, nevertheless, a vast quantity of solid work. From time to time the symptoms subsided, and at one period she thought she was cured, by mesmerism, which she then 'puffed' to whoever would listen to her, to Mary's disgust. When she died, the growth was found to be eighteen inches in diameter.

Mary to Mrs Reid   Paris, 24 March 1842

. . . Miss Smith told me Miss Martineau's complaint was polypus in the womb (it's no use making delicacy when such an important subject is in question). Is it so or not? Because they are operated on and *cured* here, but the doctor who told my friend of it says he supposes they are not in England. . . . And there is no medium between death and operation (which is not even very painful). . . . If there was any probability of saving Miss Martineau and money could do it, I need not ask—I know you would be too happy. What I dread is the obstinacy, ignorance and prejudice of people's friends. I only make one request, which is that Miss Martineau's brother-in-law shall state the case medically. I will show it to the first surgeons here for these cases. . . . I have been so struck with the ignorance on each side of the water of what is going forward on the other. . . .[9]

Faced with such impetuosity, Mrs Reid took fright. Despite her Non-conformist conscience and her realization that there was a crying need for numerous reforms of the female condition, from gynaecology to higher education, *en passant par* the setting up of charitable pawnshops for the working-class woman, it would be some years before she could convince herself that it was what she called 'a woman's part' to be active in such matters.

Mary to Mrs Reid   Paris, 3 April 1842

. . . Dear friend, a truly woman's part, in my mind, is a truly human being's part. I am so unaccustomed in this land of freedom (whatever people may say) to play woman . . . that it never came into my head to suppose a woman was not quite as fit to be busy and do good as a man. . . .[10]

It was in this year that she became intimate with another young woman who should have had an important part to play in the artistic world. This was Hilary Bonham Carter, then twenty-two, a cousin and close friend of Florence Nightingale's. She had a marked talent for painting and drawing; during the Bonham Carters' stay in Paris in the summer of 1842 Mary took her to draw in the Louvre, introduced her to artists, formed plans for her future education and career—undaunted by the fact that, even at this early stage she was always 'needed at home', as the eldest daughter of an amiable but ineffectual mother. For the moment nothing very concrete could be done for her, although in general women's fortunes seemed to be prospering.

Mary to Mrs Reid   Paris, December 1842

. . . There is a new review here called *La Revue indépendante*. It was established last year by George Sand, alias Mme Dudevant, M. Leroux and M. Viardot. Leroux is a philosopher, and so tiresome that the review was going to the dogs. It was agreed therefore that it should go entirely out of his hands and be written by others—when lo! Mme Dudevant declared she would stick by him, and that if they gave up Leroux they must give up her too— and she being the only person who keeps the review alive, they were obliged to knock under and keep him. I don't approve of her taste, but it is a triumph to the sex. . . .

And Mlle Rachel keeps the Théâtre Français from sinking, so I think we must not call out that female talent is persecuted![11]

Despite her interest in new writing, she was still faithful to the folk-poetry which had so excited her in the 1820s. Consequently Macaulay's 'sham' ballads, the *Lays of Ancient Rome*, outraged her.

Mary to Mrs Reid   Cold Overton, 17 September 1843

. . . I want to see the *Quarterly* on the *Lays of Ancient Rome*, which I despise and execrate (the humbugs) as much as I should a coarse figure of a dead lover. To have the impudence to suppose that he can give life to ballads whose only merit ought to be life is as presuming as to concoct a man, like Frankenstein, and nothing shocks me more than the stupid public, whose want of real feeling can have accepted such stuff with applause. They have no taste, no cultivation, no feeling for nature. They would mistake a piece of clockwork for a human being. . . .

I saw a curious canting article in the *Edinburgh Review* of some months back, attacking Wordsworth's Christianity. 'Pon my word, these reviews are worse than the Holy Inquisition! . . . I'll wager it is by one [James] Stephen, whom I spent three days with many years ago at a country house and thought a very third-rate person. There will be no living ten years hence. Well, 'there's a heaven aboon all', as Meg Merrilees says, and we shall die before men are banished from society for not making God after our own image. . . .[12]

Since the '20s, however, when Fauriel's Greek ballads had loomed so large in her life, and Europe's, Fauriel himself had grown old and vulnerable. In September 1843 he was run over in the street, which added to her anxieties, and alas! her old urge to manage him despite himself.

Mary to Fauriel   Cold Overton, 26 September 1843
. . . The apartment that has fallen vacant in our Paris house is a godsend. For months I have been thinking of it, and coveting it for you. Come, even if you do not care for the idea, even if it is a great sacrifice on your part, *take it*, to please me, and you will surely have your reward, because you will save such a deal of time* and have more time to work. And what put it in my head in the first place is that you might be ill again. . . . I promise that moving shall not cause you the slightest trouble—M. Mohl and I will do everything. . . .[13]

Mary to Mrs Reid   Paris, 10 March 1844
. . . I have been much tormented by anxiety, as M. Fauriel has been ill. He is better, but I am not easy yet. . . . You will find him much aged, alas! since you last saw him. It makes my heart ache to acknowledge it to my very self. I have a hundred schemes in my head for his comfort, but he is very troublesome and unmanageable, and as reasonable as a child of four years old. . . .[14]

Mary to Fauriel   Paris, [? Spring] 1844
. . . My dear, M. Mohl tells me that you told him I had so insisted that you could not refuse, although you disliked the idea

---

* Since he would not have to walk to and from the Clarkes' apartment each evening.

excessively. Dearest, if that is the case, I would rather you did not consent, however much I may wish it. It was only that I thought you would be more comfortable, but I would rather never see you again than make you unhappy. . . . I had thought that you might be ill, that with the years your living alone was becoming a trouble to you, and I am always a little anxious since your accident. But God knows I would not ask you to do what you would always dislike. . . .

Adieu, my dearest. I am so very sorry. . . .[15]

In the early morning of 15 July Fauriel died. Florence Nightingale, in her innocence, sent elaborate condolences which could hardly have been less consoling.

Florence Nightingale to Mary   Embley, July 1844

. . . That loving without the craving to be loved in return, which I think will be heaven, he seems to have realised on earth. . . . The force of his love lay in his serenity and steadfastness—it was a deep and deliberate feeling, no enthusiastic, feverish glow which leaves only exhaustion and languor behind and is connected with the least spiritual part of us.

How I hate emotional dissipation! it throws a gloomy shadow on one's whole after-life, and is what makes people think their latter days such dry sticks. People are not at liberty to wound themselves, because the scar which closes around hardens the place for ever; to squander susceptibility is like committing suicide. . . .[16]

Mary to Mrs Reid   Paris, 25 August 1844

. . . My mind is in such a low state that I wish for nothing, except perhaps for money enough to have bought M. Fauriel's library to send to Greece, to the public library at Athens. I might have done it, but my future is so precarious that I have debarred myself of that happiness by an effort of will. If ever I have money enough, I intend to found some public institution at Athens in his name. He rendered more service to Greece than any living man, and the fruit of his labours has been taken by others. But in time he will regain his right place. I do not deserve such a friend as M. Mohl, for all my thoughts are with *him*. . . .[17]

Once again she dropped her salons and dinner parties and buckled down to hard work.

Mary to Mrs Reid   Paris, 24 March 1845

. . . I have been in dreadful spirits since my return and so never allow myself a moment's idleness from seven in the morning till twelve or one at night. . . . I go every day to draw at a friend's— four, five, six or seven hours. I read M. Fauriel's papers about five hours a day. I am sorting them, and there is now three volumes in the press, but they go on so slowly at the printers that I fear they will not be out till summer, and if so I shall wait till the autumn to have them sold, as June or July is the worst time in the year for a book to appear. I had much trouble to collect the whole, as it came in a disorderly state; and what I am now reassembling is much worse. It is on the origin of Italian literature and on Dante. I shall not publish it till I have consulted Manzoni. . . .

You appear to like your present state of things, which I rejoice at. . . .

I greatly rejoice too in Miss Martineau's cure, but am sorry she is not content with the miracle performed on herself, which is quite sufficient to do credit to mesmerism, but will spoil all by writing about miracles in the papers. That's the way with all females: they *will* out-Herod Herod. . . .[18]

Fortunately Mohl was present and willing to help, unobtrusively, with these sad, fatiguing tasks.

Mary to Mrs Reid   Paris, 15 November 1845

. . . M. Mohl deserves much more from me than I can ever do, and my volatile nature is such that I am always in his debt and always shall be. But I should be a great comfort to him, I know, because he cannot open easily, and these strongly self-governing natures can only rest upon such butterflies as myself, for, curious to say, the strong depend more on the weak than vice versa. . . .[19]

Mohl's paradoxical strength was more and more useful, for not only did Mary become embroiled in yet another legal action to recover money, but she found that her mother's health was not improving.

Mary to Mohl   St Leonard's, 8 August 1846

. . . My mother is neither better nor worse, and the doctor has told my sister that in spite of her constant suffering, she is not in more danger than she was last year . . . so I shall leave in the middle of next month. . . . I have been studying Dante all this time with great attention, and as I have done a great deal already, I think I shall soon come to the end. I am very sorry now that I did not publish the Provençal lectures at my own expense, for they would have been printed much sooner. Besides my *procès*, I must go home to renew the lease of my apartment. . . . I *must* go, if only for a fortnight. It will distress my poor mother, but what can I do? She is so deaf that she does not hear unless one screams in her ear, and her head is so weak that she can interest herself in nothing. . . . It is hard to spend more than six months absolutely deprived of all sympathy or conversation, always thrown in on one's self, and witnessing such perpetual suffering—not to speak of sad recollections! . . .[20]

Soon after this Mrs Clarke too died. Once again Mary seemed to face nothing but sad endings, for, as she recalled much later in her book on Madame Récamier, that circle too was breaking up:

[In 1847] . . . Mme Récamier underwent the operation for cataract in one of her eyes; in the other the cataract was not advanced enough to insure success. She was to be kept perfectly quiet and in total darkness, and almost alone. Immediately after the operation, M. Ballanche was seized with inflammation on the lungs; in three days all hope was over. She crossed the street and attended his death-bed, and in her agitation and tears . . . all hope of recovering the sight of her eye was lost. . . .

M. de Chateaubriand was in 1847 incapable even of rising from his seat; his memory so much gone that he was heard to ask for a friend dead twenty years before, and his other faculties much impaired. Mme Récamier had endeavoured to conceal this from all, even from herself. She could not bear to tell her dearest friends that the intellect she had so entirely admired was gone . . . and he knew his faculties were going, and had the feeling of a poor proud man who hides his poverty. . . . In this state he was carried daily to the Abbaye; he seemed only to live during the three hours he spent with Mme Récamier. . . . Mme Récamier was persuaded to go for a short time to Maintenon to repair her strength. . . . During this absence a friend of hers* who lived in the same house as M. de Chateaubriand, went every day to spend half an hour with him,

_____
* Mary.

and then daily wrote a few lines to her; it was not until then that
the terrible ruin of his mind was completely revealed. . . .[21]

In the midst of so much death and decline, however, a more cheerful
motif made its appearance.

Mary to Florence Nightingale   Summer 1847

. . . What sort of a man is this M. Browning? What I read of his
poetry in these beastly reviews it is true I was not much charmed
with; he appears, as I recollect them, very inferior to his wife. The
greater the merit in his falling in love!—but I can't bear to see
women 'dowking', as they call it in Leicestershire. It means bending
the knees to make oneself look shorter, and they do it if they
are drawn for the Militia. Now women are very apt to do that
when their husband or lover is half an inch shorter than themselves. . . .[22]

Mary to Mohl   Paris, 4 July 1847

I shall not go out today; please come. I wrote the letter enclosed
with this one some days ago; don't open it for at least a month. I
have kept it in my bag out of a feeling which I can hardly put into
words; but I would like you to understand me at last. If you had
understood me six, seven or eight years ago, you might have spared
me immeasurable pain—but God forgive you, you have been punished enough.

Enclosure If you ever doubt me, or are vexed with me, open this
letter, written one day when your fortunes were not prospering.

Inner enclosure If you are not appointed [to the chair of Persian
Literature at the Collège de France] I shall marry you, if that would
please you, to show those old pedants that I know your value better
than they and their ape of a Minister, as the future will show. I
have thought long and hard about it; pray do the same—and take
your time.[23]

Mohl to Mérimée   Paris, 10 August 1847

My dear Mérimée, I have a favour to ask of you. Will you do me
the honour of standing at my side in an affair I shall be engaged in
at ten o'clock tomorrow morning?[24]

Mérimée to Mohl   Paris, 11 August 1847

. . . In Heaven's name, whom are you going to fight?[25]

Mary to Eleanor Frewen Turner   Paris, 11 August 1847

. . . As an aunt is like a fifth wheel to a coach, I was married this morning to M. Mohl.[26]

Mary to Mrs Reid   Paris, 15 October 1847

. . . I suppose you have learned that I have espoused M. Mohl before men and angles, as Winifred Jenkins writes it.* I was a long time making up my mind about it. The banns were published—if published may be called what was done so privately that by the means of the flunkey they were covered over the instant after—and all this four months before it took place, so uncertain was the affair and so determined was I to be able to change my mind to the last minute. I have not repented since then; I can't say I did either right or wrong. This world is not one of reality but one of imagination, and all things are to be appreciated through the state of the mind and nothing else.

I left this for Germany on 13th August, and I certainly enjoyed my journey greatly. I was three weeks at Berlin, where I saw the élite of the learned—which is the élite of all Germany, for the King of Prussia has lately passed a skimming-dish over all the land and secured almost all the cream for his sandy capital—very convenient for travellers. I was treated with great politeness by them, as M. Mohl was known to all, though not by sight. . . .

I keep my apartment, which is so dirty I must have it trigged up. . . . I shall see more company this winter than I have done. It is reasonable and wise, for I want to get out of my old self—I know it's the best receipt. I ought not to be melancholy for M. Mohl's sake, whose spirits always flag when mine do.

Florence Nightingale is coming, for two days only, next Wednesday. She is a rara avis, a phoenix. . . .[27]

Mary to Lady William Russell   Paris, 16 July 1867

. . . I married late, and was rather given to sentimental flirtation for a good many years—all with the most honourable intentions, of

* In Smollett's *Humphry Clinker*.

course. Only somehow or other such affairs go off, sometimes for one reason, sometimes for another, and I had a great many experiences in that line. But my friends gain by it; for, having a proper esteem for the sacrament of marriage, besides having by degrees grown old, I have transferred all my old habit of sentiment into friendships, and by long habit I suppose they have kept a resemblance to their troublesome brothers in being very ardent. . . .[28]

VII

1848-1852
Fighting for protégées

This, then, was to be the end of youthful dreaming. In place of Fauriel, with his 'beautiful eyes and melting voice', here was Mohl, about whose physical charms Mary was and remained significantly reticent. In place of an active life on any kind of public stage, there was now to be a life of observation and comment. In place of the writing of great books, there would be no more than the presentation, the management, of other writers and artists. In place of the dangers and excitements of the Restoration, here—ad infinitum—was the respectable safety of Louis-Philippe's France. To her friends, and probably also to herself, Mary made it plain that all passion was well and truly spent.

Mohl had always presented himself as the archetypal plain man, and he continued in the role, growling when his wife arranged dinner parties, refusing to be taken to the opera, systematically pursuing his academic studies. T. A. Trollope observed that he had always found M. Mohl, when calling upon him, so absolutely surrounded by books, 'built up into walls around him, as to suggest almost inevitably the idea of a mouse in a cheese, eating out the hollow it lives in. . . .'[1]

Nevertheless, romance was not quite as absent, perhaps, as Mary's new mood of realism may suggest. Mohl's work had its romantic side. In 1843, for example, he had had the imagination to encourage Paul-Emile Botta to excavate the royal palaces of Nineveh, which resulted in the first discoveries of Assyrian sculptures and inscriptions. In the '50s he planned 'the creation of an Arabic university at Algiers, where letters, medicine, theology and jurisprudence shall be taught by the remnant of learned Mahomedans'[2]—a very new idea at the time. And the collection of Oriental classics that he brought out over ten years, as well as the *Shah Nameh*, his life-work, constituted an exciting step forward in the West's understanding of the East, and eventually gained him the presidencies of both the French Asiatic Society and the Académie des Inscriptions. He was clearly a man of some vision—and one who, once attracted, was faithful to the end. Why, Queen Victoria asked him many years later, had he given up Germany for France, since he loved his native country so much. 'The truth is, Ma'am,' he replied, 'I was in love.'[3]

Nor were Mary's activities after marriage quite as earthbound, as flatly 'reasonable and wise', as she gave Mrs Reid to understand. Some of her regular guests were, of course, Mohl's fellow-scholars, whose passions, as in many such circles, were apt to centre on academic in-fighting and scandal. (Electoral campaigns for seats in the Institut were followed with as much excitement as parliamentary elections today.) But there were others whose varied interests gave a good deal more scope for a study of human nature and its social manifestations in a period of interesting change. Catholicity was, now even more than before, Mary's strong point—a happy ability to be interested in people of the most diverse tastes and creeds, and scandalized by almost nothing but stupidity. So 120 Rue du Bac became a kind of crossroads at which the most unlikely acquaintances met and were observed. Mrs Gaskell, a convinced Unitarian as well as a gifted writer, was a great favourite of Mary's; but so too was the Catholic politician Montalembert. Churchmen such as Dean Stanley and Archbishop Temple felt thoroughly at home with her; so, equally, did unbelievers like Ernest Renan and George Eliot. She never ceased to be drawn to art and artists; but her close friends also included scientists such as Liebreich and Helmholtz (who married Mohl's niece Anna) and the economist Nassau Senior. In the Rue du Bac her strait-laced sister, and others like her, rubbed shoulders with wicked and witty persons like Lady William Russell (a contemporary of Mary's who, like her, had been brought up on the Continent) and the philanthropist-littérateur-politician Richard Monckton Milnes who, among his other activities, made a well-known collection of erotica for his library at Fryston.

Old friends—Louise Belloc, Ampère, Mignet, Dr Roulin, etc.—continued to be valued; but they were constantly supplemented by younger people who caught her imagination and provided amazing subjects for study: Florence Nightingale and Hilary Bonham Carter, of course, but also Thackeray's charming daughter Annie, who herself became a writer, the Duchess of Colonna, one of the few women of the nineteenth century to make a career as a sculptor, and (in very different veins) the poet Swinburne and the new critics Taine and Schérer. She loved to observe the workings of great statesmen; but at the same time she continued to enjoy the company of children, both as subjects of study and for their own sake. 'At luncheon Mme Mohl used to call out, "Young ladies . . . whose turn is it to ride with me?" and those whose privilege it was were greatly elated. They scampered along through brake, through brier, regardless of obstacles. Once they were galloping in high glee when they saw a turnpike, and they had none of them any money. The gate was open, and they rode full tilt through it, to the consternation of the keeper. . . . The next day M. Mohl gave a double toll to the turnpike-keeper, because, as he told him, "My wife is a queer body, and she may very likely do the same again." '[4]

'Wise and reasonable' is precisely what she never became, particularly in little matters of economics or politics; but in personal relations she had a sort of instinctive wisdom—a fact attested by the lengthy periods her servants stayed with her (one, Julie, was her cook for over twenty years).

Married to Mohl, she was able to be even more independent than before. 'Married folk should always separate when they visit,' she told Mary Simpson, 'because they each are then making friends and amusement for each other, and when they remeet they are the more entertaining. In this country [England] it is supposed they adore each other so much that they never need do anything to amuse each other; but that I totally deny, and why people should cease to play the agreeable because they live together, I know not.'[5] So during the summer, while Mohl refreshed himself at the Athenaeum or with the Orientalist Max Müller at Oxford, she toured the houses of her disparate friends, dining with Thackeray, amazing George Eliot and G.H. Lewes when they first met her, taking such a liking to Holman Hunt 'that I comprehend people should put up with his unpunctualities.'[6]

The apartment at 120 Rue du Bac, into which Mohl moved in 1847, seemed to epitomize permanence and stability. 'Mme Mohl,' wrote Mrs Gaskell, 'lives on the fourth and fifth stories of a great large hotel built about a hundred and fifty years ago, *entre cour et jardin*, "cour" opening into the narrow busy Rue du Bac. "Jardin" has a very large (ten acres) plot of ground given by Cardinal Richelieu to the Missions Etrangères—and so not built upon, but surrounded by great houses like this. It is as stiffly laid out in kitchen gardens, square walks, etc. as possible; but there are great trees in it, and altogether it is really very pretty. That's at the back of the house, and some of the rooms look on to it. On the fourth story are four lowish sitting rooms and Mme Mohl's bedroom. On the fifth (slopes in the roof): kitchen, grenier, servants' bedrooms, [spare] bedroom, workroom, etc.; all brick floors, which is cold to the feet. My bedroom is very pretty and picturesque. I like sloping roofs and plenty of windows stuffed into their roof anyhow, and in every corner of this room (and it's the same all over the house) French and English books are *crammed*.'[7]

Mohl's work, with its satisfactions and irritations, provided a solid background to Mary's more erratic exploits. As he wrote to Hilary Bonham Carter on 1 May 1847:

... The Collège de France is a curious institution, founded by Francis I against the Sorbonne, and destined to introduce the new branches of learning which the Reform had fostered, as Hebrew, classical Greek and Latin, etc. From this time it has kept its privileges—is not subject to or connected with the university, and teaches all the sciences which find no room in the teaching which the university gives. . . . It is a very beautiful institution and ought to be the first in the world if it came up to the idea which led to its foundation. It is open to everybody. The most ragged boy may go in, and nobody has a right to ask who he is; and numbers of ladies come to hear the lectures which may interest them. I recollect that even while I was following the lectures of Chinese there attended a lady most regularly; she had a thick green veil, which she kept down (I suppose not to distract us), and nobody has ever seen her face.

I have been interrupted, and this letter has suffered for it; indeed I can hardly ever write a letter from beginning to the end. I can compare myself to nobody under heaven but one of those Capuchin friars whom you have seen in Italy, sitting all day long in their confessional, hearing the strange stories of sinners of all sorts, consoling the one and rebuking the other; only my customers are literary people, calling on me to tell me their enmities, the conspirations of their rivals, their plans and their helpless misery, their inconceivable infatuation, and all the ills which this species is heir to. Unfortunately, I seldom know a remedy for them, and can very seldom convince them that their enemies are not so black and malicious as they suppose. I don't know how I have come to be a confessor to so many people; but so it is. . . .

Then we have here a democratical organization of literary concerns which exists nowhere else. Every honour and every place is given by the votes of Academies and other bodies, so we are living eternally in the same bustle as Cambridge was in, according to your letter, for the election [to the Chancellorship] of Prince Albert . . . [8]

Thus was everyday life. Barely six months after the marriage, however, everyday life disappeared like a dream at daybreak. Louis-Philippe's government, though it exactly suited Mary's views, was less popular with other sections of the population. Its increasing repressiveness, its unconcern about workers' conditions as France began to become more and more industrialized, the failure of the corn-harvest in 1846 and 1847, which created widespread unemployment—all acted to set off yet another French revolution, in February 1848. The King was forced to abdicate and fled to England with Guizot, and in due course a provisional government was set up, including the socialist Louis Blanc, the poet and politician Lamartine, and a worker in the gas industry, Albert Martin. They announced that universal suffrage would be introduced, that the National Guard—a sort of militia, hitherto limited to the middle classes—would be opened up to other citizens, and that National Workshops would be set up to provide for the many unemployed. These, unfortunately, failed: not enough work could be created, doles still had to be paid, and 'paupers' were attracted into Paris from outside. They also created alarm among the less socialist of the republicans. A new government was then elected and proved to be considerably less socialist, which led to a socialist rising on 15 May and virtual civil war until well into June.

Mary to the Nightingale family   Paris, 1 March 1848

. . . Hitherto we are safe enough, but I have doubts as to the future. I do not say for my own person, which I really think nothing about; and if I did should not fear, having a friend or two in each party—except perhaps in the *juste milieu*, which I had come to detest.

You can't imagine how quick the whole thing came about. On Tuesday I went out to see the people go to the banquet in the Champs Élysées—very peaceful they seemed. There was a stream of people along the road from eight a.m., not very thick. On coming back the Chamber was surrounded by dragoons and *blouses* [workmen] bawling out 'La Réforme!', but one had no idea how it would end. Wednesday we heard of the change of ministry—the regency in the evening—on Thursday the Republic—all this with an accompaniment of pop-guns on all sides. M. Mohl served three nights last week in the Garde Nationale—to make a show, for they had not a ball or cartridge or ounce of powder in the whole arrondissement. . . .

Old Mme Guizot and the three children were hid at Mme Le Normant's, who was taken ill, probably in consequence of the fatigue. Mme Récamier making lamentation all day about it, I set off Friday morning with a letter to Mme Le Normant, to offer my services. . . . My offer was declined, and I came back through the Carrousel. . . . Some of the barricades were eighteen feet high and more, but there were little passages next the houses, about two or three or so—not easy to find, on account of the crowds squeezing through. They were very civil, and one man handed me over the barricade. . . .

The obstinacy of the King and of the whole set has brought us to this *blouse*-y government. M. Mohl is very gloomy on the subject; he says we are in the hands of savages. Others do naught but admire the good sentiments they hear expressed by the people. . . .

I feel very much as if I were shut up in the Jardin des Plantes, and the whole set in cages were let loose. My intense love for animals would make me delight in the spectacle, my pleasure in grace and beauty would almost make me forget their claws, and my esteem for them is such that even if they put out their claws I could not call them cruel: they must eat, and the retractile family live on live prey. The people have behaved prettily, and their moral beauty may stand in lieu of the physical beauty of the quadrupeds. But after all, they must eat, and who is to feed them? We— their admirers? It is all very pretty to see them growl over their prey at first, but if we must always furnish it, it will fatigue our pockets. . . .

On Thursday a little carpenter whom I often employ came to ask me a great service.—What?—To lend him a coat and trousers to save the life of his uncle, who was a Garde Municipale and shut up in their house in the Rue de Tournon. The people wanted to massacre the Gardes, and he could not go out in his uniform or in his shirt. The little carpenter was beside himself. He had a vast pistol hid in his jacket, which I'm sure he could not have fired. I gave him the clothes, and the man came afterwards to thank me.

It is agreed on all hands that, although all this has been prepared by secret societies, they would not have dared break out had not the Garde Municipale fired on the mob from the Hôtel des Affaires Étrangères—I think on Wednesday. That was a mistake. Many people were killed, picked up and carried about to show the mob. Instantly they ran to arms. Ferrari, who is one of the *société secrète* of the ultra-republicans, told me last night that on part of Thursday the party was in a state of vacillation, and thought they must give up the whole; then they took courage again.

I wish I could remember all I hear, but one's head gets quite addled. I can't describe what I felt on Wednesday night. . . . Next morning we were *en pleine révolution* and with my full advice and participation he [M. Mohl] went to the Garde Nationale. I have talked over two or three others to go, and think I am entitled to a *couronne civique*. Adieu. Love to all.[9]

Mary to Hilary Bonham Carter   Paris, March 1848

. . . M. Mohl returned this morning at five. It is the fourth night since Thursday that he has spent patrolling streets in the rain.—Of course, he can't do much the day after. We may calculate that there are at least eighty thousand gardes nationales in Paris at this time, whose nights are thus spent—and whose days consequently are diminished to one half of their value; and these eighty thousand are taken from the most industrious, enlightened morale of the nation—for as the service is voluntary, it is the best who go.

I dined with Louis Blanc a fortnight ago, never thinking what he was to become. He is quite a dwarf, with rather a pretty face. I took him for a little boy, come to play with the Child of the House, and was quite astonished he wanted to poke in his oar; but he was not much attended to. I thought he talked nonsense, and did not listen. . . .[10]

It was just before the Revolution that Mohl had 'heard Louis Blanc say to the crowd which pressed round him as he was getting into his carriage "I hope the time will come when we shall all have our carriages." Some one called out: "And who will drive me?" '[11]

Mary to Hilary Bonham Carter   Paris, 26 May 1848

. . . Ruin goes on every day increasing. The noble, the generous, the good Delesserts are giving up their banking-house—not failing, but paying off. Every good enterprise in the country for thirty years was invented or aided by them; but failure follows failure, like cards falling on each other. . . .[12]

From Mme Mohl's *Madame Récamier**

. . . Still the *habitués* went to the Abbaye, and a merry laugh even went round, often, at the queer stories about the Republicans, and the farces that were acted to show their absurdity; for to do them justice, they did not attempt to muzzle the press or the theatres. M. de Chateaubriand, like an old oak struck by lightning . . . sat, seemed to listen, and smiled when one of his favourites entered; but in reality he was indifferent to all. About March a bad cough which he had grew worse; in May he could not leave his room. . . . During the terrible days of June, when he was asked what he thought, he said he cared nothing about it. . . .

In spite of the constant firing, the barricades which she could not see, and the *garde mobile* stationed at the corner of every street, Mme Récamier, though blind and nervous, never missed a day in coming from the Abbaye to the Rue du Bac. Fortunately there were two unfrequented back streets, by which she persuaded the

* See Bibliography.

coachman to drive. Since her blindness she had been unable to walk in the streets. . . .

She dreaded his dying in the night, when it might be impossible to send for her in time; and it was a comfort that she had a friend living upstairs in the same house* who could give her a room, where she spent three nights. On the morning of the 3rd of July, at about seven, she was called down; in about an hour all was over. . . .[13]

She herself died, painfully, in the cholera epidemic of the following year.

In the autumn Mary devised a plan to enable Florence Nightingale to visit the Institution of Deaconesses at Kaiserswerth. Florence longed to study its nursing methods at first hand—it was one of the few nursing institutions which could be said to have methods—but had, as usual when the idea of her becoming a professional nurse was raised, met with horrified opposition from her mother and sister. Mary's idea was that Florence and her mother should come to the Mohls during their stay in Frankfurt, which was near Kaiserswerth, and that they would make an opportunity for her to visit the place and possibly even receive some training there. But the plan failed; the Nightingales had already packed their trunks and got their passports, when riots broke out in Frankfurt too. It was only in July 1850 that Florence managed to get to Kaiserswerth for a first brief visit, only in 1851 that she got for herself three months' work there, in its orphanage, wards and operating theatres, only in February 1853 that she was allowed to spend a month in Paris, ostensibly on a visit to Mary (to cover Mrs Nightingale's shame), really to study all the hospitals in that city and receive nursing-training from the Soeurs de la Charité.

In December 1848, according to the new French constitution, a president had to be elected. There were various candidates, including Lamartine and the right-wing Republican Cavaignac. The most unlikely one, it might have been thought, turned out to be the winner. This was Louis Napoleon, nephew of the old emperor.

Few presidents could have been more antipathetic to Mary—or indeed to most of the liberals who could remember the rule of the first Napoleon. But the climate of opinion had been changing in the '40s. The idea of public enthusiasm for a Bonaparte, at which Mary had scoffed on the occasion of Napoleon I's reinterment, was now a reality. A nostalgic cult of the First Empire had grown up, been fostered by various writers, and reinforced by the troubles of recent years and a superstitious feeling that Louis Napoleon was somehow fated to rule France.

* Mary.

To Mary the situation was quite clear: Louis Napoleon was an obvious and repulsive fraud, and his policies uniformly detestable. She never found cause to revise her opinion.

Mary to Mrs Reid   Paris, 20 November 1848

. . . There is scarcely a doubt that Louis Napoleon will be elected, and by the universal suffrage. Why? Not, as people suppose, for the love of his uncle—not a bit. Who stirred a finger for him when he tried twice before! But now the peasants say: 'He will deliver us from this republic as his uncle did.' They abominate the republic because they don't sell their goods, and though republics are very well in theory (when people are accustomed to them), there is something more essential, which is to make a living. People don't consider, when they see an absurd abuse of government, that if they overturn one set of men for being bad, another set may get in that is worse. Forms of government are nothing. It is those who work the system that make it good or bad. . . .

How long Louis Napoleon will last I can't say, but as the peasants who vote do it in the illusion that he is so enormously rich that he will pay all their taxes, it is not probable it will last. M. Mohl votes for Cavaignac—not that we are greatly delighted with the republic, but as it exists, we wish it to remain—but I don't believe it will. I have a strong presentiment that the Orléans family will be back before five years are over. We shall see. . . .

Lamartine is a puppy, and might have been of use had he been the least bit of a man, but he is a vain fool who thought of nothing but showing off his miserable self . . . a fellow who went flourishing about like a public singer, making speeches just like *roulades*, and no more to the purpose than *roulades* are to a real song. It's well to be you, not to live here, to get soaked through with disgust at everybody and everything. Faugh! I'll talk of something better!

The lecture which I was so delighted with is become, with many others, a book—and so interesting . . . that I am hunting for a private hand to take it to England, to Julia Smith. Don't believe, dear friend, that my first impression was other than sending it to you; but she won't *buy* it, and you will. And above all things I wish the book to be read, and so will you when you read it. It is called *L'Histoire morale des femmes*, by Ernest Legouvé. There are many things in it that can't be read aloud, but don't accuse the author of

indelicacy; it is a history of the position of women from the beginning of society, and of course facts must be stated.

More than twenty years ago I planned such a book, upon exactly
the same method, viz. historical. But nothing is easier than to
plan. . . .

I want to get it well reviewed—pray begin immediately to
enquire. . . .

I add a little P.S. in answer to one or two things in your letter.
If I understand right, Queens College is lectures for ladies.* You
say: 'Have one in Paris.' But whenever ladies can go to the same
lectures as men, is it not better that they should? All the lectures
here are gratis and, except at the Sorbonne, all open to ladies—and
generally you find some at them. Are the [Queens] lectures accompanied by examinations? The Sorbonne here is *the* University, and
the young men attend there previous to taking their degrees, and
are examined for those degrees, as they can enter no profession
without them. The other lectures are at the Observatory, the Jardin
des Plantes, the Royal Library, the Arts et Métiers. . . . There is
nothing done for the male audience more than the female. . . .[14]

She had not yet grasped Mrs Reid's revolutionary idea that women too
should take degrees and enter professions. By 1852 Mrs Reid was an-
nouncing that Bedford's instruction was 'given on the same plan as in the
public Universities, of combined lectures, examinations and exercises.'[15]
But in any case the Mohls' attention was taken up, this winter and the
following year, by crises that were more immediately pressing than the
details of higher education for girls. In unsettled Germany the future of
Robert Mohl, who was a member of the Würtemberg parliament, was
becoming increasingly insecure.

Mary to Mrs Reid   Paris, 24 May 1849

    . . . I am very anxious about M. Mohl's brother Robert . . . He
abolished all gaming houses from principle, but it will probably be
his ruin, as he was professor at Heidelberg, which belongs to the
Grand Duchy of Baden—and no one loses so much as the Grand
Duke by the said closing-up. They paid him an enormous tax,
besides. However, he did it as a duty, and rich fathers and mothers
all over Europe ought to be grateful . . . but they will neither care
nor know a word about it, and he and his children will be reduced

* It had been founded in 1845, arising out of the same movement as the
Governesses' Benevolent Institution, and was in fact less for ladies than for girls.

to very little. My M. Mohl wrote for us both that as far as we could join in his good deeds we would, by looking on his children as our own, and begging him not to torment himself about them. M. Mohl will bring back the two girls—one I shall put to school (if the parents agree). He sets off on Monday for Strasburg and perhaps for Germany. I am very anxious about Frankfurt. . . .[16]

For the next eight years Ida Mohl lived with the Paris Mohls, who virtually adopted her, so that Mary at last, at fifty-six, acquired at least a share in a daughter. As for Ida, she declared that she loved her foster-mother 'dearly from the very beginning'.

Mary to Mrs Reid   Paris, 7 June 1849

. . . I am afraid of the cholera—not for myself, but for Ida Mohl, who is with us, and other folks' children. . . . We must and ought to go—people are dying around us almost as if the plague was about, and I would go tomorrow if I could persuade M. Mohl. . . .

Germany is in a terrible state, Robert Mohl hiding himself in a quiet village on the Rhine. As to poor Maurice Mohl, the most generous and devoted of mortals, heaven knows what will become of him.

We are all so anxious here about the politics and the socialists that although the cholera is getting towards the same state it was in in '32, people think nothing about it and scarcely take a precaution. It is said that this preoccupation kept it a long time from spreading in '32. The consternation was so general that you might cross Paris at nine o'clock at night and not meet a soul in the street. Now the streets are exactly as before it spread. . . .

I am in trouble about my Italian friends. Mme Arconati is so cut up. The Manzonis are in great distress—they can't receive their own daughter, not having enough to add to their expenses—such a slight addition. . . . There has been a little want of economy and management, no doubt. People who put by part of their incomes have weathered these storms by living on their savings, but that will come to an end. . . .[17]

Fortunately, to take her mind off these sadnesses, she had another legal battle on her hands. She in her turn was now being sued by the heirs of the lawyer she had fought in the '30s.

Mary to Hilary Bonham Carter   Limoges, 15 November 1850

. . . Yesterday I spent four hours at the court, and heard Le Fèvre d'Aumale splutter all manner of accusations of fraud. . . . He is the 'adversary'—a lawyer who pleads himself. The worst of it is, my mother signed some paper long ago, which gives some colour to the accusation; and I signed too, they say, which I had no right to do, for I was not of age. However, though this looks ugly, if it's true (I have not the slightest recollection of it), they say it don't bear on the main point; the real point is a quip of the law which none but lawyers can understand. There were ten creatures all assembled and seated like inquisitors, besides odds and ends of folks on the benches, or rather on very good armchairs behind things very like counters, only perched up high. . . . I said: 'Pray make me lose if you like, but don't keep me long.' I should have added that I had two young ladies* flourishing about in Paris, and was sadly wanted, but as I only received yours today I could not.

Everyone is in a state of ecstasy at my lawyer. I had no idea he was such a great man; however, I like him very much. Oh, if you had seen my adversary today! He stretched out his arm at me, at the frauds I had practised, looked daggers, ranted—! I at first was agitated, and then inclined to laugh. . . .[18]

Mary to Miss Sturch (Mrs Reid's sister)   Paris, 25 November 1850

I have won my suit, which has put me in high spirits. 1. I am not sorry to get some money, as there is plenty of use for it. 2. I have been three times to Limoges in fourteen months, and that is no joke. In your [English] railroad habits a hundred leagues is nothing, but here, where even after eight hours railroad I had to go fourteen more screwed up in a diligence, it's a very different matter. I have now done with Limoges altogether (I hope). . . .

I hope the College goes on well. I am much interested just now in a sort of establishment here, only just beginning, called a Home for English Young Women. It is a horrible fact that there are people who catch handsome young English girls in London and send them over here for vice, because the lower-class is so much handsomer there and more delicate in complexion and shape. Others . . . come to get places as governesses, nursemaids, etc., and

* Hilary and Ida.

get snapped up; then if they want to get out of these vices, they can't. . . . As I am a very cautious and suspicious person, I shall keep an observant and searching eye on this new establishment, to be sure that it answers its purposes and there is no humbug . . . as the good people who take an interest in such matters are generally more gullible than other folk. . . .[19]

However, neither charitable plans, litigation, nor the economic problems of Europe were as prominent in her mind at this time as fostering Hilary Bonham Carter's talent. A wide variety of artists and teachers had acknowledged Hilary's gift for art. The difficulty was to get her the opportunity of practising and perfecting it, for she was the 'daughter of the house', and single, and therefore at everybody's disposal.

Mary to Hilary Bonham Carter   Paris, undated

. . . I always fight against the tendency we all have to use up other people under pretence that one is fond of them; but of course, one may do the same—and if *I* ever do, be so good as not to give way to me. It does me harm, for it makes me more selfish and unreasonable. . . . We all have but limited means and strength, and if we spend ourselves in sympathizing with nonsense, we can't have it for what people really want. . . . As if it was possible to do anything, in any way, without giving all one's best juices to it! . . . Families want their daughters to follow their pursuits at odd times and in any odd room, dining-room or other. But if you can't give the best of yourself to it, you will do nothing. . . .[20]

It was the old frustration again, and this time, on another's behalf, Mary was determined to combat it with more perseverance than she had shown in her own interest. Again and again she made plans for Hilary to come to Paris to study seriously. Again and again, at the last moment some relative, in no very desperate straits, 'had to' take priority. She arranged for Hilary to study with Jeanron, she actually took studios for her; nearly every such project had to be cancelled at short notice.

Mary to Mrs Bonham Carter   Paris, 25 December 1850

. . . Pray exhort Hilly to work, when you see her dragged about by everybody. I assure you, she is too good-natured—that is her radical defect. . . .[21]

Mary to Hilary Summer 1851

. . . My principal reason for making haste to write is that M. Jeanron declares he has made some wonderful discovery in painting, which you alone are to hear and profit from; and I do say that, if you have any feeling, you should try to come, if only for a month, as soon as you can. The poor man has so little to rejoice at in life that it would be like a drop of water to the poor 'rich man' in hell. (Pity don't seem to have been a much-indulged feeling upstairs in those days; it is a modern sentiment, I believe. . . .)[22]

Mary to Hilary Paris, 1 October 1851

. . . Do, do, dear child, come back after Christmas and work like a black. . . .[23]

Mary to Hilary Paris, 5 February 1852

. . . Will you come NOW or not at all! . . . *Don't* undertake a hundred small things in England, which you *must* do—and then you will be able to come! Give up the small things now, and do them when you go back. Have character and sense enough to make a sacrifice of a small thing to a large one. I know your imagination abhors that, as nature does a void. . . .

You will answer: 'I know all that, but I must teach drawing to Gertrude,* whose governess has a cold, and I must go and see Laura,† whose children have the measles, and help nurse them. Poor thing!—she is the most fortunate of wives and mothers! She has plenty of money, very good health, and can afford servants in abundance, poor dear! . . .

Thus and thus life slips through your fingers, and as all these are perfect whims, when you have administered to them, nobody recollects them, except that Hilly is a very useful person to have in the house. . . .

I boldly declare that when *I* ask you to come, it is to see you work. . . .[24]

Her other protégée, Florence Nightingale, was to Hilary what a trampoline is to a woolly rug. At the age of thirty-two, however, she was still supposed to obtain parental permission for all her visits (more particularly to any kind of nursing institution), which meant that she spent her time

---

* A sister.   † Her sister-in-law.

contriving half-truths and lies, in which Mary enthusiastically abetted her.

Hilary to Mary   August 1852

. . . Flo is in Ireland—she went with the old Fowlers, who wanted to visit the British Scientific Association at Belfast. *She* wanted to go on to Dublin to study a certain Sister of Charity's hospital there. By a sad contretemps the hospital had got a whole holiday and is being repaired and there's nothing to be seen, so that she can only give up the plan. . . .

As she thus loses Dublin, I think, Clarkey dear, she will certainly have leave to come to you—and will certainly set her heart upon it more and more, I should not wonder. As they had given her permission for absence now . . . she might come to you this autumn. . . .[25]

Mary to Hilary   Paris, 30 October 1852

. . . Tell Flo and yourself that the thing I like best is that she should be perfectly free to do her own foolishnesses, let alone wickednesses, if she likes—I preserving the privilege to tell her all *my* mind. I believe firmly that if she had had her own way, right or wrong, all her life, she would perhaps be less imaginative . . . but have more worldly wisdom—which is what I wish her to acquire, and she never will at home. It is only by knocking their heads that brats learn not to knock them. . . . Mrs Nightingale knows I am very discreet, so if after a time Flo tells of a fancy to go to some wicked place the folk in England will fancy she is still with me, and I will keep it snug. . . .[26]

Hilary to Mary   12 November 1852

. . . About Flo: I cannot tell you, dear Clarkey, how I am hoping with all my heart that she may come to you, and that soon. We are looking about for some good person for her to go with, and the opportunity once found will be one step towards bringing the matter to a decision. There will be no good in plotting escapes with convenient and fabulous [companions] for ever. . . .[27]

By now Louis Napoleon had granted himself absolute power. His coup d'état of 1 December 1851 had confirmed all the Mohls' worst suspicions.

Mary to Hilary   Paris, 10 December 1851

... I am low-spirited—it's nothing. I am like a tree torn up by the roots. I can't get accustomed to believe this possible; but it's absurd to talk for ever of one's feelings. . . .

But be assured that the town is as safe as London, providing you keep your thoughts entirely to yourself, if they have anything honest in them. . . .[28]

Mary to Mrs Reid   Paris, 10 January 1852

... I have quite as good an opinion of universal suffrage as you have—providing the suffrage is upon a scale within the ken of the voter. For instance, every man *ought* to have a vote for the government of his own village, because he has heard from childhood of the various capacities, virtues, etc. of the candidates. . . . All the education in the world will never make a person competent to judge of what has not been under his eyes for years. Supposing Russia or China was now our sovereign country, how could any of the most cultivated judge of the pretensions of the Chichikoffs or Scratchikoffs who might be canvassing at the other end of the globe! . . . If every peasant voted for his village chief, and the village chief for a large district, there might be some chance of their knowing what they were about. Till then . . . I must think universal suffrage madness—and so would you if you saw it at work as I do. . . .

For instance, many or most of the peasants in the socialist provinces who were or are socialists have voted for him [Napoleon]. Why? They can't tell. They have been asked. Oh, they answer, 'it's to get rid of the other.' What other? They absolutely don't know who they mean.

I might doubt this if I had not had a little carpenter two years ago, and by no means a bad man, who told me in May '48 that he had been beat by the soldiers. Why? Because he went with many others and bellowed out 'Vive Henri V!'

'Why, I did not know you were a Carlist.'

'No, I an't a Carlist.'

'Why did you do that, then?'

' 'Cause I'm tired of the Republic.'

Next thing I heard was that he was dying in the terrible prisons in the forts round Paris, because in the days of June he fought against order. He got out of prison and came to me, but the damp had killed him; he died soon after. Why did he fight? It seems he

cried out 'I will be rich, I will be rich', and was taken in arms still
bellowing this. He was an honest fellow originally, full of gratitude.
He made me a box, to testify his feelings when I had employed him
all the winter.—If that poor fellow had had to vote for one among
the hundred or two hundred people he knew, he would have voted
perfectly well; but his brain was turned by disorder and the nonsense that was preached about the sovereignty of the people. Nothing can be more mischievous than to use this word to them,
because—an abstract idea being very incomprehensible to many
people, even of a certain education—each says: 'I'm a sovereign,
therefore I must be rich, therefore I only take my own.'

But it's no use talking. . . .²⁹

Mary to the Miss Haughtons   Paris, 22 February 1852

. . . Brummagem Boney keeps everything in a pretty state here.
. . . *Du reste*, I live very agreeably in spite of it, and have some very
agreeable acquaintance among the English, who are most abundant
this year. My soirées are very gay. . . .

But I am so hot in my opinions that I am shy of seeing people
lest I quarrel with them, which I do in general if they put forth
notions contrary to mine. . . .

I never in my life was intolerant till now, but this would rouse
the Seven Sages of Greece. . . .³⁰

During Mary's visit to England this summer George Eliot (who had
not as yet published any of her novels but had been editing *The Westminster Review* for six years) met her for the first time, and was considerably baffled by her. 'Her *"make-up"* was certainly extraordinary, but I
suppose she is a superior woman,' she wrote warily to Sara Hennell in
June 1852.³¹

Meanwhile Mohl, left behind in Paris, grappled with the idiocies
surrounding him—smaller-scale idiocies at the Institut, larger ones in the
conduct of the new régime.

Mohl to Hilary   Paris, June 1852

. . . I am . . . sitting in committees daily and eating up my liver
in attempts at rooting out abuses. . . . Do you recollect the man
who gives his arm to ladies at the public sittings of the Institut? I
find he gets 240 francs a year to keep him in *manchettes* [cuffs]. As
he wears none now, they being out of fashion, I shall cut off the
pay. Then the architect gets 240 francs a year for these same public

sittings to see if the upholsterer has spread the carpet on the little staircase *secundum artem*, for which the upholsterer gets 400 francs a year, the carpet being ours—he only puts them down. At each sitting there is a locksmith who gets 160 francs a year for putting up a certain piece of wood . . . which piece might be nailed on once for all, or omitted, without a soul being the worse for it. . . .[32]

Mohl to Hilary   Paris, 1 August 1852
. . . They have done something almost incredible, even in this incredible state of things. You know that most of the professors for French schools are formed in the Ecole Normale here. The young men get into the Ecole by a preliminary examination; but this year Fortoul* has struck out of the list of candidates for entrance every Protestant and every Jew. This, however, would not hold, and the Protestants and Jews have been readmitted. My only hope is that this despotism, if it lasts, will teach the French to cling to the law which they are always so ready to despise and resist. . . . Meanwhile, things produce their natural effects. The almost entire suppression of the press produces either the reality, or at least the belief in, an enormous corruption. . . . We shall undoubtedly get the Empire, which will be only a humbug the more, but may bring on a war, not instantly, but by gradual irritation, resulting from the mistrust and jealousies it will beget, and which will give this man a pretext for avenging Waterloo, which is one of his fatal ideas, and on which he will split, but God knows with what a train of misery for Europe. . . .[33]

Mary to Hilary   Paris, October 1852
. . . I gave a dinner-party Tuesday, which all but crucified M. Mohl, because we were twelve people (in all), and much vittles, and a man to wait. He bore it and said nothing, but looked so dismal that I shall not do it half as often as I should like. It's very provoking to be governed by people's countenances. I had M. de Buch, the great geologist . . . and Ranke—I sitting glorious between him and M. de Collegno—and M. Roulin, M. Ampère, Miss Anna Mohl, Mr Mohl, Mme de Collegno, M. Elie de Beaumont, Mérimée, Miss S—the beauty. I wrote the names down on bits of paper; I walked round the table calculating and cogitating. . . .

* The new Minister of Education.

It went off pretty well, thanks to Ampère, but Collegno was dismal, as he had just learnt the death of Gioberti; and then the chimney smoked in the drawing-room. Still, it was rather a successful affair. . . . These things are like all other *chefs-d'oeuvre*: a little touch of chance, a something beyond the reach of art, often makes them go off better than all calculations and precautions. . . .

I had a wonderful longing to invite Mignet to dine with Ranke on Friday; but I thought of Mr Mohl's dismal face, and refrained. If you can remember to tell this to him when I'm dead I shall be obliged to you, as he thinks I have my own way in everything. It will do him good to know that I would have had a dinner-party once a week if I had followed my fancy, and he will rejoice at what he escaped. . . .[34]

Mary to the Miss Haughtons   Paris, 1 November 1852

. . . I have not written sooner, because I have been wandering . . .

We travelled in a humble way in *Stellwagens* (something between a diligence and an omnibus) . . . through Styria and Carinthia— through places that had never seen an Englishman, let alone a woman. We enjoyed this more than all; true, we had a charming young man of a Tyrolese who helped us along. In one place we could get no *Stellwagen* because there was only one, and the man who owned it only gave places to people he liked. This was such a new way of doing business that we were reconciled to the inconvenience by the curiosity.

The conductor of one of our Wagens told us that when we got into Carinthia the people in the inns (such inns!) would all go and hide themselves;—and they actually did in one of them! . . .

It was pretty cold in most of these high valleys, they being along the north side of the crest of the Alps which separates southern Austria from Venice and northern Italy; but as it was September nobody thought of a fire. There are no chimneys, only stoves, eight feet square each way—they take up half a room. The kitchens have an enormous oven in the middle, about a little higher than a table. On this a wood fire is lighted—no charcoal—and the smoke goes up in the roof all about, to find a hole which is sometimes on one side. The odd thing is that though the kitchen is in a manner one large chimney, the smoke never makes one's eyes smart— it all keeps to the top, and makes the whole as black as if it were painted. . . .[35]

Mary to Lady Eastlake   Written in 1879, referring to 1852

. . . My sister, to whom I was greatly attached, lost her only daughter, who was still young, and who left seven children, the youngest only six months old. From that time my sister never left them, and I made a sort of vow that I would never spend a year without spending some months with her; for this lost daughter was more like a younger sister to me—my sister had married so young. . . .[36]

Mohl to Hilary   December 1852

. . . It gives a vivid impression of the uncertainty of life. To wash a child's ear, having a scratch on one's thumb, and to die from the inoculation of this virus!—it is abominable! . . .[37]

VIII

1853-1858
Miss Nightingale, Miss Bonham Carter, Mrs Gaskell

In the new year, however, putting aside her family troubles and the disagreeable political situation, Mary returned to the battle for Florence's freedom and Hilary's backbone.

Mary to Hilary   Paris, 9 January 1853

. . . Flo should know once for all that she can always come here when she likes—but I think I had better not meddle in the family, as making a coolness between the Mama and me would do no good to her. . . . Not that I am of Mrs Nightingale's opinion at all. I think Flo has as good a right to do foolish things as anybody else. And there's the mistake—parents want their children never to do foolish things. . . .[1]

Mary to Hilary   Paris, 15 January 1853

. . . I am delighted to learn you have been at work and have almost finished two portraits. Let them be good, let them be bad, but *finish* them. That's the malady of amateurs—they never finish, because they are not obliged. . . .[2]

Florence had at last been offered a post (as Superintendent of the Institution for the Care of Sick Gentlewomen in Distressed Circumstances, at 1 Harley Street) where she could exercise the skills acquired at such great cost. This time, however loud the outcry from her mother and sister, she was determined to accept.

Florence to Mary   8 April 1853

. . . My people are now at 10 Burlington St, where I shall be in another week. Please write to them there, and if you can do a little quacking for me to them, the same will be thankfully received, in order that I may come in, when I arrive, not with my tail between my legs, but gracefully curved round me in the old way in which Perugino's Devil wears it. . . .

It is a Sanatorium for sick governesses managed by a Committee of fine ladies. But there are no surgeon-students nor improper patients there at all—which is, of course, a great recommendation in the eyes of the Proper. The Patients,—or rather, the Impatients, for I know what it is to nurse sick ladies—are all poor patients, poor friendless folk in London. I am to have the choosing of the house, the appointment of the Chaplain, and the management of the Friends, as the Committee are at present minded. But Isaiah himself could not prophesy how they will be minded at eight o'clock this evening. . . .[3]

Mary was delighted at this step forward, and advised her to 'trample on the Committee and ride the Fashionable Asses roughshod round Grosvenor Square.' In June, while Mary was in England, Florence snatched a last visit to the hospital of the Sisters of Charity in Paris, before embarking on the Superintendentship. There she caught measles.

Florence to Mary   Paris, 28 June 1853

. . . I had it in the cell of a Soeur de la Charité. They were very kind to me—and dear M. Mohl wrote to me almost every day, and sent me tea (which, however, they would not let me have) and he lastly, in his paternity, *would* have me back . . . and established me in the back drawing-room. . . . He is *so* kind, and comes often to see me and talk, which I suppose is very improper, but I can't help it. . . .[4]

Mrs Gaskell to Catherine Winkworth   Lea Hurst, 11–14
                                                         October 1854

. . . Oh Katie! I wish you could see her! . . . She went to Kaiserswerth and was there for three months, taking her turn as a Deaconess, scouring rooms, etc. Then to Paris where she studied nursing at the Hospitals in the dress of a nun or Abbess and was besides a month serving at a bureau in an arrondissement in order to learn from the Sisters of Charity their mode of visiting the poor. And now she is at the head of the Establishment for invalid gentlewomen; nursing continually, *and present at every operation.* She has a great deal of fun, and is carried along by that, I think. She mimics most capitally the way of talking of some of the poor

governesses in the Establishment, with their delight at having a
manservant and having *Lady* Canning and *Lady* Monteagle to do
this and that for them. And then at this Cholera time she went
off,—leaving word where she could be sent for ... to the Middlesex
Hospital, etc. I came in here for the end of her fortnight of holiday
in the year. Is it not like St Elizabeth of Hungary? The efforts of
her family to interest her in other occupations by allowing her to
travel, etc.—but the clinging to one object! ... [5]

Mrs Gaskell to Emily Shaen   Lea Hurst, 27 October 1854

   ... Speaking of the cholera in the Middlesex Hospital, she said,
'The prostitutes come in perpetually—poor creatures staggering
off their beat! It took worse hold of them than any. One poor girl,
loathsomely filthy, came in, and was dead in four hours. . . '. Then
again, I never heard such capital mimicry as she gave of a poor
woman who was brought in one night, when F.N. and a porter
were the only people up—every other nurse worn out for the time.
Three medical students came up, smoking cigars, and went away.
F.N. undressed the woman, who was half tipsy but kept saying,
'You would not think it, ma'am, but a week ago I was in silk and
satins; in silk and satins, dancing at Woolwich. Yes! ma'am, for all
I am so dirty I am draped in silks and satins sometimes. Real
French silks and satins' . . . .
   She and I had a grand quarrel one day. She is, I think, too much
for institutions, sisterhoods and associations, and she said if she
had influence enough, not a mother should bring up a child herself:
there would be crêches for the rich as well as the poor. If she had
twenty children she would send them all to a crêche, seeing, of
course, that it was a well-managed crêche. That exactly tells of what
seems to me *the* want—but then this want of love for individuals
becomes a gift, and a very rare one, if one takes it in conjunction
with her intense love for the *race*, her utter unselfishness in serving
and ministering. . . . [6]

   Mrs Reid, equally impressed, asked Mary to recommend 'another
Florence Nightingale' to help in the administration of Bedford College.
Mary was much amused.

Mary to Mrs Reid   Cold Overton, 15 June 1853

. . . I shall not find another Florence Nightingale for you—for this reason, that all Florence Nightingales like to carry out their own systems and not other people's—and that this one has not the slightest idea of being managed by all these ladies, though she may not say so. But as she complains of their sillyness it is probable (don't say so!). It is scarcely natural that a person of energy sufficient to leave a quiet home will turn quiet enough to carry out other people's ideas. Only consider that the very spirit that makes this college such a delight to you, and [makes you] give up your time and attention and money, is the organizing it according to your own ideas. You would not do that for other people's ideas. If you want someone for your college, she must be the very contrary to Florence Nightingale. . . .

My sister is a surprising woman. She says herself that this affliction,* which she never could have contemplated, is without any bitterness. She is sure God alone could have upheld her—she can't understand it herself. Neither can I without such a solution. . . .

There is a difficulty for reasoning people like me to believe without understanding, but it is some years since, by an effort of reason, I have brought myself to the conviction that reason is a faculty that can only understand itself, and that there are possibilities it can't arrive at. I believe that is Kant's idea . . . but I arrived at it myself.

This brings me to Auguste Comte, who, as far as I can make out, *will* explain everything. I have not read him, because my passion for metaphysics (of which I read an enormous quantity between the ages of twenty and thirty) is gone. I believe it is the natural passion of youthful thinkers. It is only after much knocking one's head against the sides and top of our cage that we arrive at the conclusion that a cage it is, or a den—that the mind or soul or 'pure reason' or whatever you chuse to call it is shut in something it can't get outside. I therefore have not patience to read Auguste Comte, though . . . a very good metaphysician; Gioberti explained his system to me enough to give me the ideas I have of him.

I don't know him personally. He passes for crazy at times and, I have been told, has been shut up. Also that he commits marriages,

---

* The death of her daughter.

for he has disciples. Whether they stand good in law and allow the children to inherit . . . I know not. But as the sole and real object of the ceremony is to make people keep to it, and as it is for the interest of the children it should be kept to, it's to be hoped he takes charge of them all if the marriage he blesses is only for the satisfaction of the two parties.

Leroux, another philosopher, who has twelve ill-brought-up illegitimate children, inspired much enthusiasm in an interesting girl. He offered her to come under his tent, as marriage was against his principles. However, she would not, and I hope she found another less attached to his principles. . . .[7]

Mary to Hilary   Paris, October 1853

. . . I am certainly much better, though not well yet. . . . I should not have got soaked in the rain yesterday, nor wetted shoes and stockings. . . . *D'abord*, I forgot my *caoutchoucs* [galoshes], which was a great help to all these disasters. And for why? Because I lost my heart to a charming creature with a very black beard, and a short upper lip, an elegant figure, and such manners! We talked almost all the way from London to Paris (such a lovely face!)—and how do you suppose I could look after such low things as galoshes! So I didn't, and not being able to exist without Pale Ale, went, in such weather as I almost never saw in Paris, to the Faubourg St-Honoré—to three places, before I got the right sort.

This charmer of mine . . . had no twang whatever, and did not say 'my country'—but still I thought him American (why, I don't know) . . . Just before we parted, and I had given him my address, he said—in rather a melancholy tone—that he wished I had not such a distaste to his countrymen. I said: 'But I have said nothing against Americans.' 'I am not an American, but Irish.' I bore up pretty well, considering. I said: 'I never said "distaste"; "disapproval"—yes.'

However, we had not time to enter into delicate disquisitions: the commissioner was running away with some of my luggage, and he with some other. . . .

I wondered and hoped I should see him, and he came on Thursday. I was very poorly, but he sent word he was leaving Paris. This *was* a death-blow, but I had him in. After a little conversation he told me he had followed my advice; he had gone to Sichel for his eyes, and should come back very soon. (I revived.) I said something. He answered: 'I shall only take time to embrace my children—' (Oh help! he was married!) And something made him say 'My wife—' (Confound her!) I did not cry 'D—!' but said, in a sweet tone, 'I hope I shall have the pleasure of seeing her.' What were the Spartans compared to me, I should like to know! . . .

However, he's a delightful man, and I hope I shall see him again. . . .[8]

Mary to Hilary   Autumn 1853

. . . Pray tell me how your sprain is. I am afraid you have neglected it, and that has made it so difficult to cure. Oh, the wickedness of neglecting one's self! Suicide is nothing to it: one is buried and done with—people are very sorry and get consoled. But sick folks are the plague of one's life. They absorb more capital than a war. Their relations are generally annihilated. And then, the money! the doctors! the rubbers! the water-packers! the travels! the lodgings at watering-places! the bottles, the gallipots, the plaisters, the blisters, the powders, the pill-boxes, the night-lamps, the sauce-pans, the messes, gruels, semolinas, tapiocas! I could commit suicide myself to get out of their way—wicked, cruel, extravagant, selfish, absorbing wretches. . . .[9]

In October 1854 Florence Nightingale passed through Paris on her way to the Crimea, grasping the great opportunity opened to her now that the authorities were beginning to appreciate the plight of the thousands of sick soldiers left virtually without care—and the fact that Miss Nightingale might be the person to organize care for them. In Paris she assembled the heterogeneous and difficult party she was taking with her and stayed at a hotel 'where M. Mohl had arranged rooms and supper. Uncle Sam, writing to Embley, described Florence and Mrs Bracebridge going from room to room trying to fit the party in, followed by Mr Bracebridge, who, carrying a large box with all the cash in it under his arm, was highly excited, constantly interrupting Florence with exclamations and irrelevant reminiscences, and reproaching her for being so confoundedly silent. Mr Bracebridge was followed in turn by M. Mohl, who implored him to come downstairs and eat his supper like a good boy.'[10] The party then travelled on to their heroic and horrific task.

Mrs Gaskell to Parthenope   Manchester, 21 July 1855

. . . I have been so sorry to see by your letter . . . that you have
still such cause for anxiety. . . . Babies ad libitum are being
christened Florence here; poor little factory babies, whose grimed
stunted parents brighten up at the name, although you'd think
their lives and thoughts were bound up in fluffy mills. But it's the
old story 'for we have all of us one human heart', and these poor
unromantic fellows are made, somehow, of the same stuff as *her*
heroes of the East, who turned their faces to the wall and cried at
her illness. . . .[11]

Manchester's fluff and grime presented a strong contrast with the
Mohls' Paris life, of which Mrs Gaskell and her second daughter Meta
had had their first real taste in February of that year. From their very first
meeting in 1853 Mary had taken to Mrs Gaskell as to few other women.

Mary to Mrs Reid   Paris, 17 May 1853

. . . I am so fond of her that I invited her to come and stay. . . .
To my taste she is the most agreeable literary lady I have yet seen.
(Of course, I don't speak of my dear friend Miss Benger, because
one's friends are out of the pale of comparison, and one is no judge
of them.) Mrs Gaskell has a great quantum of good sound sense
and discrimination—a great addition to talent, and by no means a
necessary accompaniment—and no vanity. . . . She was staying
with Mrs Schwabe, who had the measles and could show her
nothing . . . which was an absolute piece of good fortune to me, as
it made me see so much of her. . . .[12]

Mary to Mrs Gaskell   Paris, 6 May 1853

. . . Many thanks for *Cranford*, which I read over again with
quite as much pleasure as the first time—a great trial, that is, when
one has but four or five months between and remembers everything. And moreover M. Mohl read it instead of doing his work in
the evening. . . .[13]

Now, in 1855, Mrs Gaskell's stay with the Mohls, the first of several,
proved to be a blessed, and very necessary, change from the mental and
physical fogs of Manchester, where she not only pursued her literary
activities, but acted as welfare-worker within her husband's community,

taught in Sunday School, ran a large house and small farm, supervised (with admirable sympathy) her daughters' growing-up, and endured both the criticism of the over-godly and the tastelessness of the over-rich. She came more and more to look on Mme Mohl as a touchstone of sanity.

Meta Gaskell to her sister Marianne   Paris, February 1855

. . . There is going to be a dance here tonight—everything is in confusion—the great red cushions of the salon being beaten and shaken till the room is clouded with dust. They have been polishing the dining-room floor till I anticipate a fall in every waltz. . . . Tomorrow we dine at the Scheffers',* to meet Mme Viardot and Mrs Hollond—and afterward go on to the Geoffroy St Hilaires'— where I am afraid we shall have to talk zoologically—and be kissed. . . .[14]

Mrs Gaskell to Marianne   Paris, February 1855

. . . Ices, and a man to wait, and *galette* ad lib, much to Meta's joy. She danced all evening; the rooms were crowded, and I can't tell you half the people. . . . Saturday: atelier, and then a short walk along the Quais; then to dine at the Scheffers' (such a good dinner!). . . . Thence to the Jardin des Plantes, a great soirée got up in my honour (no kissing) but cups of rich chocolate and cream cakes, which made Meta wish she could have kept either her good dinner or her good tea to another day, for she is perpetually hungry. We hardly ever have more than twice to eat in the day. . . . In the evening Bertha Smith, Hilary Bonham Carter and two members of the Institut to dinner. Wednesday: M. de Circourt, Lady Mary Fielding. . . . Oh! and one day I saw the Duc de Broglie and his daughter, said to be very like her grandmother, *the* Mme de Staël, who had the same dark red hair, dark red fiery eyes, etc. . . .[15]

Mary to Mrs Gaskell   Paris, November 1855

. . . I saw Mme Belloc two days ago. She has finished [her translation of] *Cranford*, and is correcting the proofs; she has taken great pains with it.

I wonder whether you will be able to judge which of your works

---

* Ary Scheffer, the painter, was an old and close friend of Mary's, and Meta had artistic ambitions.

will suit the French? I should think not. They are a queer people, and as unlike the English as if they lived at the Antipodes. . . .[16]

Hilary to Mary   January 1856

. . . Oh, had I been able to take in and comprehend and follow more courageously some of the counsels you have given me, I should have been a better, and a more really useful, creature than now. I have been so stupid—so slow to perceive—rolled up like a swaddled child in my own ways of seeing and thinking. It seems to me, now that my youth and strength are gone, as though the meaning and importance of many things you have said shine out clearly and fully before my eyes. . . .[17]

Mary to Hilary   21 August 1856

. . . I remember the day when Mrs Nightingale bothered and fretted because Florence did not faddle after the poor in her fashion. Florence is a great artist. She has a strong creative individuality. . . . It is only since she has burst out like a thunderbolt in her own way that she has done anything worth while. What folly and cruelty to have made her for years give up her individuality under pretence that she must live for other people. . . .[18]

Mrs Gaskell, fortunate in being married—and to a liberal-minded, encouraging man—had never been required to give up her individuality. For once, in 1857, she may have regretted not being controlled by some prudent person, for in her *Life of Charlotte Brontë*, published that year, she had been so carried away by sympathy for Charlotte that she had accused a certain Lady Scott of debauching Branwell, spoken her mind about such people as the Carus Wilsons, and drawn down on herself various threats of libel actions.

Mary to Mrs Reid   Paris, 16 June 1857

. . . I thought the whole book a masterpiece, and I do still, and when the present nonsensical fever is over, the whole public will be of my opinion. Distance plays the part of time in these matters, and I can judge better from afar. I propose myself much fun in calling Lady Scott 'the Immaculate' to all my religious friends, just like the Holy Virgin, and I have not said a word about the book to my people in any letter, that I may get all out at once and pounce on 'em like a cat.

I love Mrs Gaskell for the very honest indignation in her book. As to prudence, worldly prudence, I despise the virtue—though I practise it for my own interest. I like her faults better than my virtues (of that sort), and you'll see if it does not add to her fame. The folk in Mayfair say 'She's capable of anything (the Scott); she'll get the upper-most.' No she won't, in the long run. I have not been so ardent about a game since '48 as I am at this Scott-versus-Gaskell, and I enjoy the idea of taking her part in England—not with an absurd zeal, which spoils everything, as Talleyrand says, but *sneeringly*. . . .[19]

Mary to Mrs Walter Bagehot (on her marriage)   29 November 1857

. . . From his article on Lord Brougham it is evident that Mr Bagehot is very clever, and that is a great element of happiness *en ménage*—at least *I* think so. When one finds one's mental amusement at home, every day is a day of festivity. If one is poor one don't mind it—for what could one get better for any money? If one is rich, *ça ne gâte rien*—! But it is not necessary to be rich, as I know. . . .[20]

It was as well that her home and social life prospered, for the Second Empire, as a régime, continued to be thoroughly antipathetic. At home the Mohls could choose their company with care; to one of her regular visitors, the publisher Charles Kegan Paul, 'it seemed that the only bond of union among the distinguished people at her house was hatred of the Emperor Napoleon III'[21], although they still welcomed Mérimée, for old friendship's sake, despite the fact that he had gone over to the enemy. The tone of the Empire, its love of vulgar display, disgusted them, as did similar developments in England; and they never ceased to be irritated by the fact that Napoleon III, ambitious, dictatorial and underhand as they felt him to be, managed to pull the wool over England's eyes. Another old friend, Victor Hugo, had left France in disgust in 1853, and remained in solitary indignation in Guernsey until the Empire was overthrown. As early as the 1850s the Mohls were convinced that it *would* be overthrown, sooner or later.

From Nassau Senior's
*Conversations with M. Thiers, etc.**   8 March 1858

Senior I spent the evening at Mme Mohl's. I spoke of the unpopularity, or worse than unpopularity, into which Louis

* See Bibliography.

Napoleon seemed to have fallen, as far as I could judge from the conversation of the few people whom I had seen.

Mohl It is much greater in the class of society which you do *not* see. The *ouvriers* have been principally struck at. They were already angry at the high price of apartments and of food. Like all uneducated persons, they exaggerate the power of government, and think that the emperor could give them cheap lodgings and bread and wine, if he liked. Instead of doing so, he inflicts imprisonment and banishment on persons who, perhaps, were *émeutiers* in 1848, but have been for years well-conducted *pères de famille.* . . . I do not think he was ever so unpopular among the working classes in Paris. The natural effects of that unpopularity will not be prevented by compression. He is compressing an elastic gas. Some day the resisting force will be greater than the compressing force, and then woe to those who are near to the explosion.[22]

Mary to Hilary   St Leonard's, 4 June 1858
. . . We went by Brighton to Chichester to see the tomb of my grandfather, Captain Hay, of my uncle, of my brother. All died long before I was born. . . . We found out an old lady who had been servant when my mother was visiting in 1807—such a nice woman; and a churchwarden, a glazier, who would take no money. Whenever I have to do with people of that class here, I fall so in love with my countryfolk that I'm ready to cry with tenderness; but the moment I mount up into the gentlefolks, my tears are dried up. Their vulgarity, their stupid admiration of riches, rank, and success, make me quite sick. . . . I was reading a book called *John Halifax*. The author wants to show her blame of * the love of money and finery, and shows all the time the importance she attaches to it. . . .[23]

Mary to Ida Mohl   Summer 1858
. . . I left your uncle in London, perfectly enchanted, in the first place, at being there, and then at finding the Athenaeum open, and all the boys, or most of them, there. Of these 'boys' the youngest is fifty-five. The age of the oldest is unknown, but Crawford, one of the most delightful, is eighty-four. . . .[24]

* i.e. disgust at.

Miss Florence Nightingale.
at Embley.
December 28th 1857.

5. Florence Nightingale in 1857, by G. Scharf

6, Self-portrait of Hilary Bonham Carter, c.1830

7, Mrs Gaskell, pastel by Samuel Laurence, 1854

Mohl to Hilary   Beaumont St, near Regent's Park, Summer 1858

. . . You know I always delight in London, even when it is as empty as now. There is really nobody, except a few who congregate at the clubs, as their households are broken up, and they go and come to town like strangers. I stumbled on Monckton Milnes, who came from Normandy; he only traversed the town. . . .

I was down at Oxford for twenty-four hours to see newly bought manuscripts. . . . Got an apartment in All Souls, as Max Müller is the only resident fellow there, and has at his disposal a porter, a cook, a butler and twelve idle servants. There has never been such an establishment of monstrous abuses. I dined at [Dean] Stanley's, where I found Madame and her daughter-in-law, who had held me for a myth, because my wife is always gallivanting about alone.

I had to come back on Holy Sabbath—no small matter. The only available train was at seven o'clock in the morning, and so the college door had to be opened at half past six, a thing never seen in All Souls, but achieved after all, with some difficulty. The substitution of the sabbath for all religion in this country is one of the most curious phenomena I have seen anywhere. . . .

It is the incredible number of great interests concentrated there and known all over the world in their own sphere . . . which makes London what it is. I believe that not even Rome, in the time of its greatest power, was to compare to London in riches, in power, and in multifarious influence in the world; and happily, on the whole, this influence is humane and healthy . . .

But its extent makes it difficult to live in; it takes me an hour, in a fast-driving omnibus, to go to the mission-house in Bloomsbury Street, and if one misses the person, half one's day is done for. I am studying the Post Office here. I tried to become acquainted with Rowland Hill, but could not. It is incredible what they have done, particularly in the internal arrangement, to insure the rapidity and security of the deliveries. There are many other subjects I wished to be able to see, ragged schools amongst them, but cannot. I am rather scandalized at the luxury of the people, which goes, it seems to me, far beyond want and comfort; but with all its faults, this is a very great nation as nations go, and approaches a state of civilization nearer than all the others, even the Chinese, as far as I can judge. . . .[25]

Mary to Hilary   Cold Overton, Summer 1858

. . . I have been drawing in pastel from busts, and find it very improving; I do them so quick to what I did. I find the best way is to do over the same, or nearly the same, thing as quick as I can (not carelessly), and after a few I have wonderfully improved in quickness. The fact is, we all try to do the *finesses* first, whereas the masses ought alone to occupy us, and the *finesses* come afterwards. It seems ridiculous, at my years and discretion, to be finding out how to improve; my only comfort is that Michael Angelo wrote at eighty about some discoveries he had just made, and painted himself as a child in a go-cart, as an emblem of his learning-state. Oh, if we could but live two hundred years and be young at a hundred, how much better it would be! . . .[26]

Mary to Hilary   Cold Overton, September 1858

. . . Is it not disgusting that you do not set to and work, instead of twaddling for ever? That head* is too well done for you to faddle away your talent as you do. . . . Why not reserve so much a day for yourself, which nothing can break through? . . .

I see the same in this house—the endless tweedling of nosegays in jugs and a nameless collection of useless nonsense.

Ever yours, as cross as two sticks,
Mary Mohl[27]

It was at this period that Florence Nightingale, a national heroine after the Crimea but now buried in constant, gruelling administration (devising hospital systems, army medical systems, nurse-training systems, the entire health-system of India . . .)—work which, she believed, probably rightly, only she could do—retired to her rooms, shut out nearly all company, and entered on the undiagnosable illness which lasted for the next thirty years. In December 1859 she was considered near death: 'Aunt Fanny feared her sinking, she could scarcely take food, for five nights was quite without rest. The distressing oppression of the breathing comes on so much more that it wakes her if she but doze.'[28]

From the first Mary thought her isolation unhealthy (even if it did set her free for a superhuman amount of work), and was convinced that if *she* were allowed near Florence, she would soon argue her out of it: 'I wish *I* could talk to her. I can't help thinking a little talk and fun would do her more good than the solitary-confinement system you have established,

---

* Which Hilary had modelled.

seeing no one but the clergyman and the business people about Barracks. I believe the constant tension on one subject is bad for her.'[29]

However, Florence was opposed, at first hand, only by such malleable characters as Hilary Bonham Carter. Mary instead became involved in quite another project: the consummation, rather by luck than good management, of her old ambition to write for publication.

IX

1860–1865
Authorship

In January 1860 she wrote a criticism for the *National Review* (it was reprinted in the same month in the *Edinburgh Review*) of a biography of Mme Récamier recently published by Mme Le Normant, the *salonnière's* niece.

Mary to Hilary   Paris, Spring 1860

. . . I received a beautiful letter from Mrs Reid the very day after my last to you, full of praises. . . . Mr Senior wants me to publish my article with the suppressions; perhaps I have already told you so. I have an exceeding mind to put it into a book, with some more history of the female sex here. I have had such whacking compliments from several—Miss Darwin among the rest (a most discriminating woman)—that it puts me *en verve*. But it don't last. . . .[1]

Mary to Mrs Gaskell   London, 7 June 1860

. . . The advice I intended to ask was this. My article, which you are so kind as to praise, was twice as long [when first published], and I had cut off a great deal then. In short, I could make a book with the greatest of ease—to show that the position of women in France was different from elsewhere. I have not the slightest pretension to make it out better than here or worse, but to show a curious historical fact which explains from far back what often appears anomalous in the manners of the country. I don't declare this pedantically, because, after all, I may see the fact bigger than it is. But all history of manners is curious—more curious, it strikes me, than histories of battles, whose variety consists chiefly in cold steel or hot gunpowder or hotter cannonballs; yet people never seem tired of them. But human feelings, and the varieties in life and manners that the human imagination has occasioned, have many more windings and turnings. But I have no notion of acting to empty benches, and if I thought my book would not be read except by my intimates, I would not write it. That is what I wanted your opinion on. The rough copy of my article is here, and if I have time I will copy it out clear and get you to read it. It is not half what I have to say (the historical part), but you may have some idea of what I mean when you have read it. . . .[2]

Mrs Gaskell to George Smith (the publisher)   February 1860

. . . I want a stronger and more practical opinion than my own . . . to get her to write a book as she purposes. She would do it well—and has that sort of knowledge of *good* French and English society which few finely-observing women possess. I mean she has—oh, I don't know what I mean in this hurry. *I* think she *ought* to write it, out of benevolence to her species—but do you think it would be 'acting to empty benches'? . . .[3]

Mary to Mrs Gaskell   London, 8 July 1860

. . . I *dare say* you are right as to my repeating too often the same thing, and I am *quite sure* you are right as to the mistake it is to do so. When I have finished, I shall ask unscrupulously for your advice, and you will give a good scratch with a pencil when you see any ungraceful testimony of opinion; for I agree with you that a thing should be always *let seen*, and not shown. I wish the animal who writes to be as invisible as the mechanism of our bodies. Nature has shown us the finest example of grace, hiding the hideous muscles under a beautiful skin; but one is weak and awkward, you know. I always think of my dear Dr Johnson's answer when a lady found fault with one of his explanations in the dictionary: 'Ignorance—pure ignorance, madam!' You know I am a Johnsonian, like Miss Matty's sister.

I greatly enjoyed Oxford, and London too. I never was made so much of, which is due to this same article. The best compliment I received was from Mrs Monckton Milnes, who on reading it thought it was her husband's, and told him so. I never should have had the perseverance to write for two whole months, had it not been for my indignation at seeing Mme Récamier so ill understood, thanks to Mme Le Normant's book. . . .

Could you give Anna* your new book to translate? I would ask
Robert to look over it. He is a most disheartening person and
would, like all the Mohls, cut off every one's arms and legs for fear
he should walk a little awry. But I have surmounted them all, and
don't care a snap for their dampings. The worst of it is that these
Germans all know English. When I spoke of it to Mr Mohl before
Anna, 'Oh,' says he, 'they all have regular translators at Leipsic;
it's impossible to get anything'—as if these had been, like eternity,
without a beginning! I could have given him a good scratch, like a
pussy.

I gave myself no end of trouble with my article, and talked so
much about it in the house that Mr Mohl did nothing but laugh at
me—I might as well have played the flute—so I never showed it
him; he is so discouraging. . . .[4]

Mary to Hilary   Paris, 14 October 1860

. . . I wish I could consult Flo about my book. This is the query.
It enters into my plan to show the two centuries in French history
when the women had the most influence: viz. the twelfth, when
chivalry began, and all at once they were sung and obeyed; and the
seventeenth, when the *précieuses* remoralized France to a certain
degree—at least they were the first to bring decency into books and
conversation. Their influence lasted the whole of the century; it
ended, one may say, with Mme de Maintenon. Now, I have my
own views on this lady, different from the ordinary ones—though
people have begun to do her some justice—and I am much tempted
to enter into many particulars of her life and letters to show her
character . . . and that her influence was precisely a proof of what
I saw as to the love of the society and the conversation of women
being a taste peculiar to the French, which nothing can prove better
than an all-powerful monarch† marrying a woman of forty-eight,
three years older than himself, when all the young beauties were at
his beck and call.

I must not have a critic that is too severe, as they discourage me,
and I throw it aside and can't work. It is a thing not sufficiently
considered, that animal spirits are the first ingredient for doing
anything. Criticism entirely stops the current, at least with me. I'm

* Anna Mohl, Ida's sister.
† Louis XIV.

convinced that is why art is so brilliant at its birth: there are no critics. . . .

But it is twelve o'clock, and I must go to bed. . . .[5]

Mary to Mary Senior   Paris, 12 November 1860

. . . My thoughts are just like jelly-fish; they come out in a messy, disgusting, pulpy state, and when I want to lick them into shape and put bone into them by words, I turn sick at the sight of them and waste paper enough, if spread out, to reach to China. . . .

M. de Loménie was here yesterday. He has just *accouché* of a new review. It is called *Revue nationale et étrangère*; it is to rival Buloz' [*Revue des*] *Deux Mondes*. He sent me the review in the morning; luckily it was already cut. He took it up and read me all the best morsels, giving proper emphasis, and saying 'N'est-ce pas que ça n'est pas mal?' 'Voilà qui est bien tapé!' 'I wonder what Buloz will say to this!' Nobody ever enjoyed their own writing so much before; his *amour-propre* is so *bon enfant*. He used to write for the *Deux Mondes*, and they made him correct his articles. He did it once; he did it twice. At last he grew outrageous and told me to say to Buloz that he must call on him if he wanted anything more; but I never saw Buloz, and I'm sorry I did not write and tell him to come to me, for Loménie got out of humour, and a bookseller called Charpentier just seized on him in the moment fit for temptation, as old Nick does, and persuaded him to be the leading manager of a new review, and now he has entered Pandemonium I feel remorse. He is very honest and kind-hearted; both his good and bad qualities will make it a *métier de galère*. You English can have no idea of the difficulty of writing against a government without giving a word that can be a handle. It was this *adresse* that he was so delighted with in his article. . . .

I will tell Loménie your good opinion. It's like watering a thirsty plant to give him a compliment. What a charming passion vanity is! (I don't mean sour, saturnine vanity . . .)[6]

Mary to Mary Senior   November 1860

. . . I have finished one morsel of my book. . . . I am afraid it will give a very bad opinion of me. It is very immoral, because I say that love was then incompatible with marriage. Don't tell anybody.

I wrote to my friend, Hutton, who spoke to Chapman and Hall; but the despicable wretches *will* see it first. Sometimes I think it's abominable, fanciful stuff, and then I think it's very good. I have lent it to a friend, and am quite quaking to hear what she says, and yet I'm such a goose that I put off sending for it, because I know if she thinks it stuff I shall not have the power to write another line. It takes away one's animal spirits—did you never find that? I do nothing without my animal spirits. I can't get off my chair when I am bereaved of them, and can't understand how some people live on in a sort of routine, without seeming to like or dislike living. . . .

No one doubts war in the spring. . . . He [Napoleon] is putting everything in preparation; horses by the thousands are out at grass all ready; more troops are adding; certain immense clothing establishments are overdone with work. . . . Meantime L.N. puts an end to passports between England and France, to become popular there . . . and the English are silly enough to be quite charmed with this dust thrown in their eyes. . . . Oh, we are a nice set! and I sometimes think we richly deserve to have a trial of French pillaging on our land. . . .[7]

Mary to Hilary   Paris, 13 January 1861

. . . Rendu has published a second edition of his book about the education of the lower classes in England. He wants to send it to the *Westminster*, to get it mentioned, I dare say with praise; but that I care nothing about. I wish you could tell whoever writes on the subject to say that nothing can be more impudent and unjust than the mania foreigners have of comparing the misery of London to the misery of other capitals. It is like comparing the dirt of a cesspool in one house to the cistern of clear water in the next, and concluding that the inhabitants of the first are very dirty and those of the next very clean. One knows that all the *canaille* of all the world may go to London, and that for our own subjects we have no passports, no gates, no books at the police, to inscribe everyone who takes a bed in every house. Here passports have been refused all over the provinces, even to workmen, for the last four years, unless they had great recommendations, etc. And as nobody can circulate in the whole country without leave, nor ever could, and all vagabonds are immediately sent back to their *dépôts de mendicité* in their departments, it's easy enough to keep it [Paris] clean. In Vienna it is even more difficult to make a sink of the metropolis, as a sort of imaginary cordon is drawn at a good number of leagues round the town, and unless the passport permits it, no one can pass this. . . . These facts I know, and I dare say the other large towns have something of the sort.

I told Rendu, who smiled as usual, and paid little attention. His book has good things in it, and after all those who point out our failings are much more useful than our flatterers. . . .[8]

Mary to Monckton Milnes   Paris, 17 January [probably 1861]

. . . We are all in turmoil and anxiety here about the war. The nation is sulky, the financials enraged, the army all agog, the haters (of which I am a very epitome) glad—for whenever our gentleman does a foolish thing we are in hopes he will plunge into a slough and we are willing to get into it up to the ears so that he should be smothered—that's my amiable state of mind.

When I think of all the abuse Louis Philippe had the courage to endure in 1840, rather than go to war, and when I think of the trouble every woman has to rear a male brat and how this fellow makes cannon fodder of them by thousands merely to turn away attention from his insolent and stupid despotism, and of the thousands who will perish, not only by cannon but by pestilence, famine and misery, then indeed I think with astonishment of the stupidity of human nature. . . .[9]

Mary to Hilary   Paris, 19 January 1861

. . . Mr Mohl says I have drunk of the poison called ink. *He*'s a comfortable person for encouraging one. I'd rather show it [her book] to the water-cart-man than to him. . . .[10]

Mary to Lady William Russell   Paris, 10 April 1861

. . . I have been so absorbed these last five months with writing a sort of sketch of past French society . . . that I seem to have been in a dream all the winter. . . .

The last seven weeks I have had two English nieces to preach and nag at—'Hold up your head! Answer in a soft voice! Don't look crusty! Don't see-saw when you walk!' Then I stick myself before the glass, walk up and down as stiff as a poker, make one of them do the same after me. . . . All morality I eschew; like Lord

Chesterfield, I think of nothing but deportment. Can you, who are a philosopher, explain why the tournure and manners of so many English of good connections, liberal education, etc., etc., are so bad, compared to those of the same rank on the Continent? Is it shyness, or pride, or the mania for cooping up the girls in school-rooms, like wild beasts in a cage, till they are pulled out to be looked at by the public? I think that explains it enough. . . . The *gêne* they feel never seems to leave them, unless they turn pert and flirty—and that is worse—and what I hear called *fast*. Oh, that I detest worse than all, and it is just as far from ease and simplicity as the former. . . .[11]

Mary to Eleanor Martin (her great-niece)   Paris, 23 May 1861

. . . Mrs Green is going to America. Her husband went last week to go and fight the South. On Thursday night he said, 'I can't stay away; I must go.' 'Very well, William; I'll go to Caen tomorrow morning' (they have a country house there) 'and sell the furniture, get rid of the lease, and follow you in a fortnight.' On Friday she was at Caen; the furniture was placarded; on Saturday she came back. . . . Her sister has sent her two sons, her brother his only son. It's the grandest thing I ever saw. I would go to America if I were twenty years younger. I never wished to go before—I hated it; I now have the highest respect for it. The slaves will be all free before twenty years are over. Oh, if your dear mamma [Selina] had seen it, how glad she would have been! . . .

Napoleon III, not content with his military and political exploits, had now cast himself in the role of classical scholar and had had built a Roman trireme, which was intended to progress majestically down the Seine.

The trireme won't budge, and our rascal had catapults made to imitate the ancient ones; but nothing can persuade the trireme to swim or the catapults to throw a stone. So all this show-off is for nothing—what ducks they are not to mind him![12]

Mary to Mary Senior   Paris, 31 May 1861

. . . The wretch of a publisher, having kept my manuscript I don't know how long, says it can't be published before October. Now I had just as soon put it in the fire; I may be dead by that time. He talks some stuff about the season, forsooth—as if books were fish and could only be ate at one time! Now, if there was anything I cared about it was promptitude; if any one promised me anything—Paradise itself—next year, I wouldn't thank them. I hate next year! . . .[13]

By now the Baron Haussmann was, at the Emperor's command, clearing away the little winding streets of Mary's Paris, and creating a grand Imperial city.

Mary to Mrs Gaskell   Paris, 2 June 1861

. . . Paris is all coming down. There won't be an old *hôtel* left six years hence. The Île Notre Dame is to have nothing but barracks on it; it breaks my heart. This fellow is jealous of all past history. Six thousand people are turned out of house and home. You English make me sick! You say, Why do you bear it? You helped him at first, and now he has six hundred thousand soldiers and you are paying for it. Yet such is your folly, you like him better than L. Philippe, though L.P. kept the peace. It will appear so strange in history that it will not be believed—but folly always has that effect at a distance. One says that it is impossible that people could be such fools.[14]

Mary to Mary Senior   London, 13 June 1861

. . . I am quite easy about my book, for I see it would not be read now—my chef-d'oeuvre. Ah! so it's to come out in October. . . .[15]

The writer William Greg, who worked with Chapman and Hall, had advised on her manuscript, which should have eased her path but did not, as she explained to Mrs Gaskell, who was also struggling with a literary project (probably *Sylvia's Lovers*).

Mary to Mrs Gaskell   Frystone, 27 August 1861

. . . Pray tell me if you are getting on with your story. I corrected my proofs in London with the utmost trouble, as I liked my bad English better than Mr Greg's good. Now mind, he has been very kind and useful, but one's ideas never can be expressed exactly by another. Oh, the trouble I have taken! I remained exactly a month longer in London to correct these proofs. I know you won't like it, but I had great pleasure in writing a part of it. . . .[16]

She was a better critic than writer; out of all her wide-ranging speculations and experiences emerged an unsatisfactory little book, in which she clearly did not say all she meant to and did say a good deal she did not mean. It was not helped by Greg's well-meant advice: the liveliness of her letters is 'corrected' away, and her occasional attempts at fine writing do nothing to mend matters. The section on Mme Récamier herself is probably the best; there she had first-hand knowledge to impart. The following chapters on the eleventh century, Provence, Mmes de Rambouillet, Scudéry, Sablé, Longueville and Maintenon are 'too much devoted to a single idea'—her old criticism of Thierry's work—and the final chapter comparing the contemporary positions of women in England and France spoils a pithy observation by expanding it into an unconvincing 'argument'. There was obviously a price to be paid for avoiding the professional dedication of a Mrs Gaskell or a Florence Nightingale, with all its difficulties and dangers.

Florence to Sam Smith   South Street, 2 June 1861

. . . Every day, from five to six p.m. to eight or nine the next morning I am totally disqualified from anything . . . by that 'grasping' action of the heart which poor Bunsen, who had it, said was like 'being hung'. . . . In addition to this, on an average of two days in the week I am totally unable to do anything . . . I must stay in bed, for if I tempt myself by getting up I am entirely laid aside for three or four hours by the exertion of dressing. . . . And the main part of the suffering of a long illness is the morbid mind of a person who has *no* variety, *no* amusement, *no* gratification or change of any kind. . . . I am always thinking I might do more, or I had better not have done what I did do. . . .[17]

Mohl to Eleanor Martin   32 South St, 27 September 1861

. . . I have remained in Sir Harry Verney's house during his and her absence, to be near Flo Nightingale, who sends me every morning a message if I can see her or not between four and six o'clock. . . . It is a comfort to her to talk to me about everything she likes, as she never sees anybody but the sanitary doctors and the people of the Council of India. She is always in bed and very weak, but not more so than I saw her three years ago, only she is fat, which is I believe no good sign, in so abstemious a person. It is wonderful to see this poor, bedridden lady working to organise the sanitary condition of India, creating boards of work in India and of control here. Whenever her instructions have been followed, cholera has ceased, as at the pilgrimage of Conjeeveram, where it had been inveterate, but has not appeared these four last years, because she has found them a magistrate who executes her instructions and gets the pilgrims to pay for the sanitary measures. I found her the other day writing to the Governor General about the measures to be adopted for keeping the cholera out of the great fair of Haridvar, up in the Himalaya, where the Ganges breaks out of a rock, and where it rages every year. The India Board furnishes her with every paper she asks for. Her principal work now is to organize the sanitary arrangements all over India. . . .[17]

Mary to Mary Senior   Cold Overton, 29 September 1861

. . . I enjoyed my visit at Monckton Milnes' so entirely that it gave me an inordinate appetite for more. I met there a lady who knows you—Miss Ellen Tollet. . . . When she saw I took an interest in discourses heard in the byways of society, she read me bits of a certain journal kept by her sister . . . not about the converse of great stars but about country people. I never heard anything more racy, more full of life and reality. . . .

We had many agreeable men, Holman Hunt among others, whom I like so well that I comprehend people should put up with his unpunctualities. I stayed there ten days, and spent my last pennyworth of strength. I came here to fall down, I may say, like the exhausted warrior who has only breath to announce the victory and drops down dead. Is there such a one, or do I dream it? My memory is so bad that I often invent quotations, and am ready to die for their exactness. But I must not go falling down at Mrs Clive's. I hate sick people, and myself more than any. I respect cats; when they are ill, they hide themselves and die unseen. . . .[19]

Mary to Mrs Grote   Paris, 3 December 1861

I had a visit of eighteen days from Lady Augusta Bruce. . . . I have now two musical nieces who play on the piano. My spouse hates music, and is heroic enough to say so, which, I think, puts him on a par with Hannibal, or any of the great ancients; as I have a particular fancy for that Carthaginian, I show it by comparing him to my spouse. I love his unquellable hatred of the Romans; I always hated them too.

Our scamp has done a nice thing. I enjoy the Mexican affair;* it is L.N.'s Moscow. I hope he'll send more and more men; serve them right. Perish armies if their death shows a principle—and the glorious principle of not falling like brigands on people at the other side of the globe! I hope some day the Chinese will cut all our throats over here; I should wish it if my own brother was one of them. The only history I read with gluttony is Boney's return from Russia; it is almost the only one where Justice, a tedious old dawdle, seems ground young and brisk. But I have no notion of two weights and two scales, of thinking right or wrong according to my partialities; only one must see all the bearings of the case, and that is difficult. But even Scamp's partisans are embarrassed by the Mexican affair.

I envy you the acquaintance of John Stuart Mill. I wish you would use all your powers to persuade him to come and see me when he comes through Paris; he is a man who thinks for himself. . . . They are scarce enough, and whether one always agrees with them or not, they are of the real stuff one loves to see. . . .[20]

Mill's *Enfranchisement of Women* had been published in 1853 and his *On Liberty* in 1859. *The Subjection of Women* did not appear until 1869. Mary's own views on women, as conveyed in her book, had by now elicited a response from Florence Nightingale.

Florence to Mary   London, 13 December 1861

. . . I understand the characters of Mme Récamier, Mme de Staël and Mme de Maintenon, etc., etc. as I never did before. But to your conclusions. E.g. you say: 'Women are more sympathetic than men.' Now, if I were to write a book out of my experience, I should begin: 'Women have no sympathy.' Yours is the tradition—mine the conviction of experience. I have never found *one woman* who has altered her life by one iota for me or my opinions. Now look at my experience of men. . . .

A woman once told me my character would be more sympathized with by men than by women. In one sense, I don't choose to have that said. Sidney Herbert and I were together exactly like two men—exactly like him and Gladstone. And as for Clough, oh

---

* Napoleon's very unsuccessful attempt to annex Mexico.

Jonathan my brother Jonathan, my love to thee was very great, passing the love of women.*

I do believe I am 'like a man', as Parthe says. But how? *In having sympathy*. I am sure I have nothing else. I am sure I have no genius. I am sure that my contemporaries—Parthe, Hilary. . . .—were all cleverer than I was, and several of them more unselfish. But not one had a bit of sympathy. . . .[21]

Mary Senior criticized the book from a different standpoint. As the attractive daughter of the economist Nassau Senior she mixed happily with all sorts of scholars and artists and, judging from her own experience, objected that in England women were treated with more respect than Mary had suggested.

Mary to Mary Senior   Paris, 2 January 1862 (alas,
                                                        one's always getting older)

. . . I ought to have put in my preface that the manners of the present day and in the rising generation, both in France and in England, are perfectly left out by me. I deal only with the past. . . .

But I don't think *you* are a judge. It puts me in mind of the *fermier-général* in 1778 when all Paris was talking of bettering the rights of man, etc. The *fermier-général*, who was enormously rich, said: 'Mais pourquoi donc changer? nous sommes si bien!'

I don't deny that women are well off in tolerably civilized places, when they are young and pretty and clever, but . . . I, who lived in the country in my youth, among very well-bred, old-fashioned and broad-landed country squires, have seen over and over what I say. The men talk together; the lady of the house may be addressed once in a way as a duty—but they had all rather talk together, and she is pretty mute if there is no other lady. And I see that it is just the same now: they have no notion that a lady's conversation is better than a man's. The widower of a friend of mine, a clergyman, was quite astonished when Mr Mohl said English women had more cultivation than the men, and you could talk to them on more subjects. He was so bothered that when he got alone with Mr Mohl he returned to the subject, and could not believe he was serious. (His wife gave out more sense in a quarter of an hour than he in a year.) And he did not invent this—it's the common opinion.

My friend — will have £12,000 a year; his sisters will have £200,

* She had worked with these two men and, it has been argued, worked them to death, on her great sanitary projects.

and they won't have a sou of his (unless they marry) until he dies. Another friend of mine married at twenty a woman ten years older than himself. He was a widower at three-and-thirty, and took especial care to hunt after a wife as fast as he could. He won't let his daughters go out, because *he* hates going out. His son may do anything he pleases, yet he is younger than the eldest [daughter]. These girls are handsome. I don't say it's essential for girls to marry, but they ought to have the choice. No! they are women!— why should *they* be independent! . . .

Ah, Minnie, you are like the *fermier-général*!

And what don't I see in all the novels about mamas trying to fish up husbands for their daughters, and the contempt thrown on all these women! Poor souls! if I had a daughter whose brother was to have £10,000 a year and she £200, I should fish too. Poor thing, she is brought up to a fine house, to be turned out or become dependent on a pert sister-in-law, and her father spends more every year on his dog-kennels than he will give to her. And if the poor anxious mother had brought up her daughters to make their own clothes and to dress shabbily, the papa would have been mortified. They are his playthings, but as to thinking of their future well-being, he never does. You always see the mama sneered at because she wants to marry them well; the papa is never ridiculous. He thinks they are there to make his tea and amuse him when he is old and gouty, and that is what they were born for.

As I have no daughters, and have married my adopted ones to my entire satisfaction,* I am in a good position to speak out. It will absolutely please me to be a little abused, because I shall be delighted to answer. I had a lawsuit in England and one in France. I lost the former because I was never allowed to speak to my lawyer: it bored him, forsooth! I gained £2,500 in the latter. I went to Limoges, took a lawyer with me and followed it up. *He* talked it over with me, and he was one of the most successful lawyers here.

I have done justice to the good feelings of the men in England when they *like* a lady. But as a sex they think women inferior— they have no money, they are to obey their husbands. Of course there are exceptions; but public opinion puts them in a very different position here. Especially, it never comes into anyone's head that women are born to nurse and look after their menfolk. . . .

* Anna married the eminent Helmholz, Ida a Hungarian Count von Schmidt-Zabierow.

Hilly . . . is a slave to her family and her kind heart. It's all very well when it's for Flo, whom she dotes upon, but for a parcel of brothers, sisters, uncles, aunts, cousins, etc. it is very provoking. She is like someone that has been boned, as meat is. She is like a molluscous animal; she has lost all power of enjoyment—all the sharp and crisp edges of her impressions are so blunted by constantly giving up all for other people that she cares for nothing. . . .

What a blessing it would be to be a foundling! Really, as a French lady said one day: 'Je voudrais que tout le monde fût bâtard.' All because she [Hilly] is single, she is to be at all their becks and calls. 'What can *she* have to do!—she has neither husband nor child!' So her soul is not her own; it's only married folk who have a right to such a possession . . .[22]

Now that Hilary, once so gifted, had become 'molluscous', she so irritated her cousin Florence that she found herself 'obliged to amputate her own limb' by refusing to let Hilary slave for her, even if such slavery had in the past released her for much valuable work.

Mary to Florence   Paris, 5 February 1862

. . . You say you were obliged to 'amputate your own limb by sending her away', but my dearest, if she is as useful to you as a limb, why should you amputate her? Keep her as she is—you keep your limb with all its sores. . . . I'm sure of this: she loves you better than anyone else does, and it would be balm to her poor worn-out spirit if she thought she was useful to you. . . .

I know you want her good above all things—I *do* know it. And so do I want it, but I question whether the thing she likes best in the world is not being with you and being useful to you. When she is with me I want nothing from her except to be exact at the dinner hour and not to talk all the evening—oh, that I cannot endure! I only want her to work for herself,—and the first years she did so; but the last she spent much time in faddling at Aunt Mai's and Uncle Nicholson's and Mrs Martin's—and now I am not sure this is not necessary for her happiness, this faddling after other people. I'm a selfish body and can't abide it—but we an't all alike, luckily. . . . Now, if she is a limb to you, you are the very person for her, for she dotes on you—it is a pleasure to her, and an honour. I agree with you: she *ought* to do for herself. But I am not sure her nature can now bear it. I give it to you as a problem—think about it. I am quite sure her mind was strengthened by being with you. . . . Her judgments were stronger, she was more discriminating; her twaddle about the family was certainly great, but so it always was. I observe that all who live much *en famille* get into it—and they have not always a husband who very unceremoniously says: 'Well well, I've heard that three or four times before' (my case—and it's very wholesome and generally wanted) . . .[23]

Mary to Florence   London, 11 September 1862

. . . Oh, selfish people are much easier to deal with than these molluscous self-wasters. . . .[24]

Mary to Florence   London, 28 September 1862

. . . I was as vexed as a pig in a high wind at being again obliged to go away without Hilly. . . . When she was eighteen, I said to her mother it would be well worth while for her to study properly. . . . Since then she has always attempted what she had not learned to do, and the conceit of her family as to their knowledge on the subject would have sufficed to prevent anything like work. But poor thing, it would be cruel to say all this now. She must do as well as she can. All I want to try and prevent is her murdering herself for her stupid family, and doing them no good either. . . .[25]

Florence to Mary   26 September 1862

. . . I give the women up. I think they are hopeless. I don't know one now who can attend to a sentence of five words, e.g. 'Tom has made a mess.' Half the women whose attention is not ready will not hear the nominative, and the other half whose attention is not steady will not hear the accusative. I once tried this experiment. . . .[26]

Mary to Mary Senior   Paris, 5 January 1863

. . . Be it known to you that the French women of 1862 are not the same as those of 1762; they are much less clever than the English ones now, and that I attribute to the neglect of the Englishmen, who have thrown English women on their own resources. Perhaps you will say, how is it that their admiration made the women so clever two centuries ago, and that neglect makes them clever in England? *D'abord*, they were charming as well as clever, because they were admired; in England they are *not* charming when they are clever; barring the exceptions, they are very disagreeable, because neglect makes people disagreeable. But it don't always make them stupid; they study and grow to a certain degree independent, but in a cross, crusty way. And those that don't, the ordinary misses, have a particular way of saying 'Gentlemen so and so', 'We can't go without a gentleman', 'Gentlemen don't like it,' that always makes me long to box their base, grovelling ears. . . .[27]

Florence to Mary   19 January 1862

. . . You say there is no female Newton, Kant, Descartes, Aristotle or Shakespeare. Very true—but Shakespeare is a *one* against all mankind, so is Descartes, so is Aristotle. 'But why are all the *ones* men?' you will say. I think it is obvious why. It would be an absolute miracle if they were women. . . . We read that Socrates spent twenty-four hours wrapped in thought exposed to the sun, as long as the sun did shine. Now if this had been a woman, either she or her mother would have been thinking about her complexion. We read that Descartes thought till one o'clock every day in bed for the sake of being undisturbed. Now I don't approve of his being in bed, but still I say that a woman who thinks it right, absolutely right, to allow herself to be disturbed by every tomfool or fooless, especially if the fool or fooless is of her family, puts it out of her power to be a Descartes, just as much as she would put it out of her power to live if she shut her head up in an exhausted receiver. . . .

I remember John Stuart Mill . . . attacked something in my book which he fancied pointed against female physicians (it did not). Now I do think that women had much better try their hands on the 'Sanitary' before they go to the 'Medical'. I am not going to trouble you with the long debate between him and me, but one of the illustrations I gave him was that Dr Elizabeth Blackwell would be inferior as a third-rate country apothecary of thirty years ago in England. And he said that was quite an unfair argument because among the very few women who had yet tried it was not likely there should be as yet one genius among them . . .

If I had such a mean idea of women as you have I should strike work; at the same time I must say that I have often sadly wondered why I have so little influence over women, because I have the two elements of feeling toward them generally the most inspiring to them, namely an unfeigned, not a got-up, belief in their capacity and a love for them so great that I will overcome my own nature to tell them their own faults. Yet women have always deceived me, men whom I trusted—never. . . .[28]

Mary to Mary Senior   Paris, 13 October 1862

. . . I have spent five days at Mme de Circourt's. . . . M. de Belvès came . . . It's one of those patterns of friendship peculiar to this country. He's perfectly devoted to madame, and monsieur likes him better than any one else, and is ready to go to the world's end with him. . . . I have another belief which I tried to insinuate in that chef-d'oeuvre you wot of, viz. that it is only platonics that have this lasting principle in them. I don't speak against marriage, because that has another element of duration than intense liking; it is a useful partnership of interests, and therefore it does without the exquisite sympathy. Of course, if it combines both, it is all the better; but it seldom does, because people marry without ever thinking of it. . . .[29]

Mary to Mary Senior   Paris, 20 January 1863

. . . As far as I can make out we may hope to see you in a month or two—and won't we go to the play! . . . *Le Fils de Giboyer** goes on night after night, filling the house and moreover the reviews, for it has been much talked of and abused. Up to this I have kept it to go with you. They say it's incomparably acted. When will you come? Tell me! for I'm like a child keeping a cake and passing my tongue over my lips at the thought of it. . . .[30]

Early in 1863 Mrs Gaskell made another of her escapes to Paris and the Mohls' apartment, partly, as usual, to get away from family and nonconformist concerns, partly to avoid hearing what reception her newly published *Sylvia's Lovers* received—'for she is not like me, a parvenu in literature, who likes to talk and hear talk of her newly acquired notoriety, whether good or bad. It bothers her, and she gets enormous compliments here, which she don't know how to pocket and thank for'[31]. Most of all, perhaps, she needed to recover from her heroic exertions on behalf of the Lancashire cotton workers, many of whom had been laid off because of the cotton famine caused by the American Civil War, and were suffering greatly.

*By Emile Augier, satirizing the regime.

Mary to Mrs Reid   Paris, 28 February 1863

... I hear so much about the workers in Manchester. They have worn her out, and her children too. .... So these human beings worth so much, will be all sacrificed to the improvident good-for-little manufacturers [mill-hands], who used to earn eighteen pence a week and never laid by a sou. I would not stir a finger for them: let them learn to think for the morrow, as other people do! Even Mrs Gaskell, who is very fond of them, can't deny their self-indulgence and other faults. ...

Mrs Gaskell had a constant headache for six months at Manchester, which went away as soon as she was here, but returns in the night very often, when she wakes in a bustle to hurry off to the committees and poor folk. And she still faints for a quarter of an hour [from time to time] when she is in Manchester, and hurried or too late. When she gets over this, she gets better. She has very often been out from nine in the morning to seven at night, and so tired that she could not eat—the children in the schools often fighting and so troublesome and impudent, but not *bad*. Her three daughters who are at Manchester are so worn out that their father means to send them away for a time.

I scarcely doubt that slavery will be ended in time by all this—and if we had fewer operatives in consequence, it might be a blessing in the long run. ...[32]

Mary to Hilary   March 1863

... Flo's ... imagination is so great a part of her life that if a crack is come to some of the images she has stood up there, all of fine china, she sees the crack for ever and can't look at anything else. I am convinced it is partly this malady, partly her solitude—My poor sister was saying to me the other day that she tried in vain to chase from her mind the irritating recollection of Mrs Tom's tricks—they were always returning and giving her malevolent feelings. .... Curious enough, Flo said to me: 'Do what I will, my mind is always hanging on my Aunt and all those grievances. I do what I can to chase it away, but it *will* come back.' They both have an intensity of feeling verging on madness. ...[33]

Mary to Mary Senior   Paris, 12 December 1863

. . . I was very low. . . . To comfort myself I have been often to the Italian Opera. . . . There's a new play, *Montjoie*, by Octave Feuillet, much talked of. I must find out whether there are any *scènes scandaleuses* before I can take my niece of sixteen, just out of her village; or if I can explain things by a secret marriage, as I did about *Norma*, whom I married to Pollione, without banns, long before the opera begins. I was more bothered about Lucrezia Borgia; but she was a very wicked woman, and her son passed off in the crowd of her crimes. . . .[34]

Mary to Monckton Milnes   Paris, 22 December [?] 1863

. . . It is said that Eugénie is enraged at the Bellangers (the favourite à la Dubarry) being again indispensable to the Emperor's happiness—not that she is given to jealousy, but that she can't bear such low creatures to be in favour. She would not mind if it were a fine lady. They have pulled down the best part of the galerie du Louvre, under pretence that it was in a bad way (a lie), but it is his whim to make it up again. They have altered three times the bit they have built up—that I have seen with my eyes. They are going to build a new bridge about thirty feet off from the Tuileries bridge because he don't like the bridge to be opposite the garden, and they will pull this one down if he lives ten years more. There will not be a stone left of the Paris of my youth. By the bye, did you ever see the Hôtel St Paul—an old house in the part of Paris opposite the Jardin des Plantes? It still has three *gargouilles* stretching four feet over the street. In the court there is still a square turret and *meurtrières* to pour boiling oil on the assailants, and various other remains of 1400. It is one of the remains of the Middle Ages most astonishingly preserved because at a fag end of Paris, and turned into a manufactory of jam and jelly. . . .[35]

Mary to Lady William Russell   Paris, 23 February 1864

. . . You want to hear about Germany. . . . I am told our queen holds to Germany against Denmark, that the prince holds to Denmark, and that the ministers are for Denmark because they think it wise to go with the next heir. But as Lord Palmerston is going on for eighty, and the queen is about forty-three, he need not, I should think, trouble himself about the heir. . . .[36]

The Schleswig-Holstein question was now adding to anxieties in Europe, but the vulgar excesses of Imperial Paris seemed to Mary to be increasing. People, she said, were now 'overflowing with court, or rather ministerial, ball scandal.'

Mary to Mary Senior   Paris, 13 March 1864

... Certainly the *bals costumés* are something out of all proportion with the state of morals and manners of the mass of the nation. ... The thing most talked of *au dehors* by ladies in whispers, and not mentioned by gentlemen before them, was the Marquis — disguised as a cock, with wings flapping and outstretched, and to act this character *au naturel* he hopped after some ladies after the fashion of a cock in a farmyard, paying more court to the hens than would be considered proper in a biped without feathers. ...[37]

Mary to Ida von Schmidt   Malvern, 22 July 1864

... You are very much mistaken if you fancy that the English do not trouble themselves about peace or war. I never saw London in such a state as it was from the time of Lord Palmerston's first long speech, which finished by owning that the Danes were in the wrong, till the evening, when the majority of eighteen decided that there was not sufficient cause for censure. We were all in a fever. ... I believe that the real reason why we have not had war is that the Queen would not. But her influence is so occult that no one ever alludes to it without saying 'so people say on the Continent'. ...[38]

This summer, on a visit to the Monckton Milnes, she had met Sir Richard Burton, the exotic cosmopolitan traveller and translator of the *Arabian Nights*, and his wife. Strange tales were told about their relationship.

Mary to Monckton Milnes   Autumn 1864

... Do you know, I think the ménage Burton *se sont distribués les rôles*. He acts as a ferocious mussulman to her lovely oppressed and impassioned slave, and I suspect they chuckle over our simplicity instead of fighting in their secret apartment, and if she told you that he had beat her, I would believe it unhesitatingly. ...[39]

Mary to Monckton Milnes
                    Mme Arconati's, Lake of Como, September 1864

. . . My spirits are at zero. The rain falls in torrents, the wind
blusters, the thundering rolls on at a distance, the clouds overhead
are of all shades till they get black, besides large grey ones that scud
along the opposite mountainsides. The lake rolls crested waves,
and silver serpents come down the mountains into it. This house
is on a high promontory rock—an old convent built by poor friars;
the rocks are a part of the house. I'm on the fourth floor one way,
ground floor the other—a terrace for each floor, with twisty old
myrtle trees. When it don't rain I go downstairs by these, but now
it pours I go by a stone staircase which is stuck in the rock. Inside
of the house is damp, and a scorpion was on the white-brown wall
last night—the first live one I ever saw. The whole lake is covered
with thick mist. I have a very large room with no curtains, a floor
of spotted artificial marble, no carpet, four chairs. The windows
rattle and the house has an echo that makes me think all night the
monks are coming up the scorpiony stairs. . . . I'm so cold; as to a
fire, no one thinks of such a thing. Very few books, as they come
here for [only] two months. Oh lack, I wish I was in Paris or
London or Fryston with you to make me laugh. Mme Arconati is
an old and dear friend, but not jovial. . . .[40]

Mary to Monckton Milnes   Milan, 22 September 1864

. . . We came here that I might see Manzoni once more. I used
to play at blind man's buff at his house when I lived here many
years ago. I have seen him since. . . . The last time his favourite
daughter was dying and his mother, whom he doated on, was there
with three other daughters—all now dead. It is a trait of his
character that he never once recalled that visit, though many
circumstances made it a remarkable epoch, but I know he *could*
not, he has such a dread of suffering and feels so acutely that he
could not bear to think of it. He has all his life put his hands before
his eyes to avoid what was too painful, till the habit has so grown
that the acute sensibility which caused it has the effect of insensibility. I might write three sheets about him . . .[41]

Memories of an even earlier past were evoked this autumn, for a book
of reminiscences about the old Barbauld-Aikin circle was published.

Mary to Mrs Reid   Paris, 1 November 1864

. . . You are now the only person I know that remembers my dear Miss Benger, whose picture is in my drawing-room, done by Miss Smirke, another dear friend. . . .

I was a girl of fifteen—very shy, very ignorant, but still able to admire. . . . Miss Benger took me to see the rare collection that lived in those small houses so modestly at Stoke Newington. I'm sure it was very kind of her to take such a raw, ill-licked cub as I was to such people. . . .[42]

But this rare mood of nostalgia passed, dissipated by Mary's excitement at what was currently being published—and particularly Mrs Gaskell's *Wives and Daughters*, which was now appearing in the *Cornhill*.

Mary to Mrs Gaskell   Paris, 28 December 1864

. . . I got the numbers long ago and read the story in two days (such a treat!) and sent them on to Anna, who is most grateful. . . . I have this very evening read the last number of the *Cornhill*, and am as pleased as ever. The Hamleys are delightful, and Mrs Gibson—oh, her tricks are delicious! But I am not up to Cynthia yet. Molly is the best heroine you have had yet. Every one says it's the best thing you ever did. Don't hurry it up at the last; that's a rock you must not split on. . . .[43]

Mary to Mary Senior
(*now Simpson, on her marriage*)   Paris, 7 March 1865

. . . I hope you won't give up your translations to keep house; though housekeeping is very laudable, the other's your best friend. One's pursuit always is; it sticks so close to one. No disparagement to the connubial tie, which I greatly esteem, but I have observed that *that* is improved by not being the only occupation in life; it is all *agrément* when one don't make it the sole stick to lean upon. . . .[44]

By now the correspondence with Mrs Reid had dwindled almost to a standstill—a fact which Mary had taken very calmly, assuming that Mrs Reid had merely become as engrossed in Bedford College affairs as Florence Nightingale was in her sanitary concerns. She was therefore disconcerted to receive, at this late date, a letter from Mrs Reid reproaching her with 'cooling'.

Mary to Mrs Reid   Paris, [?] 1865

. . . One time Florence Nightingale was so fond of me that no company was to her what mine was. She would walk with me for hours in the Park and would comport herself as if she would give anything in the world that I should stay a few days longer. But when her all-absorbing pursuit came over her all this vanished. She still liked me, but did not want my company. How absurd I should have been had I not accepted this. Well, I did the same with you— I never struggled with the college nor with the sick women. I have not the slightest taste for nursing—fact is, I mortally dislike it. I wish well to girls, but they bore me. Well, both you and she must feel, and do feel, that I'm a bit of a wretch not to care about such interesting things except wishing them well.—Mrs Chapman one day declared if I were American I should work for the slaves. Now I hate slavery, but as to spending all my life about it, I could not. It is not my vocation, I can't help it. . . .[45]

Mrs Gaskell was now suffering greatly from the heart disease which killed her towards the end of this year. Nevertheless she made a special effort to fulfil her engagement to stay with the Mohls in March 1865, having promised herself the two treats of their company and uninterrupted work on the rest of *Wives and Daughters*.

Mrs Gaskell to Emily Shaen   Paris, 27 March 1865

. . . I have no watch, there is no clock in the house, and so I have to guess the time by the monks' singing . . . and bells ringing (all night long, but especially in the morning). So I get up and come down into the smallest and shabbiest of the sitting-rooms, in which we live and eat all day long, and find that M. Mohl has had his breakfast of chocolate in his room (library) at half past six, and Mme Mohl hers of tea at seven, and I am late, not having come down (to coffee) till a little past eight. However, I take it coolly and M. and Mme come in and talk to me—she in dressing gown and curlpapers, very, very amusing, he very sensible and agreeable, and full of humour too. . . .

Then, after breakfast, which lingers long because of all this talk, I get my writing . . . and write, as well as I can for Mme Mohl's talking, till 'second breakfast' at about eleven. Cold meat, bread, wine and water and sometimes an omelette—what we should call lunch, in fact, only it comes too soon after my breakfast and too long before dinner for my English habits. After breakfast no. 2 . . . very often callers come—*always* on Wednesdays, on which day Mme Mohl receives. . . . When we dine at home it is at six sharp. No dressing required. Soup, meat, one dish of vegetables and roasted apples are what we have in general. After dinner M. and Mme Mohl go to sleep, and I have fallen into this habit; and at eight exactly M. Mohl wakes up and makes a cup of very weak tea for Mme Mohl and me. Nothing to eat after dinner—not even if we have been to the play. Then Mme Mohl rouses herself up and is very amusing and brilliant; stops up till one, and would stop up later if encouraged by listeners. . . . She generally has a dinner-party of ten or twelve every Friday, when we spread out into all the rooms (and I am so glad, for continual living and eating in this room and no open window makes it very stuffy) and 'receive' in the evening.

Guizot has dined here, and Mignet and Montalembert, since I came; and many other notabilities of less fame. But everybody stays up the first half of the night, as I should call it. When we go out for the evening, we go to dress directly after our dinner nap and tea; and just cross the court-yards—even in snow—or step to the Porter's Lodge opening into the Rue du Bac, and send him for a coach. We 'jigget' to some very smart houses . . . and in general have a great deal of very beautiful music from the masters of the Conservatoire, quartettes and quintettes; make a buzz of talk, look at fine dresses. And I come home hungry as a hawk about one a.m. . . .[46]

Mrs Gaskell to Marianne　　　　　　　London, 24 April 1865

. . . I *was* so well that first three cold weeks in Paris; but the close overpowering heat, and the real want of food, and lowness of diet, have made me so weak, I almost get out of spirits about ever being fit for anything again; which, I know, is nonsense, especially remembering how well I was three weeks or a month ago. . . .[47]

Mary to Mary Simpson　　　　　　　Paris, 18 May 1865

. . . I am now under the expected stroke of a great misfortune. My dear Miss [Hilary] Carter I may never see again. For twenty-five years our friendship never paused. I can't bear to think of it.

The doctors say there is no hope; but I go on thinking they may be mistaken. I wrote to ask if I should be a plague to the family if I went over and took a lodging next door, that I might see her when she liked. Florence's answer is: 'Don't come; you could not see her. She could not even be told you are there, as it might agitate her. She may not read any letters, she is so weak.' As I know what a torment over-zealous friends are, I have kept quiet; but it is a hard thing never to see her again. . . .[48]

Mary to Florence   Paris, 16 May 1865

. . . Three or four years ago, when I was with her at Kensington and she was in the greatest anxiety to finish her statue, M. Mohl went to London and she chose to invite a certain Mr Spottiswoode to breakfast with him on the Monday at nine. She received a letter on Saturday night from Laura, who had come to London with Jack, because, forsooth, he was going to shoot in the Highlands. They had arrived on Saturday and Laura, to hasten the wonderful shooting satisfaction, sent him off on Sunday morning and wrote to Hilly to say she could not bear to sleep alone at a hotel (she only had two maids and her children with her!) and that she wished Hilly would go and sleep at the hotel on the Sunday night . . . and would you believe it! Hilly, fagged to death, went on Sunday night to sleep at the hotel, and got up before seven to come back and receive M. Mohl and Spottiswoode at breakfast! If Laura was such a fool, why did she not keep her husband till Monday! No—Hilly must be maid-of-all-work. . . .[49]

Florence to Mary   London, 8 September 1865

. . . There is *not a single person*, except yourself, who does not think that Hilary's family were quite right in the most monstrous of slow murders—and that Hilary was worth nothing better than to be sacrificed—and all for what? . . . The fetichism of Family is a worse fetichism than that of Sunday. Because that only rolls its Juggernaut car one day of the week—the other, every day in the week. I shall never cease to think, as long as I live, of you and M. Mohl as Hilly's *only* friends. . . .[50]

Hilary died on 9 September 1865.

Mary to Emma Weston   Cold Overton, 1 October 1865

 . . . In June I came to London and saw her. She was much better, and I indulged in hope, but no one else did. . . . The last time I saw her she kissed me tenderly. 'Clarkey dear, you know you are my good mother.' Her eyes filled, and I felt I was going to give way, so, arming myself, I said: 'Come, come, let us talk of art'—a subject always near to us both. . . .[51]

Mary to Florence   Cold Overton, 22 September 1865

 . . . I had a letter today from poor Elinor Carter,* and I could almost have laughed a bitter laugh, she says so innocently: 'Mama is pretty well, and bears it better than I expected.'
 'The devil she does!' I could willingly write.[52]

Florence to Mary   London, late 1865

 Darling, I cannot bear you to think that I preach 'Stoicism'. It is unworthy of your acumen, you have got that from Parthe. I think, just as much as you do, that to take care of oneself is the eleventh commandment. If poor Hilly could speak, she would tell you that I have worried her to death to make her live, to make her keep reasonable hours, stick to her art at reasonable hours, instead of muddling away the whole day and then working at night in the snow in a solitary penthouse, with diarrhoea upon her. But it is no use returning to all that. Let me say about the Stoicism. It is because people *don't* take care of themselves that I am so disturbed.
 I admit that I cannot see the soundness of mind—it seems to me a kind of delusion like poor Hilary's—when I see people sacrificing the objects of life in order to live . . . and giving up the things which they themselves wish to live for, for fear these should shorten their lives.
 As to myself, if you mean me, if you think that my living the Robinson Crusoe life I do is the effect of Stoicism, there never was a greater mistake. It is entirely the effect of calculation. I cannot live to work unless I give up all that makes life pleasant. People say: 'Oh see: the doctors have said these eight years she could not live six months—therefore it is all a mistake.' They never say: 'She

* Hilary's sister.

has lived eight years when the doctors said she would not live six months, by adopting this kind of life, sacrificing everything else in order to work.' . . . I have ceased to try to make anybody understand this. I do hope I am getting wiser in this respect—*not explaining*. I have felt a good deal that, so far from my family taking pains to understand my reasons, they set other people to torment me upon a misunderstanding. . . . This very year they did so. They set people to write to me—'I can no more believe that your present life is what is best for you than I can believe with Mr Gladstone it is healthy to live over a churchyard.' I never said it *was* 'best for me'. All I said was, it was best for the work—or rather it is the only way in which the work could be done, with the present habits of people of my class. . . . And the most curious thing is that the very people who accuse me of stoicism then preach stoicism to me and say . . . you ought to bear these things with perfect serenity. . . .

Indeed I ought. And I *am* miserably weak, in mind and body. However, I really have given up explaining things, and that is a gain to serenity. I don't think that for four years I have even tried, except to you. . . .[53]

X

1866–1872
Collapse of an Empire

By 1866 the comparative stability of Europe in the '50s and early '60s was disappearing. The French economy was now being affected by Prussian ambitions and the Austro-Prussian War.

Mary to Mary Simpson   Paris, 15 May 1866

. . . People think of nothing but this probable war, which has paralysed everything; the very pastrycooks declare they sell no cakes. I don't believe it has such an effect in England, but the failures here are enormous. It is wonderful to me that mankind are such intense fools they can't or won't declare they will not have a war that ruins everybody. . . .[1]

Mary to Ida von Schmidt   Paris, 21 December 1866

. . . There is general uneasiness in France, and the people at the Bourse say that this state of things cannot last. The Péreires pay no dividend this year for the *crédit mobilier*. Louis Napoléon is beginning to be no longer considered a profound genius. . . .[2]

George Eliot to Mrs Richard Congreve   Biarritz, 16 January 1867

. . . We stayed three days in Paris and passed our time very agreeably. The first day we dined with Mme Mohl, who had kindly invited Professor Schérer and his wife, Jules Simon, Loménie, Lavergne, 'and others', to meet us. That was on the Saturday, and she tempted us to stay the following Monday by saying she would invite Renan to breakfast with us. Renan's appearance is something between the Catholic priest and the dissenting minister. . . . [3]

Mary to Ida von Schmidt   Paris, 24 May 1867

. . . Everything is going down here, and the money we have invested in Italy and Spain gives no interest, and the Austrians are such fools that I am afraid they will let themselves be beaten again. . . .[4]

Mary to Mary Simpson   Paris, 3 June 1867 (cold and rainy,
                                         sitting over the fire)

. . . I shall go to London, please the pigs, but I can't say when, because it is so cold that I have put off my journey till the latter end of June. Lady Augusta made a sort of engagement with me when she was here, but I can't make up my mind to move. I've grown old, my dear, though I fight the good fight against it, and hold high my banner, and run up and downstairs like a lamplighter. I am only weak, and that is a great bore. I am no more fit to die than to command a fleet, just because I don't like it; I'm ridiculously and basely fond of living. . . .[5]

Mary to Ida von Schmidt   Paris, 6 June 1867

. . . Paris has gone quite mad. The Emperor of Russia has turned everything topsy-turvy. . . . He went on the very evening of his arrival to the *Grande Duchesse de Gérolstein*, to see Mlle Schneider dance the can-can. It seems that I saw her dance it a week ago— and it did not strike me as at all improper! It was Mérimée told me it was the can-can. . . .[6]

Mary to Lady William Russell   Paris, 16 July 1867

. . . The Emperor is gone. While he was here there was no peace, nor no coach to be had, the whole town cared for nothing else. . . . I think his chief charm was that he telegraphed from Cologne to get a box to see . . . a burlesque on the German court, very much tasted* I dare say, by the Russians, but it ought not to be tasted by the Emperor of Russia, as his grandmother or great-grandmother, the Empress Catherine, made love to the soldiers; and so does the Grande Duchesse, to one in particular. . . . The Emperor also went to Mabille, in spite of all that could be said about the proprieties, and though the Parisians pretended to be shocked, I believe it was these *inconvenances* that made him so popular. . . .[7]

*i.e. relished.

8. Madame Mohl's Paris salon

9. Madame Mohl in later life. Sketch by W. W. Story

Mary to Lady William Russell   Cold Overton, 7 August 1867

I should have written long ago had I not been in trouble. I found my dear sister, whom I love better than any one in the world, had fallen down a week before my arrival, and though the bone is not broken (at least so the country surgeon says), the muscles of the thigh were so stretched and lacerated that the pain for days was dreadful. One of her sons was with her, but she forbade his writing to any one. Her nerves were so *agacés* that she could not bear any human face, and my coming down was discouraged under pretence of change of servants. . . .

My dear sister is considerably older than I am. I never spend a year, happen what may, without coming to her, always in a fright lest it may be the last. You may suppose, therefore, the trouble I have been in; for though my husband has a much greater place in my life, though he is my best friend and an incomparable companion, I have an indescribable tenderness for her that I have for no one else, nor ever had except for my mother. Yet she is much fonder of her sons than of me, and in fact I am but a very secondary person in her life. It's odd, but it's true nevertheless. . . .[8]

This summer Florence Nightingale too had her troubles, though of a rather different sort. Her Aunt Mai, who had been relieving her of all domestic cares, and thus freeing her for her great administrative tasks, had at last decided that duty called her to look after her own family. Florence complained bitterly.

Mary to Florence   Cold Overton, 3 September 1867

. . . I too have had horrid experience of motherhood, and don't pretend now to be stronger than nature. She is the cruellest tyrant we have—my dear sister would see me drawn and quartered to save her sons a headache; as to justice and morality they are totally nil. I am perfectly shocked to see it. . . . I am perpetually employing all my ingenuity to amuse her. Her son Charles is as stupid, as tiresome—! And she is fatigued with me and delighted with him— he's always in the right if we differ. I'm always in the wrong. It's like a girl with her lover. Depend on it—Nature is so powerful, when she wills a thing, that we must give way, we Platonists. Take your aunt with this spell upon her—allow for it. . . . Try to think coolly on what I say. . . .[9]

Curiously, Mary now found herself acting once again as a sort of substitute mother, at the age of seventy-four, when Ida's small son Nandor was sent to boarding school in Paris.

Mary to Ida von Schmidt   Paris, 30 October 1867

. . . I fetched the little one yesterday, and took him to Mme Boissier's, thence to the Val de Grâce, and on the way thence to Mme Tastu. When he is here I can do nothing, so I go out visiting and take him with me. . . .

I have found a way of fixing his attention. I give him a card for each word he reads well and without hesitating. I tell him to look at it well first, for if he does not read it properly he will not win the cards; but if he wins them all, then I will buy him a toy. I am sure that if I had him for three months he would read easily; but I should die of it. . . . The fact is, that if there were no schools the whole of the grown-up population would be either killed or extinguished, and if schools have only a moderate number of faults we ought to be very glad of their existence. . . .

I shall send for Nandor on Christmas Day, because it would be too sad for him to be at school, and again on New Year's Day. Next Monday I intend to invite some children to play at blind-man's buff and lunch in the dining-room, before I put down the new carpet. . . .

M. de la Boulaye . . told us last night that during the last few years experiments have been made in America, in certain colleges, to bring up girls and boys in exactly the same way, and their faculties were exactly equal, varying only according to the individual. . . .[10]

These new attitudes were gratifying. In practical terms, however, they had still produced few results, and Florence—overworked, obsessive and isolated in South Street—was more impressed by the second fact than the first. A pupil of hers who had been the matron of the Liverpool workhouse hospital had recently died, and there was, it seemed, not a single trained, intelligent woman to replace her.

Florence to Mary   February 1868

. . . I don't think anything in the course of my long life ever struck me so much as the deadlock we have been placed in by the death of one pupil, combined, you know, with the enormous Jaw, the infinite female ink, which England pours forth on 'Woman's Work'. Hilly used to say that all the demand I made on my country was for one young woman with a head. That, it seems, is not to be found. . . .[11]

Florence to M. Mohl   London, 16 February 1868
. . . All the winter she had 1350 patients, three hundred on the floor, and to fight for every necessary of life for them. She was never in bed until half-past one in the morning and always up at five-thirty. . . .[12]

Florence to Mary   [? Summer] 1868
. . . My people never made any sacrifice for me at all. When the world said it was right for me to stay at home, I was to stay at home—when the world applauded my going to the Crimea, I was to go to the Crimea. I don't suppose any one of them ever gave five minutes thought as to which *was* right.

But I assure you I don't let these things 'corrode' into me now— you told me not. . . .[13]

Mohl to Eleanor Martin   London, 8 October 1868
. . . Florence . . talked with all her old animation. On the whole I think her rather better than six or seven years ago, when I recollect well to have turned round under the door to look at her, thinking I would never see her again. But her work is too much for her. Not only has she that enormous business of sanitary organisation in India, but to keep up the War Office to the new sanitary regulations and the incessant correspondence about nurses she has sent out to towns in England and to the Colonies. Then she has to form new nurses, to fight with towns and countries about infirmaries, workhouses, water-supply; it is an endless, ever-renewed, almost hopeless fight with indifference, ignorance and waste. . . .

I came from Oakham second class, to escape from the silent swells, and found in the waggon at Peterborough an old lady with a parrot, a young one with a black cat and another with a beautiful baby; all very talkative, rather screamy and so I had plenty of occupation on the road. . . .[14]

Mary to Eleanor Martin   Paris, 1869 [?]

. . . I dined at some Americans' last Thursday, to meet M. Longfellow, the American poet, and a most agreeable person he is.

There was a thick and short English man in a morning coat and tightish cravat, whom I took by his clues for a Catholic priest from England, and asked Mrs Perkins (the lady of the house) about him. She answered that he was no Catholic but a Sacramentalist and preached in English in some chapel in Paris to a numerous English audience. She said little about his doctrine, but it's a new division who fuss about sacraments, it seems—and so do the Catholics, so I suppose they are near akin—but he don't call himself a ritualist. M. Mohl was not there . . . or I would have asked him to rummage into the man's doctrine. His name is Gurney. . . . Did you ever hear of Sacramentalists? In my youth good clergymen were content to look after the poor and did not pester one with sifting out new doctrines. Nothing is so plain and straightforward as Christianity if people will take it as it is. . . .

I sat by an old American friend of mine, Tom Appleton, who believes in spirits knocking about tables and says they are just as silly and tiresome as live people and why shouldn't they be! This was too much for me, but he and the Gurney got into talk about these Spirits, and I could not understand a bit what they were at, in fact I was a long time before I could persuade myself that Tom Appleton was serious. . . .[15]

Mary to Ida von Schmidt   Paris, 15 September 1868

. . . I sent this morning for the little fellow [Nandor], who is here and quite well. As it is Sunday, I don't choose to tease him with reading, for I have observed that everywhere except in England people love Sunday. It is a festival, a day of rejoicing. . . . In England every one dislikes the thought of it. . . .

He speaks French much more easily; he pronounces so well that one would hardly know he was German. Your uncle says that I attach an absurd importance to this, and it so happens that he himself is the cause, for I think that in the present condition of Germany, it is a great advantage for him to be settled, and so honourably, in France; and it would be an inestimable advantage for him if he spoke French like a Frenchman. . . .[16]

Mary to Eleanor Martin Paris, 1870

... Never say to a child 'Look at your brother, so much younger and so much wiser!' You will plant eternal jealousy into the child's heart, which nothing will ever eradicate; let sympathy act slowly. Besides, he had better keep his faults than have a gnawing at his little heart that will destroy his family feelings, and make him look upon himself as an outcast. ... [17]

Mary to Ida von Schmidt Paris, 7 May 1870

... Mr Mohl has made up his mind to take Nandor to Heidelberg on July 1. I love him very dearly, and you need not fear lest his stay here should have in any degree diminished my affection for him ... You should not talk to him of things above his comprehension; the minds of children ought not to be stretched any more than their limbs, and it is better to teach them words than ideas. This was the old fashion, but it is also the fashion of nature, who gives us memory before reflection.

I cannot give an opinion as to your new notions on the education of girls at Vienna. I am sure, however, that they are foolishly brought up everywhere, for fear of knowledge doing them harm, whereas the emptiness of their heads is the real evil—and the absence of rational ideas. If I ask my way in the street of a well-dressed woman, 'I don't know' is the invariable reply. If a woman wants to stop an omnibus, she always chooses a steep slope on which the poor horses can hardly stand. ...

In short men have contrived to make women as incapable as possible, except where their paltry little interests or ludicrous sentimentalities are concerned. ... What they ought to learn is not Latin, but how to live. But how are they ever to learn that!—always watched, always kept in leading-strings. ... [18]

In France 1870 had started encouragingly with the advent of Ollivier's liberal ministry, but by July 19 war had been declared on Prussia—ostensibly over Bismarck's attempt to seat a Hohenzollern on the Spanish throne, but also because of the war-hysteria whipped up by the press of both Prussia and France.

Mary to Lady William Russell Cold Overton, 31 July 1870

... I forget if I wrote you the real story of the Hohenzollern affair. I will risk repeating it. The Duchess Stéphanie of Baden's daughter married a Hohenzollern-Sigmaringen, the Stéphanie being first cousin to Queen Hortense, and the same sort of person—one niece, the other daughter, to Joséphine. They were like sisters. The daughter of Stéphanie was much brought up with Louis Napoleon ... L.N. proposed a little while ago to his old playfellow's second son to marry the daughter of the Duchess of Alba, niece to the Empress Eugenie, and promised to help him to the crown of Spain. ... The young man refused, but the idea had taken root in L.N.'s head. He proposed then the eldest son, leaving out the condition of the marriage. . . .

Meanwhile the industrious peasants of the south of Germany and the Rhine will all be ruined, the cattle taken, the corn trod down. Oh, I could cry! . . .[19]

Mary to Monckton Milnes   Paris, undated, but probably 1870

. . . Nothing can be worse than the state here—at least to my feelings, because I wish the French to be beat to get rid of L.N., yet I am in the greatest affliction about Paris, which I love, and am afraid of the siege. In short, I see trouble every way. The killed and wounded soldiers whom I don't know I can bear well, for they each went with the hope of killing others and had no business to go. But I am troubled for so many others and for the town I so love. It is an amazing *bon fine* to finish the empire, and I can comprehend that you all, who have neither friends nor Penates there may take it easy. I can't.

. . . P.S. L.N.'s vanity is such that I am convinced the immense noise this makes comforts him very much.[20]

In this emergency Florence Nightingale's strengths came into prominence once again. She had been called in to organize the sending of medical supplies to both sides in the war.

Florence to Mary   London, 16 August 1870

. . . Stores, ammunition, clothing, guns, *everything* is falling short—false muster rolls of battalions—men returned at nine hundred strong, who never were more than five hundred. . . . And this, my dear, is what would happen at *our* War Office, if we were to go to war, which God forbid—except that ours is incapacity, not pillage. . . .[21]

Florence to Mary   London, 18 August 1870

   . . . After the fighting come the miseries of the poor people, and
a victory is only less dreadful than a defeat. . . . England does talk
such intolerable 'bosh' about Prussia. Now, if you take all the great
names in Science, in Literature, in metaphysical and religious
philosophy, in art, of the last eighty or ninety years in all Germany,
will you tell me how many of these came out of Berlin? Yet the
higher civilization is to be subjected to the lower, and England is
to rave about Prussia. . . .[22]

Florence to Mohl   London, 17 November 1870

   . . . They are performing operations with common butchers'
knives and without chloroform near Orléans since November 8th or
9th. . . .[23]

Florence to Mohl   London, 23 November 1870

   . . . Here at last is the copy of the things and cash we have sent
to the German side from September 1 to November 12, which you
were so good as to say you would put in the Cologne Gazette. This
does not include, of course, what we have been doing for the
French sick prisoners in Germany (we sent £5000 of things last
week alone). . . .[24]

   For the duration of the war the Mohls remained in England, where
they had been staying when it broke out. In September indeed M. Mohl
had what Florence referred to as 'your *péritonite*'; she advised him to follow
the doctors' advice, 'even if it is to go on a régime, even if it is to go to bed
for a day or two and eat slops.'[25] Mary too—she was now seventy-seven—
was not well and, to add to her miseries, her nephew Thomas Frewen had
just died.

Mary to Mary Simpson   London, October 1870

   . . . My illness was brought on in great part by my tormenting
myself about the war, which entirely took away the capacity of
eating, and brought on a catarrh of the stomach. I was so weak I
could not stand. Then, to finish me, my nephew died on Saturday,
and I want to go to my poor sister. . . .
   And Paris goes on worse than ever. Sometimes I think I shall
never go home—and to be without a home and ill is no joke. . . .[26]

   She did not go home until the end of the Commune, although M. Mohl
returned in March 1871. In England she mixed with all her old friends

and several new ones, and convinced Mary Simpson, at least, that 'she had the power of throwing off her anxieties, both in society and in reading. . . . There were other French exiles who contributed to the interest of society that year. The Viardots, who received every Saturday evening and had beautiful music. . . . Ivan Tourguenieff, Taine, Lanfrey and many others.'[27]

Mary to Ida von Schmidt   London, 18 February 1871

. . . The delay in receiving letters . . . can be a source of profit to nobody.

. . . I got one on the 15th from the Haughtons. . . . They have suffered greatly, as they could not eat horse. During the last month the bread was so abominable that if they had not had a little provision of sea-biscuits they must literally have died of hunger. The shells were whizzing round their house in the Rue Gay-Lussac, near the Panthéon, and poor Eliza, who cannot get up or down stairs, expected every moment to be struck. . . .

They went to the Rue du Bac. The garden was full of shells, but none had struck the house. My two maids slept in the cellar or the kitchen next to it, but Julie—the heroic Julie*—would not leave our apartment, because if a shell had burst in, she might put out the fire and save our possessions. How then can people say the French are all demoralized! . . . However, we are very ignorant as to what is going on . . . Julie is more heroic than epistolary. . . .

I am very economical, not knowing what income we shall have. We must make up our minds to railroads paying nothing for years, and that the war indemnities will be enormous. No matter: if I lose half my income, it will be worth while to have got rid of Bonaparte. . . .[28]

On 3 April, as soon as she became aware of Mary's fears of ruin, Florence Nightingale wrote to offer her £1000 at half an hour's notice.[29]

The assembly which was elected after France's surrender in January 1871 was largely Orleanist or even Bourbonist, and chose Thiers as its leader. In Paris, on the other hand, the socialists were more and more dominant, resented the terms of the peace which the Assembly negotiated, and set up the Commune, even adopting the old republican calendar and the red flag. The civil war that ensued was probably the bloodiest conflict of Mary's rich experience in that line. A first-hand account soon came from Annie Thackeray.

* The cook.

Annie Thackeray's journal　　　　　　　18 March 1871

. . . Came from Le Havre. Saw the German helmets gleaming in the villages—blossoms on the fruit trees and the snow lying on the ground everywhere. The fortresses and outlying fortifications all round Paris terribly grim. . . . Everyone in black—empty streets. Drove to Mantes next day. German notices on the walls. To St Cloud, burnt, utterly destroyed—sunshine—people singing. Frenchman, to me: 'Listen to 'em! Their country's in ruins, and they sing.'

22 March

To Mme Mohl's in the sunshine; met hurrying crowds of figures who looked as if they had come straight out of the French Revolution. Massacre in the Place Vendôme. Charlotte and I were out together—we rushed across the fire of the guns to escape. We took refuge in the Church of St Roch. Rue St Roch crowded with people turning out to fight, others running away, while others stood joking on their balconies.

Determined to leave Paris. Railway in the hands of the Blues. Reds advancing. Our train moved out of the station just as the fighting between the Blues and the Reds began. . . .

Home, calm silence, no guns. Most horribly frightened now it is all over. To bed, quite done up.[30]

Mohl to Lady William Russell　　　Charenton*, 23 March 1871

. . . I set off to go to the Rue Pigalle. As long as I was in the Faubourg St Germain all went on well, although I saw many shops closed; but on the other side I heard the *rappel* beaten everywhere, and every open place was occupied by National Guards. I went through the Palais Royal, which I found entirely deserted; all the shops closed, and not a soul about. The iron railings of the garden were shut, but at last I found an outlet to the Rue Vivienne, where people were shutting up even the coffee-houses; and as I arrived on the boulevard, which I tried to cross at different places, but was warned off, I heard firing lower down, and a crowd running by, crying 'On nous assassine.' So I gave it up, and came home through the Rue Richelieu. The firing had been in the Rue de la Paix. . . .

*Name of the famous madhouse, in which Mohl, now returned to Paris, felt that he was living.

The Prussians now declare they will bombard Paris, and we may possibly hear tomorrow the batteries of St Denis opening on the town. . . .

Holy Easter, 1871

. . . I will imagine myself sitting at eight o'clock at your round table, you writing a letter on green paper, and I eating tongue to open my appetite, and telling you that I sent a year ago a Jew from Adrianople to Saba to get rubbings of inscriptions of the defunct Queen of Sheba, of Solomonian memory, and her ancestors and descendents. . . . When I left, in August, we had no other news of the man than a little mention of him in a letter from the Governor of Aden. In February I found in the Augsburg Gazette another mention of him and his doings, but a rather discouraging one, as it is said that he copied the inscriptions in Hebrew characters, to be afterwards retranscribed in Sabean, which is a proceeding calculated to make the whole affair worthless. A few days ago the man walked into my room and brought me above five hundred inscription, copied, not in Hebrew, but in orthodox Sabean. He could not make rubbings with paper, as the Arabs would have murdered him instantly; and notwithstanding all his precautions, he would have been ten times murdered if he had not been a Jew, and as such protected, hid and fed by the Jews he found, who are sadly oppressed by the Arabs, but able and willing to shelter him to a certain degree. I am delighted at his success, and hope to publish this budget of news . . . in the Asiatic Journal, as soon as the printing office is delivered from its savage occupants.

And now my tale is told, your green letter is sealed. . . . Mrs Arthur has eaten her prawns, Arthur has replaced the four little plates symmetrically, your man has brought mulligatawny; so let us enjoy ourselves. . . .

17 April 1871

. . . The town becomes every day more empty, five hundred thousand having emigrated. The consumption of flour has fallen from eight thousand tons a day to five thousand, which will give you an idea of the place. Yesterday, going through the Rue de Beaune, I found to my wonder a quantity of fowls and two big cocks wandering about and crowing as if they were on a dunghill. The French Academy has given up its sittings *faute de combattants*;

ours [the Académie des Inscriptions] is going on valiantly with sixteen members; and I held on Friday a sitting of the Société Asiatique with eight members, of which I was very proud. . . .

26 April 1871

We are living far from high. . . . Little meat and fish is coming in. They say the Prussians will buy the Colonne Vendôme and rebuild it at Berlin. But this must be a joke, and a very grim one it is. . . .

30 April 1871

. . . Yesterday evening there was furious fighting, and I saw high flames rising from some unfortunate village—I suppose Clichy—which they together must have burned. This morning is deep silence, as if all the batteries had gone to church; but it will certainly not last long. . . .

Mohl to Emma Weston   1 May 1871

. . . The composition of the Commune is wonderful. Some are old conspirators, journalists or *hommes de lettres*, some journeymen bookbinders or such like, some street musicians, some doctors, some lawyers. . . . How they made their way we do not know; most likely they were deep in the obscure socialist conspiracies which are constantly going on. . . .

They have got hold of a good and bad idea—the necessity of great municipal rights—but they ride this hobby-horse to death in their folly. Their conception of a commune is insane. They want to make a state of it. For instance, they appropriate to the town of Paris all the great establishments of the state, and declare that they will indemnify France for them and buy from it the Louvre and its galleries, the Jardin des Plantes, the Bibliothèques, the Facultés. They have got a minister of foreign affairs. They pretend to be at the head of the federation of the republican communes of Europe. They claim all the legislative powers of a sovereign state, and want to change the distribution and property of capital. And this is what gives them their most sincere adherents—workmen who have been addled by insane discussions about the rights of capital and work. Then there are thousands of deserted soldiers, of Fenians, Poles, Garibaldians, and all the riffraff of cosmopolitan demagogy—many thousands of condemned criminals, who were not allowed to reside

here, and have now flowed into Paris—and a great mass of indifferent or unwilling Parisians, who have been accustomed during
the siege to obey military orders. These are, I believe, very much
disheartened. . . .

Mohl to Lady William Russell   10 May 1871

. . . I came in contact with the Commune yesterday, quite
unexpectedly and against my will. A certain French-Chinese
bishop, Monseigneur Perny, a sort of *savant*, has published the
first volume of a French-Chinese dictionary. He was his own
printer, and has worked for the last two years in an apron and paper
cap, like an ordinary journeyman at this immortal work. Unluckily
for him, when he went out he donned a wide-brimmed hat with a
gold cord and wore a gold chain and cross round his neck with
other ecclesiastical frivolities—which proves that he is not a man of
sense; he did not see that if one has the luck to possess an apron
and a paper cap, it is not the moment to leave them off and to put
on the Order of the Holy Ghost or such like. In short, he went out
in this costume of the age of barbarism and despotism, and was
caught in the street by the National Guard, who adore religious
liberty, and clapped into the Conciergerie, where he has been kept
in secret for the last five or six weeks with other bishops, ready to
hand when they want to shoot a few to avenge any casualties among
the Federates at Versailles. . . .

At last a member of the Commune . . . advised the Asiatic
Society to lay claim to him. . . . It is just possible that this may be
of use to the poor man . . . but I fear not; for arrests are arbitrary,
and no one knows by whose orders. . . .

Mohl to Lady William Russell   14 May 1871

. . . The beasts have now emitted a ukase, that every one of us is
to take a *carte de sûreté*, which every armed ragamuffin in the street
is empowered to ask to see, and if you have not got it, to arrest you.
I won't take any, as I do not recognise their right to command me,
and I would rather remain at home until the devil has got them,
which I hope will be shortly. . . .

. . . The state of the town is indescribable. At every crossroads there have been barricades, of which the remnants fill the streets, the pavement is frequently covered with dried or drying blood, the houses battered and half-ruinous; at every corner a sentry who orders you to walk in the middle of the street, that you may not be able to throw petroleum on the houses. I did not understand what the first sentry told me, and crossed over to the opposite pavement; but he reiterated his orders and threatened to shoot me, which quickened my dull understanding. It would really be ignominious to have been shot as a suspected incendiary. . . .

I came back by the Quai, but when I came to the entrance of the Rue du Bac, I found an enormous barricade, over which Mérimée's house had tumbled, closing up the street with a ruin thirty feet high. The whole offered a dismal spectacle. All that part of the Rue de Lille between the Rue du Bac and the Rue Solférino . . . is one mass of ruins. The Hotel St Aignan has entirely disappeared, the others are wrecks burned out, half the walls fallen, the rest black and tottering. They had all been absolutely covered by petroleum pumped upon them. . . . The ruins are yet smoking, and the firemen stand upon them, directing streams of water on this boiling mass. The façades still stand in part, without any back, and may at any moment crush the firemen who stand behind and beside them. . . .

While I am writing the whole of the horizon is again red with fire. . . .

27 May, 1871. Three o'clock

. . . When I saw that the danger of pillage was over, I collected together the money, papers and plate I had hid, to have all under my hand in case of fire. But this danger too is rapidly passing away, as the whole population is watchful about it, to a degree which it is difficult to imagine. I believe nobody, certainly no woman, could carry a bottle or any such vessel in a street where she is unknown without danger. . . . The fury of a frightened population is quite ferocious, and really the shooting off-hand of people who carry no arms is a real public danger, and a very bad example. . . .

Five o'clock

. . . The firing goes on. I wonder that these last quarters
can hold out so long. In the Palais Royal the palace is entirely
burnt. . . . Most people I see are become so restless they gad about
without any purpose, only from being unable to keep in any one
place. On me it has another effect: it makes me thirsty to an
incredible degree. I never drink between meals; but now it is as
if I was devoured by an interior fire, and I drink water all day
long. . . .

Mohl to Lady William Russell   29 May 1871

. . . It was all over at eight o'clock. The remnant of the beasts
surrendered unconditionally; four court martials will judge them.
. . .[31]

As soon as Mary heard this news, she hurried back to Paris, escorted
by Dean Stanley and his wife.

Mary to Mary Simpson   Paris, 13 June 1871

. . . I should have written last week if my poverty (of strength
but not of will) had not governed me—like the poor apothecary in
Romeo and Juliet, for whom I have often felt as much compassion,
by the bye, as for the lovers. . . .

We arrived here at one in the morning, and got to bed at three.
My poor spouse looks wretchedly; he had waited from half-past
eight to near twelve at the railroad, when he went back. We got
there at past twelve, tried in vain to get a coach, and at length,
leaving the luggage, set out on foot along the dark muddy streets;
yet we were all three as merry as crickets, and felt no fatigue. As we
trudged along, we called to every wheeled thing we could discern,
but they were obdurate. At last a little omnibus, which was plying
to some station, was persuaded to bring us here.

We were all curiosity to see the ruins. But after all, they were
not half so numerous as we expected. But on crossing the Carrousel
the Tuileries were invisible. True, it was very dark, and the town
is as yet lighted like a small country town. We did spy every now
and then a monstrous heap of stones.

Our porter opened the ponderous door much sooner than I
expected, and we got upstairs and ate our dinner very merrily at
two in the morning. Mr Mohl, however, seemed impervious to all

fun, and looked like a man who had been hung and cut down before his last gasp. He was better the next morning, however, and the house rang with his old laugh. . . .

Nothing strikes me more than the alteration in people's faces and deportments. One of my maids, about twenty, is grown so thin and hollow-faced it is fearful. The other is exactly the same. The porter hid himself in the cellar and would never open the door. The consequence is, he looks extremely well—I may say better. Cowardice is a healthy regimen. . . .[32]

Mohl to Lady William Russell   Paris, 15 June 1871

. . . Literary work is beginning again here, and I am very busy after my long idleness. Only we have all lost our memories, and I have become slightly idiotic. It was seldom the uneasiness of one's personal security which was the cause of this mental depression, as the danger of an unobtrusive individual in a large town is never great. But the cessation of all civil life, and the feeling of living in an enormous madhouse where the patients had overpowered the keepers, and where the most dangerous of the insane were the masters, and kept plastering the walls with their wild decrees and lying despatches, was intolerable. . . . I learned at the printing-office that there alone they had consumed five thousand reams of *papier d'affiches.* . . .[33]

George Eliot to Barbara Bodichon   Shottermill, 17 June 1871

. . . How about dear Madame Mohl and her husband? I have been wondering through all the horrors whether M. Mohl had returned to Paris, and whether their house, containing too probably the results of much studious work lies buried among ruins. . . .[34]

Mary to Mary Simpson   Paris, 28 June 1871

. . . Rain seems to have undisputed empire here. As to the fever and dead bodies and dangers I was threatened with, it is perfect nonsense. The streets are crammed with people; everybody is in black, but that is the chief difference. I have not seen any one in colours. The shops have nothing but black bonnets, except a flower or so to show it's not private mourning. It's really curious. . . .[35]

Mary to Mary Simpson   Cold Overton, 5 August 1871

... I arrived here half-dead with fatigue—not so much with the journey as with a sort of battle at Peterborough, where the platform must have had at least eight hundred people on it, with three or four porters, and I had to run from my Great Northern to get into my Cross Midland [train], hauling hold of one porter, who, as he was stronger than I, managed to get away. I had three packages in my hand, two in the van, and three minutes allowed for changing. I never ran quicker in my best days. ...

I found my poor sister better than expected. Only one niece here. I am able to return to my writing, and am so glad. It is the first time for eleven months, and I begin to hope I have not grown stupid, and that the brain has escaped the general wreck. ...[36]

Mary to Mary Simpson   Cold Overton, 11 August 1871

... When you come [to Paris] we will go to the play every night; but I don't think the theatres are in a good state in September, because all the university people are away. However, you must decide that yourself; I can only keep you *au courant* of what is going on. ...

The Prussian government want to make Mr Mohl the head of the new university they establish at Strasburg, because his position in Paris, they think, would make him of more consequence at Strasburg. But he answered that nothing would induce him. He did not, I suppose, say what I know to be the truth: that nothing would induce him to be anything under the Prussian government. ...[37]

Mary to Mary Simpson   Paris, 22 December 1871

... I'm much better, and as a proof am full of absurdities, a fact that can't be helped. ...[38]

Mary to Lady Augusta Stanley   Paris, 6 January 1872

... We are pretty comfortable as far as mere living goes. Everything is much dearer; but our losses have been far less than I expected, and the wonder to me is, that after such a dreadful year, such a dreadful waste of life and means, such sums to be paid— first to the enemy, and next for the extravagancies of the imperial

government—that things are as good as they are. Such a waste of
the poor animals—the cattle so diminished in number that my
London kitten won't lap milk, forsooth, because it is so different
from what she had at Florence Nightingale's. She goes about
mewing for better, which they call cream here. . . .[39]

Gradually, however, her old spirit began to come back to life.

Mary to Eleanor Martin   Paris, 20 January 1872

. . . I have a dinner party pretty regularly, once a fortnight, on
Friday—twelve or thirteen people. The intervening Friday people
come in the evening without invitations and very pleasant it
is. . . .

I have made a point, even when this winter I was at my worst,
of cultivating society—which, being my especial talent, I will not
bury, for in the present state it is far more useful than giving away
money. The quantity of people in good circumstances who have
kept away for various causes must, of course, deaden everything,
though less than I should have expected. And every little does a
little good, were it only to feed the poor horses and hackney
coachmen; it is far better to give them employment than [charitable]
help.

Besides, I agree with my dear old Johnson: civilization and
society are greater moralizers than preaching—at least in large
towns. I can't judge of villages—though, from various observations
which I have made in England, I am convinced that if sociability
between the various grades of society were more cultivated, it
would be by far the best way to prevent the ever-increasing hatred
between the democracy and aristocracy. When I was young your
grandfather* was the friend of all his tenants, yet he did not spoil
and pet the beggars as Tom did. He used to invite the farmers'
wives to tea now and then. These were remains of old-fashioned
manners. It never came into their heads to be wanting in respect
and good feeling—and benevolent habits of thought are more
cultivated by seeing one another than by separation. However, the
manners now in England are so totally different from the old ones
that I am not fit to live there; I found that out last winter.[40]

* Mr Frewen Turner, Eleanor's husband.

Mary to Lady Augusta Stanley   Paris, 19 March 1872

. . . I am quite a new person from what I was when I saw you here. In November and December I was very bad. I made a great effort to force myself into life. I saw the tendency in Mr Mohl to fall into low spirits because of the foolish, the absurd, the unjust feelings against Germans. I determined at least to fight against it as far as I could, and did all in my power to keep up society and goodwill—never refused to go out, however great the effort. . . .

Mr Mohl don't know how much his spirits depend upon the *bienveillance* of others. No one knows it—and he would be hurt if he did. We all depend dreadfully on each other. We live in a world of looking-glasses, and it is our mind, not our face, that is given back to us by the reflection. If we see a dingy look at us, we grow dingy. A benevolent look is better than a cordial. . . . Our very being seems composed of how we stand in the minds of our fellow-creatures. Some call it weakness, and so it is; but I question whether it is not a law of our nature.[41]

On 1 April Mohl's brother Hugo died.

Mary to Eleanor Martin   Paris, 23 April 1872

. . . Poor M. Mohl was dreadfully cut up . . . He greatly esteemed his brother and was proud of him, for he was the first botanist in Europe and had offers from Petersburg, Berlin and Munich to be head of their botanical gardens. . . .

My next trouble was that I had combined a dinner party with much calculation to bring about a meeting between Guizot and the young Japanese envoy come here purposely to study the system of public education on which Guizot's ministry from '39 to '48 had made such improvements . . . and M. Mohl being President of the Asiatic Society it is a graceful and proper thing that he should help as far as he can all learned communication with Eastern nations. Guizot is eighty-five and spends his summers in the country, so that it is now or never. . . . I offered to M. Mohl to write to all those I had invited, he would not let me . . . and said *no*, he would go through it, it might be useful to the young Japanese (who is a very taking person, by the bye) and he added 'As he may not know our customs he may think it an insult to put him off, the Japanese being great martinets about manners and politenesses. . . .'[42]

Mary to Ida von Schmidt   Paris, 25 May 1872

. . . During the last month your uncle has not been at all well. The death of his brother affected him deeply. . . . I attribute this excessive grief to his mind having lost something of its elasticity; it distresses me extremely to observe this change in him. I do all I can to make his life smooth and pleasant. Perhaps my goodwill has less effect than the charms of youth, which are mine no longer. Perhaps I have lost the talisman which made every word I said, and even my follies, graceful in his eyes, and consoled him for everything else. I am more sorry for him than for myself, but there is nothing to be done. There is a certain spring in my mind which I have preserved but which is seriously impaired in him, and the result is that nothing, hardly, gives him any pleasure, while the same things amuse and please me as much as ever. I went the other day to the Théâtre Français, and I cannot tell you what pleasure it gave me. I thank God for it, which would astonish many a devout mind. . . .[43]

XI

1873-1883
'As witty and gay as ever'

In 1873 Napoleon III died. During the next decade, the last of Mme Mohl's life, the world was a very different place from the one she had grown up in. On the one hand, Britain was now conscious of its Imperial role to an extent she had always found hard to take seriously; on the other, it had taken several firm steps along the road to modernism in welfare-care and tolerance. (Forster's act of 1870, bringing in universal state primary education, and the abolition in 1871 of religious tests at universities are two examples within fields of which she herself had had some experience.) Women were still without the vote, but had gained the Married Women's Property Act; an even newer style of New Woman was now emerging in England, breaking out of her Dolls' House, invading medical schools and typewriting offices, replacing her corsets with Rational Dress, bicycling and on occasion playing hockey 'like a man'. In art the Gérards, Smirkes, and even the Delacroix and Scheffers had long belonged to the past; the first Impressionist Exhibition was held in 1874. Rossini had been ubiquitous in the 1820s; now the concert programmes contained such names as Debussy, Mahler, Wolf, Albeniz. . . . As for writers: it was a long step from Scott to Henry James, Thomas Hardy, Swinburne, Rimbaud, Maupassant, Zola . . .

For the first time, Mary began to show signs of decline. Very many of her friends were now dead or dying. Her own energy was diminishing. For her, as for Europe, it was very nearly the *fin de siècle*.

Florence to Mohl   London, 20 May 1873

. . . Every individual man who formed my committee in 1857, many of them hardly older than myself, are dead. And I hang on. John Stuart Mill's death was a great shock to me. Mr Grote used to say of him: 'Talk of Mill's logic. Why he is thrilling with emotion to the very finger ends.' That is just what he was. . . .

My training schools have assumed such pressing proportions. . . . They are always staying with me or coming to be talked to. . . .[1]

Mary to Ida von Schmidt   Cold Overton, 9 September 1873

. . . Alas, I am losing all my friends. My poor Milady [Lady William Russell] is still alive, but so suffering and complaining that it is always a toss-up how one finds her. Madame Arconati died sixteen or seventeen months ago, and the Princess Belgiojoso soon after, and I was a wretch, refusing to go to see them . . . although they begged me to do so. I shall never forgive myself. It is true that I was not well, but I could have done it. Alas, I was out of temper with them both, or I should have gone.

I shall be glad to get back to Paris, but it breaks my heart to leave here. My sister is better in body than I have seen her since her fall, but worse in mind. For the first two years she lost nothing, and took an interest in everything. This is no longer the case.

She is still beautiful. I never before saw a very old person who was agreeable—*very* agreeable—to look at, although she does not look at all young for her age. Even the loss of her teeth does not disfigure her. It is an incomparable gift, and worth every other. . . .[2]

Mary to Mary Simpson   Paris, 7 October 1873

. . . I have returned to Paris fully determined not to let myself fall into discouragement or laziness, but to fight with life, and to force it with kicks and thrusts to give me all the enjoyment it possibly can. This resolution will prove to you that my health has improved. . . .

Mme Chevreux . . . has read me some love-letters from Ampère to Mme Récamier, between 1820 and 1825. They are quite charming, and I am delighted that she is going to publish them. She is surrounded by people who discourage her, because it is not usual that a man of twenty should be so much in love with a woman of forty, and they call her a coquette. Certainly she was a coquette, but a charming one; and if everyone was perfect there would be no more books, and if there were no more books, the best thing would be to be buried as fast as possible. . . .[3]

By a cruel irony, Florence Nightingale—at fifty-five, having created the British Empire's civil and military hospital services practically single-handed—now found herself once again 'Mrs Nightingale's daughter'.

Florence to Mary   Norwood, 18 June 1875

. . . I am 'out of humanity's reach' in a red villa like a monster lobster in charge of my mother, by doctors' orders, as her only chance of recovering strength enough to see once more her old home (Lea Hurst), after which she craved. Here she is happy— happy, at least, compared with her miserable unhappiness in London.

Stranger viscissitudes than mine in life few men have had: vicissitudes from slavery to power and from power to slavery again. It does not seem like a 'vicissitude', a villa at Norwood, yet it is the strangest I have yet had. It is the only time for twenty-two years that my work has not been the first reason for deciding where I should live and how I should live. Here it is the last.

It is the caricature of a life. . . .[4]

Mary to Mohl   Lea Hurst, 15 August 1875

. . . Mr Jowett spent three days here. He is a man of mind; I think he would suit you. He may be going to Paris; be kind to him if he does. If I were at home, I should ask him to dinner. He is very fond of Florence, which would also suit you. She is here, and her conversation is most nourishing. . . .[5]

Mary to Mary Simpson   Cold Overton, 5 September 1875

. . . Odo Russell was at Knowsley, and sang all one evening. You know the marvellous pleasure a beautiful voice gives me—but I wanted some Rossini and Bellini! He is as fond of them as I am; but, forsooth, his wife had only brought accompaniments for German music and some French. Confound German music! Oh, that I should have been born under the reign of Rossini, and should have lived to see those vile Germans on the throne! *Encore*, if it was Mozart, Weber, or even some of the respectable entrancing old fellows!* But it puts me in a rage to hear people in ecstasies at the music of Beethoven—a deaf man! The next thing will be raptures over the painting of a blind man. I'll always maintain that music is above all a pleasure through the ears. . . .[6]

* i.e. Handel, Glück, etc.

Mary to Mary Simpson Paris, 28 October 1875

   ... I never felt so utterly prostrate in my life as when I got here.
... Sometimes I hope to revive; sometimes I think I'm done for.
My only hope is that by whining to my former friends they will
reanimate me by their kindness. So I am writing *des lettres de faire
part* to that effect. And this is one—to announce that I died last
September, about the 3rd, and am coming to life again about the
28th October, and am inviting them, not to my burial but to my
christening, and hoping they will be as kind to the newborn as they
were to the moribund ...[7]

Mary to Mary Simpson Paris, December 1875

   ... My poor husband has been very ill this month. I was half-
crazy the last half of November, for the doctors could make nothing
of him, he was so bad; he is a little better now. I had two nights last
month during which I thought he never would recover, and I was
so overturned those two days that my arm and hand were quite
without feeling, and my speech embarrassed. I thought I should
have a stroke. . . . It passed away when he got better. . . .[8]

Mary to Mary Simpson Paris, December 1875

   ... The doctor this morning has set my poor head right again by
telling me Mr Mohl will get well with careful management. I was
down in the abyss of despair; now I am ready to jump over the
table like the cow over the moon! . . .[9]

In the early morning of January 4th, however, he died.

Mary to Mrs Wynne Finch 4 January 1877, January 1876

   ... He had been struggling for breath for four or five hours,
worse and worse. He stroked my face all the time, but could not
speak. That stroking has been an ineffable comfort to me. . . .[10]

Ida von Schmidt to Mary Simpson 19 July 1886, referring to January 1876

   When I arrived in Paris on the morning of the 4th, all was over.
He lay still and quiet in his bed. My aunt sat upstairs in the spare

room, rocking herself to and fro before the fire—not crying, but really out of her mind. . . .[11]

Florence to Mary   23 March 1876

. . . I think you need not—indeed I am sure—torture yourself with thinking you did not appreciate life with him. I have heard you say a hundred times that where the 'central affection' was what it was in your happy, thrice happy, life, all was right. You made him, a melancholy man by temperament, happy—thrice happy too. . . .[12]

Florence to Mary   6 August 1876

. . . Why do you torment yourself with thinking that you 'did not value him'! You were the light of his life, the brightness of his firmament. You gave zest to his life—all that it wanted. . . .[13]

Mary to Lady Derby   Cold Overton, 11 July 1876

. . . How ungrateful I must have appeared to you, so sympathizing as you have been! . . . I could not write this winter, I was so dead. . . .

I had much to do at Paris. . . . I have my dear husband's papers to look over, and they are so numerous, but . . . I have made arrangements for publishing several things. The translation into French of the great epic poem, the Shah Nameh, which he was charged to do by the French Government in 1828, as well as publishing the Persian text, was happily finished, but he had still a volume of notes, *éclaircissements*, index, etc. to do. . . .[14]

She still had a fund of lively irascibility to draw on, however, and Gladstone's policy this year roused her to something like her old self. He was advocating that Britain should send a military force to discipline the Turks who had massacred some 12,000 Christians in Bulgaria.

Mary to Lady Derby   11 October 1876

. . . I am absolutely sick of the nonsense going on. The conceit of the nation, supposing that we can make all Europe do what we think right, and what *is* right! It is perfectly absurd. As to Gladstone, it is the madness of disappointed ambition, and would not be worth minding if the public was not so ignorant and conceited as to suppose that we have the power to make all Europe humane by showing our fists at them. . . .

I remember well the movement towards 1825 or thereabouts, when the Greeks were much worse treated than these have been. But it never came into anybody's head that we alone were to go to war all across Europe to make the Turks behave themselves well— for that, I suppose, is what these absurd people are aiming at. . . . In my solitary and melancholy occupation of reading old letters and sorting papers . . . I must own to the greatest horror of war, and the terror of sacrificing our good, hardworking countrymen to go across Europe and get killed for the Russians to take Turkey— for that would be the upshot. . . .[15]

George Eliot to Mary Simpson 1877

. . . Please tell our dear Mme Mohl I am glad to have some news of her through you. The last I had was from M. Schérer, to whom his wife had sent word that she had found the dear old lady sobbing in her solitude. That left a sad impression on my mind. . . .[16]

Mary to Eleanor Martin Stors, 5 August 1877

. . . This country is in a great turmoily state. . . . The Duc de Broglie and a very large party of the higher classes have set their minds on having back as much of the old government as they can, and some say they have made an alliance with the Bonapartists to take back the boy who remains, rather than leave the republic to get on in its own way.

Thiers it was who made the peace with the Germans in 1870, when the whole country was in anarchy. He alone wandered about from England to Germany to see what he could do—that I know, . . . for he sent for Mr Mohl . . . to go and see him, and my spouse was touched to see the anguish he felt for his country. . . . He went back to France, called an assembly at Bordeaux, consented to be the man who would come forward to make proposals to the allies (no one else dared, because every one said they would be for ever hated if they talked of asking for peace). He had that courage and got the best conditions he could. . . .

He is now past eighty, but . . . has remained the same. . . . and was here the other day. . . . A grand breakfast was given to the grand electors, and a good deal of liquids to the smaller ones in the garden. I think *I* had the best of it, for my old friend came and talked to me of our early days, and seemed quite glad to see me. . . .[17]

Mary to Lady Eastlake   Paris, 13 January 1878

. . . I was talking to an artist yesterday about Correggio having sometimes, and I believe generally, painted his pictures in grey to get in the drawing, and colouring them afterwards. I have seen one (I forget where), all the greys done and only a portion in colours. This artist declares that Titian often did the same. As I have had much handling of the brush in my life, it was always a subject of great interest to me. Old Mr Smirke was very fond of me, and used to take a great interest in my efforts. He it was who first told me that Correggio had done this, but I never heard that any other colourist had, and this about Titian surprised me. My artist declared that Rubens did so also. Now, that seems to me wonderful, because there appears such a furore in his way of painting that one can hardly conceive he did it otherwise than slapdash. . . .[18]

23 January 1878

. . . All these *recherches* about colour, etc., are and have been part of my life and occupation, so I judge like a painter, and find satisfaction in a hundred details and little touches of light and shade slipping in in some queer or novel way which no one else would ever observe. It gives an intense satisfaction which others cannot even perceive. . . .[19]

Mary to Lady Eastlake   Paris, 17 August 1878

. . . I am reading over my husband's letters, and . . . am astonished that I was so unkind as to leave him every year for three or four months. He governs himself, but I see how much he missed me. My sister, to whom I was greatly attached, lost her only daughter, and I made a sort of inward vow that I would never spend a year without some months passed with her. My dear husband respected the feeling, and never complained; but now I see it. . . .[20]

Mary to Lady Eastlake   Paris, October 1878

. . . We have all been demented here with the Exposition. . . . I will make a humble confession, viz: the *produit de l'industrie* that most pleased and interested me was a large glass sort of cage full of Japanese fish. Whether they were *produits de l'industrie* or *de la nature* I know not, but they were certainly alive, and more like living jewels than anything I could compare them to. I could not tear myself away from them. . . .[21]

Florence to Mary   22 February 1879

 . . . How horrible are these Afghan and Zulu Wars—especially Sir Bartle Frere's Zulu War—not because our bravest soldiers and officers have bit the dust—not because we have now another costly and great 'little war' upon our hands—but because we shall have Zululand and the Transvaal to annex and administer, besides Natal and God knows what besides. Have we managed India so very well as to wish to manage South Africa besides? . . .[22]

Mary to Lady Eastlake   Paris, July 1879

 . . . I have written to say I will go to my niece in the country . . . Don't believe that I have not the same love, the same high esteem, the same trust in you, because I have not written; but I am like an old dried-up leaf blown about by the wind. I fall into a corner like a lost bit of rubbish—a gust comes, and all at once I am in a whirlwind. . . .[23]

She now struck others too as an old woman, but still a remarkable one. Angelo de Gubernatis, who was preparing a study of Manzoni and Fauriel and hoped that she might possess some of their letters, received a striking account of her from Renan.

Ernest Renan to Angelo de Gubernatis   Paris, 4 July 1879

 . . . Forgive my delay in replying about the correspondence between Manzoni and Fauriel which is in the possession of Mme Mohl. She is a remarkable woman, about ninety years of age, but as witty and gay as ever—talks about 1815 and 1820 as if they were yesterday—but making arrangements with her is not easy, for her memory for recent events is completely obliterated, and one has to mention a project many times over to get her to carry it out. But I think I have succeeded. This morning I saw the dear old lady coming up our narrow stairway, as briskly as any young thing, and straight away *she* began to talk about the plan.

Yes, she has the letters written by Manzoni when he was very young to Fauriel, who was considerably older. From what she told me, this is a young, unorthodox Manzoni, rather different from the respectable, orthodox patriarch in Milan. We shall see, for she is going to bring it all here, and if she doesn't, I shall give her a reminder. When we have seen what she has . . . it will be easy for you to come to an arrangement with her, for Fauriel's memory is a religion with her (not, I am sure, that it drives out the memory of Mohl). . . . It is important to lose no time, because if we lost Mme Mohl or if her memory grew even weaker, it would be very difficult to fish all this material up out of a tangle of foreign heirs. . . .[24]

Mary to Lady Eastlake   Paris, 12 January 1880

. . . The intense cold has almost killed me . . . A fortnight ago, when the thaw began, all Paris went to see the Seine caracoling like an overfed horse. The icebergs rushed along like mad, broke the bridges; the Pont des Invalides has lost the three middle arches. The people would go down to see it close up, and got drowned— there was no end to the mischief. I was so ill with the cold I could not go. I would have given anything to see the icebergs rushing along . . .[25]

Mary to Sophie Wyse   Paris, 1 March 1880

. . . I have been out of all patience about my husband's book. I particularly wish both volumes to come out before the London season is over, for this reason—the second volume is mostly on India. Her ancient civilization, her profound ideas, and the quantity of study and learning the Anglo-Indians have spent upon India, almost fill the volume. Now, no one before has been able to give an account of what the English have done to fathom the ancient civilization of India. It was the most difficult and curious part of all my husband's studies, and he gave all his attention to it. . . . And as I have one foot in the grave, I should like to hear my husband's profound researches and sharp intellect appreciated by my countrymen. The book's title is *Vingt-sept ans d'études orientales*. . . .[26]

Mary to Mary Simpson   Wormstall, 21 October 1880

. . . I am glad not to return sooner, as I much dread the solitude of Paris, but I suppose it will begin filling early in November. I have found here *Macaulay's Life*, by Trevelyan. Have you read it? I want to borrow it from you, or I must beg it from here. . . .[27]

Mary to Mary Simpson   April 1881

. . . I feel the decadence of my mind as plainly as in my body. I have as much judgment as ever I had in my life; but half our faculties are the children of memory. . . .[28]

Mary to Lady Derby   Paris, 20 May 1880

. . . I have read lately an English book, a sort of history of England and all its curious changes, by an Irishman, called Justin ·McCarthy, which is called *A History of our Own Time*. I don't say I agree with all, but it has taught me a great deal. I wonder what is thought of it in England. . . .[29]

Mary to Mary Simpson   Paris, 20 July 1881

. . . I have been absolutely roasted alive here, but had not courage to go, because I did not know what to do. I have no home in England now my sister is gone. Friends are kind, but one ain't sure one is not in their way. . . . I am a poor creature, but I run about and am as alert as ever. . . .[30]

Thus she remained until her last illness in 1882–3, when for the first time she was immobilized. Even then, as her friend Sophie Quirins told Mary Simpson,

. . . 'she read a great deal, lying on her sofa with her lamp on a small table beside her. She would read thus until twelve o'clock, without her eyesight suffering in the least, indeed latterly without needing spectacles. The winter before her death she took up Walter Scott, reading over and over again *Ivanhoe* and *Old Mortality* with renewed pleasure; also a work by Mr Walter Bagehot. I took her a *Quarterly Review* with a notice of Fanny Kemble's *Reminiscences*, which she enjoyed highly, and also read over and over again. Her memory was as vivid as ever when she went back to the past, and I spent many an hour listening to her stories of younger days. It was a perfect panorama. . . .'[31]

Florence to Mary   30 June 1881

   ... Oh indeed I love you, love you dearly. Forty years and more
have I loved you. ...

                                                2 November 1881

   ... How can I ever forget you! I stand in the Rue du Bac 120
now at this moment as much as if I were really there in the
body. ...

                                                6 June 1882

   ... Never doubt your friend's love.[32]

   She died on 15 May 1883, aged ninety, and was buried in Père Lachaise.

Bibliography

In order to allow as much space as possible for Mary's own words, I have, I am well aware, treated such large-scale subjects as Florence Nightingale, Mrs Gaskell, and the entire societies of France and England from 1793 to 1883 with ridiculous brevity. To understand Florence as a whole, it is necessary (and very enjoyable) to read Cecil Woodham-Smith's *Florence Nightingale* (1951); there is probably no better general biography of Mrs Gaskell than Winifred Gérin's (1976). Mrs Gaskell's *Letters* (edited by J.A.V. Chapple and A. Pollard, 1966) are essential reading for anyone interested in her period and circle as well as herself; the most helpful twentieth-century histories of nineteenth-century France and England are probably those by Bertier de Sauvigny, Cobban, Briggs and Trevelyan, whose details are given below.

ABBAYE-AU-BOIS CIRCLE: see Biré; Herriot; Mme M[ohl]

Ampère, A.M. et J.J., *Correspondance et Souvenirs*, Paris, 1875

Anthony, K., *The Lambs*, Hammond and Hammond, London, 1948

Aron, Jean-Paul, ed., *Misérable et glorieuse: la femme du XIX siècle*, Fayard, Paris, 1980

Artz, F.B., *France under the Bourbon Restoration*, Russell and Russell, New York, 1963

Augustin-Thierry, A., *La Princesse Belgiojoso*, Plon, Paris, 1926

—— *Augustin Thierry, d'après sa correspondance*, Plon, Paris, 1922

PRINCESSE BELGIOJOSO: see Augustin-Thierry

BELLOC, LOUISE SWANTON: see Speaight, Robert

BENGER-BARBAULD CIRCLE; see Anthony; Bowring; Crabb Robinson; Fletcher; Le Breton

BERCHET, GIOVANNI: see Santuro, F.

Bertier de Sauvigny, G. de, *La Restauration*, Flammarion, Paris, 1955

Biré, Augustin, *Les dernières années de Chateaubriand*, Garnier, Paris, 1919

BONHAM CARTER, HILARY: see Bonham Carter; Woodham-Smith

Bonham Carter, Victor, *In a Liberal Tradition: 1700-1950*, Constable, London, 1960

Bowring, Sir John, *Autobiographical Recollections*, Henry King, London, 1877

Briggs, Asa, *The Age of Improvement 1783-1867*, Longman, London, 1959

CHATEAUBRIAND: see Biré, A.

Cobban, A., *A History of Modern France*, Penguin, London, 1961

Colquhoun, A., *Manzoni and His Times*, J.M. Dent, London, 1954

CONDORCET, LA MARQUISE DE: see Guillois, A; Galley, J.B.

Constant, Benjamin, *Journaux intimes*, Gallimard, Paris, 1952

Crabb Robinson, H., *Diary*, ed. Thomas Sadler, Macmillan, London, 1869

— — *Diary*, ed. Derek Hudson, Oxford University Press, 1967, and see Morley

Delacroix, Eugène, *Journal*, ed. Hubert Wellington, Phaidon Press, Oxford, 1951

Delécluze, Etienne, *Journal 1824-8*, ed. Robert Baschet, Grasset, Paris, 1948

— — *Souvenirs de soixante années*, Michel Lévy, Paris, 1862

Eliot, George, *Letters*, ed. G.S. Haight, Yale University Press, 1955

FAURIEL, CLAUDE: see Condorcet; Constant; Galley; Guillois; Staël

Fletcher, Mrs E., *Autobiography*, Edmonston and Douglas, Edinburgh, 1875

FREWEN (TURNER) FAMILY: see Leslie

Galley, J.B., *Claude Fauriel*, Saint-Etienne, 1909

Gaskell, Mrs, *Letters*, ed. J.A.V. Chapple and A. Pollard, Manchester University Press, 1966

— — *Works*, Smith and Elder, 1906

and see Gérin; Sharps

Gérin, Winifred, *Elizabeth Gaskell*, Oxford University Press, 1976

Grant Duff, Sir J.M., *Notes from a Diary 1851-72*, John Murray, London, 1897

GREEK REFUGEES AND INDEPENDENCE: see St Clair.

Green, F.C., *Stendhal*, Cambridge University Press, 1939

Gubernatis, A. de, *Il Manzoni ed il Fauriel*, Milan, 1880

Guillois, A., *La Marquise de Condorcet*, Ollendorff, Paris, 1897

Guizot, F., *Mémoires pour servir à l'histoire de mon temps*, Michel Lévy, Paris, 1858

Herriot, E., *Madame Récamier et ses amis*, Payot, Paris, 1924

IRELAND IN THE 18TH AND 19TH CENTURIES: see Kee

ITALIAN REFUGEES AND INDEPENDENCE: see Berchet; Manzoni; Colquhoun

James, Henry (ed.), *William Wetmore Story and His Friends*, Edinburgh and London, 1903

Kee, Robert, *The Green Flag*, Weidenfeld and Nicolson, London, 1972

Kegan Paul, Charles, *Memories*, Routledge and Kegan Paul, London, 1899

Le Breton, K.M. (ed. Mrs H. Martin), *Memories of Seventy Years*, Griffith and Farrar, London, 1883

Lehmann, A.G., *Sainte-Beuve*, Oxford University Press, 1962

Leslie, Anita, *Mr Frewen of England*, Hutchinson, London, 1966

— — *The Gilt and the Gingerbread*, Hutchinson, London, 1981

Levin, Harry, *The Gates of Horn*, Oxford University Press, 1963
Manzoni, A., *Epistolario* (ed. G. Sforza), Paolo Canara, Milan, 1882
  and see Colquhoun; Gubernatis
Marmier, Xavier, *Journal 1848-90*, ed. Eldon Kaye, Droz, Geneva, 1968
Martineau, H., *Autobiography*, Smith, Elder & Co., 1877
  and see Webb
MÉRIMÉE, PROSPER: see Raitt; Trahard
M[ohl], Madame, *Madame Récamier*, Chapman and Hall, London, 1862
MONCKTON MILNES, R: see Pope-Hennessy
Morley, E.J., *The Life and Times of Henry Crabb Robinson*, J.M. Dent,
  London, 1935
NIGHTINGALE, FLORENCE: See O'Malley; Woodham-Smith
O'Malley, I.B.O., *Florence Nightingale 1820-56*, London, 1931
O'Meara, K., *Madame Mohl: her salon and her friends*, Richard Bentley,
  London, 1885
Partridge, E., *The French Romantics' Knowledge of English Literature*,
  Champion, Paris, 1924
Pope-Hennessy, J., *Monckton Milnes: the flight of youth*, Constable, Lon-
  don, 1951
Quinet, E., *Lettres à sa mère*, Paris, n.d.
Raitt, A.W., *Prosper Mérimée*, Eyre and Spottiswoode, London, 1970
RÉCAMIER, MME: see Herriot; Mme M[ohl]
REID, MRS: see Tuke, M.J.
Renan, Ernest, *Oeuvres complètes* (vol. x), Calmann-Lévy, Paris, 1961
St Clair, W., *That Greece Might Still Be Free*, Oxford University Press,
  1972
Sainte-Beuve, C.A., *Causeries du Lundi*, Paris, 1857-70
—— *Nouveaux Lundis*, Paris, 1863-70
—— *Portraits contemporains*, Paris, 1869-71
  and see Lehmann
Santuro, F., *Vita ed opere di Giovanni Berchet*, Giosti editore, Livorno,
  1915
Senior, Nassau, *Conversations with M. Thiers, M. Guizot, and other
  distinguished persons*, Hurst and Blackett, London, 1878
Sharps, J.G., *Mrs Gaskell's Observation and Invention*, Linden Press, 1970
Simpson, M.C.M., *Letters and Recollections of Julius and Mary Mohl*,
  Kegan Paul, Trench and Co., London, 1887
Smith, M.E., *Une Anglaise intellectuelle en France sous la Restauration:
  Miss Mary Clarke*, Champion, Paris, 1927
Speaight, Robert, *The Life of Hilaire Belloc*, Hollis and Carter, London,
  1957
Staël, Mme de, *De la littérature dans ses rapports avec les institutions sociales*,
  1800

Staël, Mme de, *Delphine*, 1802

—— *Corinne*, 1807

—— *De l'Allemagne*, 1810

Stanley, Dean A.P., *Life and Correspondence* (ed. R.E. Prothero and G.G. Bentley), John Murray, London, 1893

Stendhal, *Souvenirs d'Egotisme* and *La Vie de Henri Brulard*, both in *Oeuvres intimes de Stendhal*, ed. H. Martineau, Gallimard, Paris, 1955

—— *Correspondance*, ed. H. Martineau and V. del Litto, Gallimard, Paris, 1967

STORY, WILLIAM WETMORE: see James

Thackeray Ritchie, Anne, *Letters*, ed. Hester Ritchie, John Murray, London, 1924

THIERRY, AUGUSTIN AND AMÉDÉE: see Augustin-Thierry

Ticknor, G., *Life, Letters and Journals*, London, 1876

Tocqueville, A. de, *Correspondance*, ed. A. Jardin, Gallimard, Paris, 1970

Trahard, P., *La Jeunesse de Prosper Mérimée*, Edouard Champion, Paris, 1925

Trevelyan, G.M., *British History in the 19th century and after*, Longmans Green and Co, London, 1937

Trollope, F.E., *Frances Trollope*, Bentley & Son, London, 1897

T.A. Trollope, *What I Remember*, Bentley & Son, London, 1887

Tuke, M.J., *A History of Bedford College for Women 1849-1937*, Oxford University Press, 1939

Turgenev, Ivan, *Lettres inédites à Pauline Viardot et sa famille*, ed. H. Graniard et A. Zviguilsky, Editions l'Age d'homme, Lausanne, 1972

—— *Nouvelle correspondance inédite*, ed. A. Zviguilsky, Librairie des Cinq Continents, Paris, 1971

Webb, R.K., *Harriet Martineau: a radical Victorian*, Heinemann, London, 1960

Woodham-Smith, Cecil, *Florence Nightingale 1820-1910*, Hamish Hamilton, London, 1951

References

'Simpson' represents the *Letters and Recollections of Julius and Mary Mohl*; 'Corr.' the *Correspondance de Fauriel et Mary Clarke*; 'W.S.' Cecil Woodham-Smith's notes; 'Houghton' the Houghton Collection in Trinity College, Cambridge; 'RDM' the *Revue des Deux Mondes*

Introduction

I

1. Gaskell Letters, pp. 289-90
2. ibid., p. 326
3. Simpson, p. 80
4. James, *William Wetmore Story*, I, p. 365
5. To Lady William Russell, Oct. 1867, Simpson, p. 239
6. To Florence Nightingale, 22.9.65, W.S., p. 77
7. To Fauriel, 24.9.23, Corr., pp. 78-9
8. To Mrs Reid, 12.3.29, Bedford College
9. To Mrs Reid, 5.7.40, Bedford College
10. To Mary Simpson, 7.3.65, Simpson, p. 218
11. To Mrs Reid, 29.2.63, ibid.
12. Quoted in Smith, p. 120
13. W.S., p. 96
14. Simpson, p. 81
15. To Fauriel, 22.9.28, Corr., p. 275
16. To Fauriel, summer 1843, quoted in Galley, pp. 450-2
17. Simpson, p. 184
18. To Hilary Bonham Carter, 1858, ibid., pp. 145-6
19. To Lady Derby, 11.10.76, ibid., p. 354
20. To Lady Augusta Stanley, 23.7.74, ibid., p. 335

II

1. Corr., pp. 21, 22
2. To Mary Simpson, Simpson, p. 224
3. Leicester Record Office
4. To Hilary Bonham Carter, 2.6.58, Simpson, p. 141
5. Fletcher, pp. 102-3
6. ibid., p. 70
7. To Hilary Bonham Carter, 26.6.48, Simpson, p. 55
8. To Mary Simpson, 1.8.80, ibid., p. 382
9. To Eleanor Martin, 23.2.70, ibid., p. 255
10. To Mrs Reid, 24.3.45, Bedford College
11. To Lady William Russell, 1868, Simpson, p. 21
12. To Mohl, 5.8.30, Galley, p. 322
13. To Mary Simpson, 12.11.61, Simpson, p. 186
14. To Mrs Reid, 4.10.40, Bedford College
15. Simpson, p. 6
16. To Mrs Clarke, 10.3.34, Leicester D75
17. Simpson, p. 2
18. His leases and fire insurance policy of 1802 and 1809, Leicester C 88-93
19. Leicester C124
20. To Florence Nightingale, 26.11.68, British Library

21. To Mrs Reid, 2-9.1.42, Bedford College
22. To the Nightingales, 1.3.48, Simpson, p. 55
23. To Miss Wyse, 24.10.73, ibid., p. 187
24. To Mrs Grote, 3.12.61, ibid.
25. To Mrs Reid, 7.6.49, Bedford College
26. To Hilary Bonham Carter, 2.4.61, W.S., p. 114
27. To Dean Stanley, 4.3.76, Simpson, p. 351
28. ibid., p. 6
29. To Lady Augusta Bruce, 8.5.72, ibid., p. 323
30. ibid., p. 18
31. To Lady Augusta Stanley, 1870, ibid., p. 4
32. To Florence Nightingale, 5.2.62, W.S., pp. 70-1
33. To Hilary Bonham Carter, Simpson, p. 85
34. To Ida von Schmidt, 1.12.66, ibid., p. 226
35. To Hilary Bonham Carter, 15.12.50, ibid., p. 63
36. To Lady Augusta Bruce, 8.5.72, ibid., p. 323
37. To Mary Simpson, 3.6.67, ibid., p. 232
38. Leslie, *Mr Frewen of England*, pp. 16-17
39. ibid., p. 20
40. To Ida von Schmidt, 9.9.73, Simpson, p. 235
41. To Lady William Russell, 7.8.67, ibid., p. 235
42. To Mary Senior, 2.1.62, ibid., p. 178
43. To Mrs Reid, 28.9.39, Bedford College
44. To Hilary Bonham Carter, 1.4.60, W.S., p. 112
45. To Hilary Bonham Carter, 12.7.61, Simpson, pp. 3-4
46. Le Breton, p. 101
47. ibid.
48. To Fauriel, 3-4.10.29, Corr., p. 315
49. To Miss Wyse, Simpson, p. 7
50. ibid., p. 7
51. Dictionary of National Biography
52. Le Breton, pp. 53-4
53. ibid., pp. 40-1
54. To Mrs Reid, 30.1.65, Bedford College

III

1. *Oeuvres intimes*, p. 1429
2. J.J. Ampère, quoted in Partridge, p. 319
3. A. Thierry, ibid.
4. *Fraser's Magazine*, April 1864
5. To Lady William Russell, 1868, Simpson, p. 21
6. Quoted in O'Meara, p. 122
7. *Lettres à sa mère*, II, pp. 285-6
8. Florence Nightingale to Mary, 3.9.67, W.S., p. 79
9. To Lady Eastlake, 23.1.78, Simpson, p. 363
10. ibid.
11. To Eleanor Martin, Leicester D180
12. To Lady Augusta Bruce, 19.3.72, Simpson, p. 321
13. To Ida von Schmidt, 7.10.73, ibid., p. 322
14. To Mrs Reid, 15.6.53, Bedford College
15. To Fauriel, 21.6.29, Corr., p. 284
16. To Mrs Reid, 20.11.48, Bedford College
17. Journal, pp. 54-5

18. *Oeuvres intimes*, p. 1429
19. To Ida von Schmidt, 25.5.72, Simpson, p. 324
20. *Eustace Diamonds*, vol. I, chap. 2
21. To Eleanor Martin, 22.12.66, Leicester D177
22. To Fauriel, 11.8.22, Corr., pp. 34-5

IV

1. *Oeuvres intimes*, p. 1429
2. ibid.
3. To Mary, 15.8.22, Corr., p. 29
4. ibid.
5. *Portraits*, p. 130
6. Quoted in Galley
7. ibid., p. 22
8. Levin, p. 102
9. Galley, p. 150
10. Quoted in an article in the *Journal des Débats*, 4.7.85
11. *Mémoires pour servir . . .*, I, pp. 291-2
12. *Epistolario*, passim
13. *Dix Ans d'études historiques*, pp. xxii-xxiii
14. To Mary, 13.7.22, Corr., p. 9
15. To Mary, 22.6.22, Corr., pp. 3-5
16. To Fauriel, 23.6.22, RDM, vol. 48, pp. 557-8

Letters

I

1. Corr., pp. 10-12
2. ibid., pp. 15-24
3. ibid., pp. 32-4
4. *Oeuvres intimes*, p. 1430
5. *Journal*, p. 418
6. ibid., p. 97
7. op. cit., p. 1429
8. *Correspondance*, II, p. 7
9. Corr., pp. 35-9

10. ibid., pp. 25-30
11. ibid., pp. 44-6
12. RDM, vol. 48, pp. 570-2
13. ibid., pp. 568-9
14. *Oeuvres intimes*, p. 87
15. Corr., p. 50
16. RDM, vol. 48, pp. 573-6

II

1-3. Corr., pp. 57-73
4. Sainte-Beuve, *Nouveaux Lundis*, vol. 13, p. 186, n. 1
5-11. Corr. pp. 68-91
12. Gubernatis
13. Galley, p. 296
14-17. Corr., pp. 100-18
18. Bibliothèque de l'Institut, fonds 2977, quoted in Smith, p. 11
19. Corr., pp. 124-7
20. ibid., p. 142
21. 4.6.24, ibid., pp. 105-6
22. ibid.
23. 13.6.24, ibid., p. 111
24. 21.6.24, ibid., p. 149
25. ibid.
26. 21.7.24, ibid., p. 124
27. 9.9.24, ibid., p. 149
28-30. ibid., pp. 146-58
31. 24.10.24, RDM, vol. 48, p. 836
32. ibid., pp. 837-9
33-4. Corr., pp. 145-63

III

1-4. Corr., pp. 174-96
5. Simpson, p. 232
6. *Journal*, p. 226
7. *Diary*, 8.12.59, I, p. 120
8. Bibliothèque de l'Institut, fonds 2977
9-12. RDM, vol. 48, pp. 843-5

13. Galley, p. 312
14-17. RDM, vol. 48, pp. 852-9
18. Max Müller, quoted in Simpson, p. 13
19. ibid., p. 14

IV

1-15. Corr., pp. 208-79
16. RDM, vol. 49, pp. 141-2
17. Senior, *Conversations*, I, pp. 107-8
18-24. Corr., pp. 282-321

V

1. Galley, pp. 321-3
2. December 1830, quoted in Trahard, vol. II, p. 229
3. To Lady William Russell, 1868, Simpson, pp. 20-1
4. Mme Mohl, *Madame Récamier*, p. 69
5. Simpson, p. 20
6. *Madame Récamier*, p. 51
7. Quoted in Raitt, p. 24
8. To Fauriel, Bibliothèque de l'Institut, fonds 2977
9. *Madame Récamier*, pp. 100-1
10. ibid., p. 102
11. Corr., pp. 334-7
12. RDM, vol. 49, p. 146
13-17. Leicester D70-84
18. Corr., pp. 351-3
19. Leicester D78
20-1. Leicester D79-80
22. Corr., pp. 364-5
23-6. Leicester D81-9
27. op. cit., vol. II, p. 295
28. Ticknor, vol. II, pp. 124-5
29. Simpson, pp. 25-6
30. Corr., pp. 369-70
31. Simpson, pp. 29-31
32. Bedford College

33. Corr., p. 381

VI

1. Simpson, pp. 29-31
2-12. Bedford College
13. Corr., p. 381
14. Bedford College
15. Corr., p. 386
16. W.S., p. 64
17-19. Bedford College
20. Simpson, pp. 36-7
21. pp. 108-11
22. Quoted in O'Malley, pp. 131-2
23. Bibliothèque de l'Institut, fonds 2977
24. O'Meara, p. 91
25. ibid.
26. Simpson, p. 47
27. Bedford College
28. Simpson, p. 234

VII

1. *What I remember*, vol. I, p. 286
2-6. Simpson, pp. 25, 109, 114, 142, 185
7. To Emily Shaen, Paris, 27.3.65, Letters, p. 749
8. Simpson, pp. 42-3
9. ibid., pp. 51-5
10. Bonham-Carter, pp. 97-8
11. Grant Duff, vol. I, p. 228
12. Simpson, p. 56
13. pp. 112-14
14. Bedford College
15. Tuke, p. 21
16-17. Bedford College
18. Simpson, pp. 63-4
19. Bedford College
20. Simpson, p. 112
21. W.S., p. 102
22-7. W.S., pp. 102-6
28. Simpson, pp. 77-8

29. Bedford College
30. Simpson, p. 91
31. *Letters*, II, pp. 39-40
32-7. Simpson, pp. 92-110

VIII

1-2. W.S., p. 106
3-4. British Library
5. Gaskell Letters, pp. 305-7
6. ibid., pp. 318-30
7. Bedford College
8-9. Simpson, pp. 116-19
10. Woodham-Smith, *Florence Nightingale*, p. 109
11. Gaskell Letters, pp. 358-9
12. Bedford College
13. Brotherton Collection, Leeds University Library
14. Gaskell Letters, p. 332
15. ibid., pp. 333-4
16. Simpson, pp. 126-7
17. W.S., p. 107
18. ibid., p. 108
19. Bedford College
20. Simpson, pp. 136-7
21. *Memories*, p. 304
22-6. Simpson, pp. 138-46
27-9. W.S., pp. 110-13

IX

1-2. Simpson, pp. 161-24
3. Gaskell Letters, p. 599
4-8. Simpson, pp. 164-77
9. Houghton, 17/2
10. W.S., p. 113
11-16. Simpson, pp. 179-84
17. W.S., p. 115
18. Leicester Record Office, D203A
19-20. Simpson, pp. 184-7
21. W.S., pp. 66-7

22. Simpson, pp. 188-91
23-6. W.S., pp. 70-1
27. Simpson, p. 198
28. W.S., pp. 98-9
29-31. Simpson, pp. 196-7, 128, 199
32-3. Bedford College
34. W.S., p. 116
35. Simpson, p. 203
36. Houghton, 17/16
37-9. Simpson, pp. 207-13
40. Pope-Hennessy, p. 144
41. Houghton, 17/12
42. Houghton, 17/14
43. Bedford College
44-5. Simpson, pp. 217-18
46. Bedford College
47. Gaskell Letters, pp. 749-51
48. ibid., p. 753
49. Simpson, p. 219
50-1. W.S., pp. 74-6
52. Simpson, p. 221
53-4. W.S., pp. 75-7

X

1-2. Simpson, pp. 224-7
3. *Letters*, vol. IV, p. 334
4-8. Simpson, pp. 231-5
9. W.S., p. 80
10. Simpson, pp. 240-1
11-13. W.S., pp. 80-1
14-15. Leicester Record Office
16. Simpson, pp. 245-6
17. Leicester Record Office D174
18-19. Simpson, pp. 258-60
20. Houghton, 17/42
21-5. W.S., pp. 89-91
26-8. Simpson, pp. 261-5
29. W.S., p. 92
30. *Letters of Anne Thackeray Ritchie*, p. 146

31-3. Simpson, pp. 267-300
34. *Letters*, vol. V, p. 152
35-41. Simpson, pp. 300-21
42. Quoted in Smith, p. 134
43. Simpson, p. 324

XI

1. W.S., p. 94
2-3. Simpson, pp. 330-2
4. W.S., pp. 87-8

5-11. Simpson, pp. 342-7
12-13. W.S., p. 95
14-21. Simpson, pp. 351-71
22. In the possession of Frau Lisel-Charlotte von Siemens
23. Simpson, p. 377
24. Renan, *Oeuvres complètes*, vol. X, p. 806
25-31. Simpson, pp. 383-95
32. W.S., p. 95

Biographical Notes

Further information about persons who may be less familiar to readers and who are not described at any length in the text.

AMPÈRE, JEAN-JACQUES (1800-64)
Son of the famous scientist. Very Romantic both in his early ecstasies over Byron and English literature in general and in his enthusiastic polymathy: Classical archaeology, Hebrew, Chinese, mediaeval French literature, Scandinavian studies, etc. Was Professor of Literature at the Marseilles Athénée, the Ecole normale supérieure and the Collège de France, and for a period Fauriel's deputy at the Sorbonne. Devoted to Mme Récamier from 1823 until her death. Shared lodgings with Mohl in the Rue du Bac from 1831 to 1847.

ARCONATI, COSTANZA, MARCHESA (1800-71)
Milanese patriot exiled by the Austrian régime in the early 1820s. She and her husband then lived in their mediaeval castle at Gaesbeck near Brussels, set in a large beech forest. The little 'court' of other Italian refugees who were usually to be found there included the poet Berchet, who cherished an unrequited love for her for over twenty years, and her brother-in-law the General Collegno, with whom she had an affair about which she confided in Berchet. Mary's suspicions about her relationship with Fauriel may or may not have been founded on pure jealousy.

After Italy gained its independence she and her husband, who had large estates in Lombardy and Piedmont as well as Belgium, settled in Turin, and the Marquis became a member of the Chamber of Deputies.

ARRIVABENE, GIOVANNI, COUNT (1787-1881)
Economist and Italian patriot. A member of Mme Arconati's circle.

AUDOUIN, JEAN-VICTOR (1797-1841)
One of the founders of entomology in France. Started the *Annales des Sciences naturelles* in 1824 and in 1825 began his lectures on entomology at the Paris Muséum; in 1833 became Professor of Entomology at the Sorbonne. Said to be an admirable lecturer—clear, elegant and capable of arousing interest in the driest subjects.

BALLANCHE, PIERRE-SIMON (1776-1847)
Christian philosopher with a mystical conception of a universal mind and religion, expressed above all in poetry. His works include *Du Sentiment considéré dans ses rapports avec la littérature et les arts* (1801), *Essai sur les institutions sociales dans leurs rapports avec les idées nouvelles* (1818) and

Essais de palingénésie sociale (1827-9). He was devoted to Mme Récamier, and therefore a regular member of the Abbaye-au-Bois salon for many years.

BELGIOJOSO, CRISTINA, PRINCESS (1808-71)
Milanese patriot and émigrée. She was active in the Italian revolutionary movement and in 1848 raised a battalion of volunteers to fight the occupying forces. Both talented and beautiful, she spent most of her later years in Paris, where she wrote and entertained prolifically.

BERCHET, GIOVANNI (1783-1851)
Poet and patriot. Spent his early years in Milan, when it was under Austrian rule. Wrote for revolutionary papers, was a member of Manzoni's circle, then devoted to obtaining Italian independence, and probably belonged to the Carbonaria. In 1821 his activities were discovered by the Austrian police and he was forced to flee to Paris, after which he remained in exile for twenty-seven years.

BLANC, LOUIS (1811-82)
Socialist politician and historian. First became well known through his *Organisation du Travail* (1839) which demanded that the State provide work for the unemployed. His *Histoire de Dix Ans* of 1841 was a highly critical account of Louis-Philippe's régime and helped to cause the Revolution of 1848 in which he played a leading part. After the failure of his National Workshops he fell out of favour and fled to England where he completed an *Histoire de la Révolution française* (1847-62) and collected material for his *Dix Années de l'histoire d'Angleterre* (1879-81). In the Commune of 1871 he returned to France and was once again active in socialist politics.

BROGLIE, VICTOR, DUC DE (1785-1870)
Statesman. Constitutional Royalist, leader of the Opposition during the Restoration and member of the Government under Louis-Philippe. Married to Mme de Staël's daughter. Much admired by Mary for his modesty and devotion to duty.

BROUGHAM, LORD (1778-1868)
Politician and writer, co-founder of the *Edinburgh Review*. He advocated and/or effected many reforms—legal, educational and political. His 'Observations on the Education of the People', containing the advocacy of universal education which so irritated Mary, was published in 1825.

BULOZ, FRANÇOIS (1804-77)
Editor of the *Revue des Deux Mondes* from 1830. Known as a quarrelsome man, he broke not only with Loménie, but with George Sand, Balzac, Hugo and Dumas at various times, but his editorial instinct was excellent;

under his aegis the *Deux Mondes* became the most important French review.

CARREL, ARMAND (1800-36)
Journalist and Republican. Founded *Le National*, which helped to create the conditions for the Revolutions of 1830. Died in a duel with the newspaper-owner Emile de Girardin.

CHATEAUBRIAND, FRANÇOIS-RENÉ, VICOMTE DE (1768-1848)
Presiding genius of the first wave of Romanticism. Fled from the Revolution in 1791 and spent a year in America, whose wild landscapes and noble savages were leading themes in his *René* (1802), *Atala* (1801) and *Les Natchez* (1826). *Le Génie du Christianisme* (1802) preached the doctrine of Christianity as a moral and aesthetic force, stressing its power to inspire great art as well as its humanity. It was partly written in England to which Chateaubriand had fled after fighting on the Emigré side. When he returned to France Napoleon appointed him Ambassador at Rome, but he grew increasingly disenchanted with the Empire. His political career under Louis XVIII followed a similar curve: he was a minister at Ghent and later Ambassador to London, but lost favour and became disillusioned. By Louis-Philippe's reign he had retired from public life and consoled himself with Mme Récamier's devotion and the respectful attention accorded to him and his *Mémoires d'Outre-Tombe* in the Abbaye.

COLLEGNO, GIACINTO, GENERAL (1794-1854)
Italian patriot and soldier. Officer in Napoleon's army at eighteen; took part in the Russian and Waterloo campaigns. Returned to Piedmont in 1814, was sentenced to death by the Austrian authorities and thereafter became an exile, fighting in the wars for the independence of Greece and Spain. Later became a passionate geologist and botanist and qualified as a doctor of science in 1836; in 1839 was appointed Professor of Geology at Bordeaux.

COMTE, AUGUSTE (1798-1857)
Founder of Positivism (and in effect sociology) according to which society was to be studied by the objective laws of mathematics, physics, chemistry and biology. There should be no consideration of prime causes as in the 'metaphysical stage of the history of thought', which was now superseded by the scientific stage. Comte's early lectures, given in his own rooms, attracted many of the best minds of the time. In character, however, he was generally acknowledged to be intolerably arrogant; in the late 1820s he had a long mental breakdown. From 1842 he converted his philosophy into a religion, which Huxley called 'Catholicism without God': he endowed it with a catechism, a sacred library and a patron saint in the form of Clotilde de Vaux, with whom he was in love. It was true that, as Mary had heard, he celebrated marriages according to his own rite.

CONSTANT, BENJAMIN (1767–1830)
Writer and leader of the liberal opposition in the Restoration. For a long period he was devoted to Mme de Staël and followed her about in France and in exile. He is now best known as the author of a brilliant short novel, *Adolphe* (1816).

COUSIN, VICTOR (1792–1867)
Professor of Philosophy at the Sorbonne from 1815; his courses were suspended from 1820 to 1827 because of his liberal tendencies. Thereafter his career was brilliant. 1830–51 he was head of the Ecole normale supérieure and first a Councillor of State then Minister of Public Instruction (1840). He had a great influence on French education in general and the university teaching of philosophy in particular. It was he who introduced Hegel to France.

DELÉCLUZE, ETIENNE (1781–1863)
Artist, art critic, journalist and above all diarist. His Sunday evenings in the late 1820s attracted many of the same liberal young Romantics as went to the Clarkes': Stendhal, Mérimée, etc. It was at Delécluze's that Mérimée first tried out his *Théâtre de Clara Gazul* on an audience.

FREWEN (TURNER) FAMILY
John, Mary's brother-in-law, was born in 1755 and died at Cold Overton in 1829, when Eleanor was only forty-three. Eleanor herself was born in 1786, bore four children, built Knossington National School in 1855, and died in 1879, having outlived all her children. The eldest, Selina, was born in 1809, married the Rev. Mr Martin of Anstey Pastures on the other side of Leicestershire and had four children, of whom Eleanor Martin was a favourite correspondent of Mary's in later years. Eleanor Frewen Turner's sons dropped the 'Turner' from their name. The youngest, John, died of a decline in 1844, when he was twenty-six. Both Thomas and Charles (born 1811 and 1813) acquired seats in Parliament almost as of right and while they were still up at Cambridge. Thomas remained all his life one of the largest landowners in England. One of his sons was Moreton Frewen, the explorer and sportsman, who married Clara Jerome, and thus became the uncle of Winston Churchill.

GUIZOT, FRANÇOIS (1787–1874)
Politician and scholar. Professor of Modern History at the Sorbonne from 1812 to 1830, during which time he published a vast quantity of well-documented, methodical work, of which the most characteristic example is perhaps his *Histoire de la révolution d'Angleterre* (1826–56), on the development of the constitutional monarchy. During the Restoration he became a liberal leader, and his lectures were suspended 1822–8. After the Revolution of 1830 he was Minister of Education 1832–7, then Foreign

Minister, then Prime Minister. The Revolution of 1848 threw him out of power, and the rest of his life was spent in writing; his output was prodigious.

HAUGHTON FAMILY
Sir Graves Haughton (1788–1849) was an Orientalist who, as a foreign member of the Institut, was much in Paris. Mary became attached to his daughters.

HAUSER, CASPAR (dates unknown)
A strange figure, possibly an imposter, who surfaced in the 1820s–30s, claiming to be an aristocrat's son who had been brought up by German peasants but had always remained miserably conscious of his deprivation.

HUGO, VICTOR (1802–85)
Poet, novelist and dramatist—perhaps the greatest figure of French Romanticism. His first book of poems was published in 1822, his first novel in 1823. The drama *Hernani*, deliberately flying in the face of all accepted dramatic conventions, was used as a key battle by traditionalists and Romantics at its first performances in February 1830; the Romantics in the audience, led by Gautier, won, and carried the day for the Romantic Movement as a whole. After Louis Napoleon's coup d'état in 1851 Hugo left France for Guernsey, where he remained until 1870, writing *Les Châtiments* (1853), *Les Misérables* (1862), etc.

LA FAYETTE, MARIE-JOSEPH, MARQUIS DE (1757–1834)
Politician and general. Fought in the American War of Independence and the French Revolution and was the prime mover of the Declaration of the Rights of Man. During the Restoration he had faded out of public life, but returned in the Revolution of 1830 and played an important part in the events which put Louis-Philippe on the throne.

LEROUX, PIERRE (1797–1871)
Philosopher, economist, socialist-idealist. In 1824 was co-founder of *Le Globe*, in 1841 of *La Revue indépendante*. George Sand is said to have been influenced by his 'religion of humanity', which he expounded in *De l'Egalité* (1838) and *De l'Humanité* (1840). For a period tried to run a printing-house on socialist principles; it failed.

MANZONI, ALESSANDRO (1785–1873)
Novelist, dramatist, poet, leader of the Romantic movement in Italy. His *Promessi Sposi* followed Walter Scott in its historical imagination, use of landscape, interest in humble people; his dramas *Carmagnola* (1820) and *Adelchi* (1822) boldly ignored the traditional unities of time and place. In his early years he was as revolutionary in politics as in literature. Later he became reconverted to Catholicism, abandoned literature and devoted his

attention to his family and improving the agricultural methods used on his estate at Brusuglio.

MÉRIMÉE, PROSPER (1803–70)
Son of an artist. In the 1820s was part of the Romantic circle, though he cultivated an ironic detachment. In 1825 he published, as a hoax, the *Théâtre de Clara Gazul*, purporting to be dramas by a Spanish actress. *La Guzla*, another hoax, was published as a translation of Illyrian ballads. In 1829, inspired by Scott, he published the *Chronique du Règne de Charles IX*. He is now best known for the masterly novellas of his later period, particularly *Carmen* (1847), on which the opera was based. In 1834 he was appointed Inspector General of Historical Monuments and (with Viollet-le-Duc) did much to preserve Gothic and other architecture in France. Almost alone among the Mohls' friends, he accepted the Second Empire, having long been a friend of the Empress Eugénie and her family, and eventually became a Senator.

MIGNET, FRANÇOIS (1796–1884)
Historian and close friend of Thiers. Became a Councillor of State and Academician under Louis-Philippe. Best known for his *History of the Revolution* (1824) and *Mémoires historiques* (1843).

MILNES, RICHARD MONCKTON (1809–85)
Poet, politician, philanthropist, later Lord Houghton. Wrote various political and literary monographs, was an early champion of Keats, and entertained a wide variety of notable figures. For many years he was in love with Florence Nightingale.

MONTALEMBERT, CHARLES, COMTE DE (1810–70)
Liberal Catholic writer and historian. Many polemical writings advocating a liberal approach to Catholic education and the restriction of Church power in non-religious affairs. In the Second Empire he led the militant Catholic faction.

MUSTOXIDI, ANDREAS (1785–1860)
Greek writer and historian, born in Corfu. As a young man was appointed official historiographer by the (French) government of the Ionian islands, but in 1820 was sacked by the (now British) regime—and anathematized by Byron—for publishing a pamphlet on the cession of Parga to Turkey. An exile until 1824, publishing numerous works on archaeology and Classical history. Returned to Greece at its Independence and became Minister of Education.

QUINET, EDGAR (1803–77)
Liberal poet and philosopher. Under Louis-Philippe became Professor of Foreign Literature at the Collège de France, but his lectures were con-

sidered so anti-clerical that he was dismissed in 1845. Between 1848 and 1850 was active in socialist politics, and in 1851, after Louis-Napoleon's coup d'état abandoned France for twenty years.

RANKE, LEOPOLD VON (1795-1886)
Celebrated historian (and long-standing friend of the Mohls), best known for his studies of Rome.

RÉCAMIER, JEANNE, MME (1777-1849)
Salonnière, who entertained many of the greatest literary and political figures during the Empire and Restoration. She was Mme de Staël's closest woman friend, and for a short period was loved by Benjamin Constant, before becoming the pivot of Chateaubriand's life. Both David and Gérard painted famous portraits of her.

RENAN, ERNEST (1823-92)
Educated for the priesthood, but close study of the Hebrew and Aramaic texts of the Bible led him to question its divine inspiration and therefore the whole basis of orthodox Christianity. Became a distinguished Semitic scholar, published much, and in 1862 became Professor of Hebrew at the Collège de France, where he again frightened the orthodox; after the publication of his *Vie de Jésus* (1863) he was dismissed and his Chair abolished. Throughout the 1870s and 1880s he continued to publish prolifically, and in 1870 was reinstated, becoming head of the Collège in 1883. He and Taine were probably France's leading philosophers towards the end of the nineteenth century.

SAINTE-BEUVE, CHARLES-AUGUSTIN (1804-69)
Critic and writer. In the 1820s and 1830s an enthusiastic supporter of the Romantics; in 1829 published the fictional *Vie, poésies et pensées de Joseph Delorme*, in 1834 *Volupté*. Known as the 'father of modern criticism'; best remembered today for his immense series of portraits of contemporary figures.

SAND, GEORGE (1804-76)
Pseudonym of Aurore Dupin, who married the Baron Dudevant. By the 1830s she had broken away from her husband, established her independence in Paris, taken to wearing the famous trousers, and become the mistress of the writer Jules Sandeau (later she was associated with Alfred de Musset and Chopin). Her early theme (in the novels *Indiana* (1832), *Lélia* (1833), etc.) was women's right to independence, above all emotional and sexual. Later she supported Republicanism, Christian Socialism, Leroux' humanitarianism, etc. For a time she was active in journalism, but from the 1850s returned mainly to writing novels and memoirs; by the end of her life she had produced some 105 volumes.

SCHÉRER, EDMOND (1815–89)
Philosopher and critical theorist, who was among the first to declare that literary and other artistic judgments must necessarily be relative.

SCHLEGEL, AUGUST WILHELM VON (1767–1845)
Early translator of Shakespeare and enthusiast for primitive literature (ballads, Hindu writings, etc.). Through Mme de Staël, a great friend, his views helped to influence the new attitudes to these subjects which began to appear in France in the early part of the century.

STAËL, GERMAINE, MME DE (1766–1817)
In her mother's salon, when she was a girl, she had known Diderot, Talleyrand, Bouffon, etc. Her own salon in the Empire was a centre of intellectual activity and anti-Napoleonism. She had been forced to emigrate in 1792 and spent some time in England and Switzerland; Napoleon again exiled her in 1803, 1806 and 1810. During her travels she was usually accompanied by Schlegel and Constant; she did not return permanently to Paris until 1814. In her writings she stressed above all the contrast between the 'classical' literature of the South, which she held to be an alien transplant in France, and the Romantic literature of the North, its natural crop—ideas which paved the way for the breakaway from the rigid conventions which had frozen France's cultural life for many years. She also wrote the novels *Delphine* (1802) and *Corinne* (1807), stressing women's equal needs for intellectual self-fulfilment and human affection. *Corinne* contains scenes of boring English country life which echo Mary's feelings.

STENDHAL (1783–1842)
Pseudonym of Henri Beyle. Novelist and critic. His first signed work was *Rome, Naples et Florence*, published in 1817, reflecting his passions for Italy, art, music, literature and society. In the 1820s he published *De l'Amour* (1822), a *Vie de Rossini* (1823) and *Racine et Shakespeare* (1823–5) debating the virtues of classicism and Romanticism. His first novel *Armance* only appeared in 1827, *Le Rouge et le Noir* in 1830 and *La Chartreuse de Parme* in 1839.

TAINE, HIPPOLYTE (1828–93)
France's leading philosopher (with Renan) in the latter part of the nineteenth century. His very determinist theory of *la race, le milieu et le moment*, according to which all human and social development is predictable if those three factors are known, provided the philosophical basis for Naturalists such as Zola, and dominated French thinking for a period.

TASTU, AMABLE, MME (1798–1885)
Poet, much admired from the middle of the 1820s. Despite innumerable

family difficulties she published several collections of verse and books for children, besides translating *Robinson Crusoe* and other works.

THIERRY, AUGUSTIN (1795-1856)
Historian. One of the first in France to insist that historical writings should be based on a study of contemporary documents and should include the common people. Many of his sources are now considered unreliable, but the liveliness of his writing, owing much to Scott in its use of anecdote and local colour, makes it still interesting reading. *L'Histoire de la Conquête de l'Angleterre par les Normands* laid great emphasis on an Anglo-Saxon spirit which survived conquest and was sublimated in the English system of constitutional monarchy. *Récits des temps mérovingiens* (1840) explores sixth-century France; it was written after he had become totally blind and paralysed.

THIERS, ADOLPHE (1797-1877)
Statesman and historian. During the Restoration, when he was excluded from politics he published his *Histoire de la Révolution française* (1823-7), still a masterly exposition of the subject. After the Revolution of 1830 he was in the Government for ten years, until he resigned over foreign policy issues. Thereafter he returned to writing and published another major work, the *Histoire du Consulat et de l'Empire* (1845-62). In the 1860s he returned to politics, as a fervent anti-Imperialist, conducted the peace negotiations in 1871, and was responsible for most of France's economic and military reconstruction after the Commune. He was the first President of the Third Republic.

TOCQUEVILLE, ALEXIS, COMTE DE (1805-59)
One of the most original historians of the century. In his *Démocratie en Amérique* (1835 and 1840) he argues that there is an ineluctable drive towards democracy and equality and that Europe must plan its future along those lines. *L'Ancien Régime* (1856) was to have been the first volume of three examining the factors which caused the Revolution to occur in France rather than elsewhere, the way in which it grew out of the society it destroyed, and the reasons for its failure.

TRISTAN, FLORA (1803-44)
Brought up in poverty. At seventeen made a disastrous marriage to the lithographer who employed her and after five years left him, taking her children and determining on a life of freedom. Eventually she became associated with the revolutionary socialist Saint-Simoniens and Fouriéristes and began to campaign for divorce-law reform and women's rights in general with an almost religious fervour. In 1843 she founded the Union ouvrière.

VILLEMAIN, ABEL-FRANÇOIS (1790–1870)
Professor of Literature at the Sorbonne from 1816 to 1830; Minister of Education under Louis-Philippe. Original in setting literature in a historical context and also in his comparative approach to the various literatures of Europe.

Index